AN OLD SOLDIER'S MEMORIES

From a negative by Maull & Fox.

AN OLD SOLDIER'S MEMORIES

BY

S. H. JONES-PARRY, J.P., D.L.

LATE CAPTAIN ROYAL DUBLIN FUSILIERS

AUTHOR OF 'MY JOURNEY ROUND THE WORLD,'
ETC.

"Sweet memory, wafted by thy gentle gale,
Oft up the tide of time I turn my sail."
SAMUEL ROGERS

LONDON
HURST AND BLACKETT, LIMITED
13, GREAT MARLBOROUGH STREET
1897

All rights reserved

TO

LIEUT.-GENERAL SIR JOHN BLICK SPURGIN, K.C.B., C.S.I

AND

ALL OFFICERS PAST AND PRESENT OF THE

ROYAL DUBLIN FUSILIERS

THIS BOOK

Is Affectionately Dedicated

BY

THE AUTHOR

CONTENTS

CHAPTER I

PARENTAGE AND EDUCATION 1

My maternal grandfather: Admiral Robert Lloyd—A licensed pirate—A rough old salt—My father: Post-captain in 1840—My uncle: Sir Love Jones-Parry—An after-dinner leg—My uncle: Colonel Parry Yale—A hero—At school in Chester—At the Royal Naval School—At Shooter's Hill—At a private crammer's—I go to Addiscombe for examination.

CHAPTER II

INDIA 15

I get my commissions (1849): my Queen's, my Company's (H.E.I.C.)—To India by the Overland Route—At Malta, Alexandria, and Cairo—Crossing the desert—At Aden—Colonel Outram—At Madras—With the 52nd Madras Native Infantry at Vellore—Officers and men—My chums—Inviting the Brigadier to lunch—In delicate health—"Native dictionaries"—Captain Wilson—Slade—Appointed to 1st Madras Fusiliers—Sladen of Ours—A drunken apothecary—At Bellary—My new regiment—A Plymouth Brother—A Nawab—Our tigers—Visiting at Vellore—The regiment ordered to Burmah—I join it on the march—Madras.

CHAPTER III

RANGOON 38

The voyage—Rangoon—The great Pagoda—A court-martial—The 1st Bengal Fusiliers—Moselle on tap—Amateur theatricals—Sepoys' sentry-go—*The Wreck Ashore* and *Charles II.*—Mormons—Burmah and the Burmese—The granary of India—Religion—The priesthood—Marriage a convenience, not a rite—Love of tobacco—Cigarettes and love.

CHAPTER IV

PEGU 52

To re-capture and occupy Pegu—The expedition—"The Beast John" and "the intellectual Digney"—Storming of Pagoda—Pegu captured and occupied—The Pagoda described—A night attack—I go to Pegu—The Commissariat stores—A keg of arrack—What came of it—I arrive—A weak position—The garrison—Peguers, in and out—Saving the Sepoys—The enemy down on us—McClory saves my life—An attack in earnest—"Eternal Watch"—An unsafe position—Narrow shaves—"Who is Nelson?"—The old campaigner—Burning bamboos—Old biscuit to eat—British guns heard—Short of ammunition—Relieved!—The fruits of our defence—Our losses.

CHAPTER V

PEGU—SECOND DEFENCE 82

A Burmese mode of defence: Sowing bamboo skewers—Northwards, after the enemy—To Sephanghoon and Mausaganoo—The marmalade and the flies—Neill and his Minié—A poonghie house—Back to Pegu—We erect a stockade on the river-bank—The enemy stockade themselves—A critical position—Death of Sale—Captain Nicolay—Royal Navy boats—On the *qui vive*—Burning jungle—Arrival of convoy—I have a nasty accident—Review of the Second Defence of Pegu.

CHAPTER VI

OUR JOLLY MARCH 93

"Go to Shoaygheen" (with gunpowder and food)—No road, only jungle tracks—We start—Feeling our way—Fording rivers—Sagacious elephants help us—A jungle on fire—Big trees tumble—A mass of wild birds—Tigers about—Shoaygheen at last—A Burmese burial-ground—Accident to Neill of Ours—To Tonghoo.

CHAPTER VII

TONGHOO 98

Tonghoo described—Compared with Pegu—Our new Colonel (Apthorpe)—Our new cantonment—We officers the centre of attraction for the natives—Those two false teeth!—A merry race—Mad dogs—Burying the local archbishop—A feminine fight—Our men and the native women—I am very bad with dysentery—The story of Maima and Fatima—"Don't go"—The wife of the bandmaster—The bandmaster's dream—Grateful Maima—The dream and its sequel—The king's road between Tonghoo and Pegu—Appointed to survey and report on it—Interesting incidents—Natives and the telescope—Nearly drowned—A domestic tragedy—Attached to the Sappers—Poor Bond—I again get dysentery, and am ordered to Europe for three years—Prince Ernest of Leiningen—Two anecdotes.

CHAPTER VIII

LONDON TO CONSTANTINOPLE 121

London in the early Fifties—Evans's in Covent Garden—The Argyll Rooms—The Haymarket—At Cheltenham—A severe winter (1854-5)—I decline an A.D.C.-ship, and join the Turkish Contingent—At Vienna—Lord John Russell—At the Opera—Trieste—Too warm a bath—Pilgrim Turks—At Athens—The "Maid" Smyrna—Up the Dardanelles—Pera—The Sweet Waters of Europe—Mutual admiration—Whyte Melville—Wilde Brown and Tame Gammell—The first English officers commissioned by the Sultan—Selecting a site for the camp—Drainage of the Embassy—Fighting the cholera—Am gazetted Deputy-Assistant-Quartermaster-General — My beastly horse—Florence Nightingale—Passing the boots—We are to embark for Kertch.

CHAPTER IX

THE CRIMEA 142

"Rats are awful"—Tied up in a sack—Kertch—The museum, and the tomb of Mithridates—Making a plan of the place—The Turkish officers—Paying the Turkish soldiers—Our position at Kertch—My duties—A brave enemy—Effect of frost on the sea—Our Christmas dinner—The admirable Percy—The extreme cold—At Yenikali—I am made Assistant-Quartermaster-General—A severe storm—"A mass of icicles"—In battle array—Protecting our position—Scurvy and its cure—Our recreations—Armistice signed—Interesting relics—Irregular horse—Peace—Farewell dinners—To Constantinople—Sam Slick's daughter—At Balaclava and Sevastopol—Turks not cowards—"Better than most of the Christians in those parts"—The Turkish soldier.

CHAPTER X

HOMEWARD BOUND 163

A project surrendered—Travelling in uniform—At Venice—At Milan—We bespeak an opera—A prolonged tour—At Chamounix—London in 1856—The Junior United Service Club—John Parry, Albert Smith, Fechter, Jullien—Vauxhall and Cremorne—Koenig and Puzzi—Mary Keeley and Miss Bateman—A crush at the Alhambra—In Wales—I fall in love—I join the School of Musketry at Hythe—Engaged !—*Liber Veritatis*—" Deeds, not words "—"O. H. M. S."—Ordered to rejoin—Marriage—London to Suez—"India in a blaze "—My wife returns to England.

CHAPTER XI

LUCKNOW 172

In the Red Sea—Sleeping on deck—At Madras—Praises of Neill—His death—At Calcutta—Stories of Neill—Travelling *dâk*—At Allahabad—At Futtypore—We reach Cawnpore—The recent tragedy—" Revenge it !" " We will !"—I am attached temporarily to 75th Regiment—Crossing the Ganges—Twenty-thousand camp

x CONTENTS

followers—On the march—On gun-guard—Incidents of the march—Fighting at Maragungh—News from Lucknow—The Alumbagh—Its defence—The Dilkoosha—Occupying the Martinière—Bank's Bungalow—A murderous fire—An Amazon—A narrow shave—The Shah Nujjif—The Naval Brigade—Lord Pelham Clinton—Burning huts—Sir Colin—We join the Regiment of Details—A real battle—"The fire was hellish"—A compliment from Sir Colin—My servant Solomon—"Never out of fire"—The 32nd mess-house—We occupy the Moti Mahal—An old chum—The evacuation of the Residency—We are the last to leave—End of the relief of Lucknow.

CHAPTER XII

ALUMBAGH 204

A blow to our prestige?—Our position—"Outram my man"—No means of transport—Boy officers—The Enfield rifle—Musketry drill—"Guard, turn out!"—Firing day and night—An attack in force—The Monkey-god—The Begum—Target practice—The country settling down—News from Lucknow—Attack on Alumbagh—A battle in a dust-storm—At Dilkoosha—We hold the Kaiser Bagh—At Lucknow—The city fairly ours—A jolly bathe—"Such a sight"—A rascally ex-Minister—A pathetic incident—"Take them to the rear"—Loot—An old Crimean friend—Our barouche—Palais Royal trumpery—Another dust-storm—The Queen and the army—In camp at Nawabgunj—Lord Ellenborough—The natives and English policy—The Queen's and the Company's officers—At Durreabad—At Fyzabad—At Sultanpore—I have low fever—Second attack of fever—At Allahabad—At Calcutta—Third attack of fever—At Madras—Before the Medical Board—"Entitled to a good rest"—At Bangalore—My wife joins me—Musketry instructor—Cholera—A grievance—A year's leave on urgent private affairs.

CHAPTER XIII

ENGLAND—MALTA—RETIREMENT 278

I exchange into the 8th King's—To Templemore—To Malta—Acting Inspector of Musketry—On an opera committee—Behind the scenes—A furious *prima donna*—"Art is art"—Music—A musketry story—I retire from the army—I refuse appointments in Militia and Volunteers—Some reflections on army matters—Favouritism.

CHAPTER XIV

HOME. 1868 282

In Wales—I take up farming—I become a magistrate—Some curious cases—High Sheriff in 1871—Judges and chaplains—I am made Deputy-Lieutenant—An accident, and a Journey Round The World—My book on the latter subject—The Primrose League—District inspector—My first district—Chairmen—Sermons—My second division—Three years' work as political speaker—A crowning incident of my life—My dear old comrades—Left alone with sweet memories.

AN OLD SOLDIER'S MEMORIES

CHAPTER I

PARENTAGE AND EDUCATION

"Voilá l'espayce de hom ker yer swee."—*Trilby*.

LIKE another illustrious personage connected with the Principality, I was born at Carnarvon. For this I take no credit to myself. Good and sufficient documentary evidence exists to enable me to fix the date of the important event as April 28, 1830.

Those of my readers interested in my pedigree are referred to Burke: I hope they will understand it. For my own part, as will be seen in a note to Nicolas' *History of Welsh County Families*, I was content to believe in my descent from Adam, but since reading Darwin I now claim kinsmanship with the biggest and oldest Vertebrate ever created. Please note *Vertebrate*, as I do not own connection with anything that has not a backbone.

Apart from pedigree I have been lucky enough to see both my grandfathers. Of my paternal one, Mr. Jones-Parry of Madryn Park, little need be said, as I cannot even remember him. He was a shrewd man of business, and was said at one time to own land in every county in North Wales. Of my maternal grandfather, Admiral Robert Lloyd of Tregayan, Anglesea, volumes might be written, and I am always somewhat surprised that the gentlemen who write naval notes have never once come across any of his achievements.

Admiral Robert Lloyd was the most splendid *licensed pirate* I have ever heard or read of since the days of old Benbow. His services are well worth recording. From an extract I have before me, I find that he was born March 24, 1760. In March 1779 he served on board the *Valiant*. Then on the *Fairy*, 18 guns, Captains Berkeley Keppel and Brown. He was wounded in a sharp action which preceded the capture of that sloop by the French frigate *Madame*. After much other service he was promoted to the *Latona*, Captain Thornborough, and fought under that officer in the celebrated action of June 1, 1794 (Lord Howe's victory). He rejoined Captain Thornborough as first lieutenant in the *Robust*, 74 guns. He served in Lord Bridport's action, and was severely wounded in the expedition to Quiberon.

In 1796 he commanded the *Racoon* in the North Sea, where, after a short fight on January 11, 1798, he took *Le Policrate*, French privateer, and on the twenty-second of the same month *La Pensée;* he had previously captured *Les Amis*.

Captain Lloyd captured on October 20 following *La Vigilante*. On December 6, 1799, he sunk a French lugger and *Le vrai Décede* and *L'Intrépide;* in this latter engagement he was severely wounded in the head by a half pike. After serving in various places he was appointed, on February 11, 1812, to the *Plantagenet*, and between September 8 and December 17, 1813, Captain Lloyd took not less than twenty sail of vessels measuring in the whole 12,500 tons. Afterwards he captured a large number of coasters, and accompanied the expeditions against Washington and New Orleans. On his return to England he brought home the bodies of Generals Gibbs and Packenham. He became a Rear-Admiral in 1830, and a Vice-Admiral in 1837.

I have heard my mother say, that so great was the damage he did to the French that a price was set on his head. He never wanted men to man his ships, for to sail under him meant certain prize-money. He declined knighthood when High Sheriff of Anglesea in 1820, because the honour was not bestowed in recognition of his naval services.

Although rough and brusque to others, to me he was gentleness itself; he used to call me his man "Friday," and I was allowed to attend him when dressing. I worshipped him from afar, for I had a lurking dread of a man who I was told had killed so many. When silently watching the mysteries of his toilet, I noticed, before he put on his wig, the fearful gash that ran from end to end of his skull—a French delicate compliment paid him as he boarded *L'Intrépide;* also an ugly red mark on his side, which probably dated from Quiberon.

He was a rough old salt, and swore worse than our soldiers did in Flanders; he told the Bishop of Bangor that it was "a bad habit he had acquired since he came on shore."

His stories were endless: one in particular well bears repeating. It was of a storm through which he not only weathered his ship, but towed two prizes he had captured. The violence of the storm used to increase in proportion to the amount of port wine the old Admiral had imbibed. On one occasion when he was High Sheriff of Carnarvonshire, he, as was the custom in those days, dined with the Judge. Now, his lordship was a very sedate personage, and his port wine was good: hence the Admiral's storm arose by mighty leaps and bounds. The description was thrilling, and, when it was all over and the ships safe at anchor, the Judge gravely remarked: "You must have been truly grateful to Divine Providence for such a miraculous escape." "Yes," said the Admiral, "I did think the Almighty d—d considerate on that occasion!"

When seventy-two he married as his second wife a lady of twenty-seven, who took care of him, limited his grog, and checked his swearing. I am thankful he had a peaceful old age.[1]

My father was the second son of old Jones-Parry of Madryn; he was sent when quite a small boy with his elder brother (Sir Love) to Westminster. I remember his telling me how they used to ride pillion all the way to Westminster from Madryn in Carnarvonshire, and that on the first occasion his sorrow at leaving home was somewhat lessened by the fact that he and his brother had blue spenser suits with silver buttons and light blue beaver hats. Can any one picture anything more touching and comical than these two little fellows riding all that great distance in such a costume?

My father was intended for the army, and was borne on the roster of some regiment as a lieutenant before he was twelve years old. He remembered that the Colonel used to call sometimes, and give him a sovereign—whether as a present or in lieu of pay does not appear. One fine day his elder brother (attracted by the money or by the uniform of the gallant Colonel) changed his mind, and desired to be a soldier; so his name was substituted for my father's, and my father had to go into the Royal Navy.

At the age of thirteen years and six months he fought on board the *Triumph*, Captain Sir Erasmus Gower, in the action of Camperdown, and was very severely wounded. As far as I can remember a shell burst over the wheel, and killed and wounded several sailors; a large splinter struck my father, injuring his throat and arm.

I well remember his telling me that whilst he was in the cockpit another middy came down. When the latter's turn

---

[1] Admiral Lloyd served from 1782 to 1787 on board the *Hebe*, during a portion of which time Prince William Henry (William IV.) was borne on the books as a midshipman.

arrived the doctor asked him where he was wounded; the poor boy faltered, and the good kind doctor said, " Oh, I see you've had a very narrow escape; come, drink this, and then go up and do your duty like a man." The medicine was a dram of rum. My father never mentioned the name of either, but told me the middy lived to become a good sailor. As to the doctor, I feel sure he scored up above. After this severe wound my father was sent home, and was of course made much of.

On October 1, 1804, he assisted in capturing a French privateer. I think he saw more service, but I have no record of it.[1] He received blood-money for his wound at Camperdown. He retired as a post-captain in 1840.

My father naturally came across Captain Lloyd at various seaports. He thus became acquainted with my mother, who was an only child, and they made a runaway match.

I am reminded of a funny story my father used to tell about some sailors, who in those days were very particular as to the style of ship they took service on. If a frigate was not trim and taut, they would have nothing to say to her. The *Gorgon* was in harbour flying signal for hands. Two old salts took a boat, and rowed alongside, scanning her yards, figure-head, etc., critically. At last they got to the stern. "What's her name, Bill?" The other, who was a poor scholar unfortunately, spelt the name by letters backwards, which made it "Nogrog." "By the powers! No grog!—that won't suit us," and off they went.

Another story that impressed me was as follows: My father and a lot of other jolly fellows were dining at an inn in Portsmouth. The window looking on the street was wide open. The noise of a terrible commotion reached them, and one named Barlow, jumping up, put his head out of window, and said, "Only fancy, there's a row on,

---

[1] According to James's *History of Naval Wars*, my father distinguished himself at Acre.

and Billy Barlow not in it." He sprang into the street, and was never heard of again. It was supposed that it was a press-gang row, and that Barlow got knocked on the head in the scrimmage, and was thrown over into some basin or dock to prevent further inquiry. It reminds one of the strange disappearance of Grimaldi's brother.

My father's last ship was the *Royalist*: he accepted post rank in 1840. I remember him very well. He was passionately fond of children, though somewhat strict with his own, as was necessary with a large family. The raising of the corner of the table-cloth meant silence, and he used to have our pockets sewn up if he found we kept our hands too much in them. My father was a magistrate for the counties of Denbighshire, Flintshire, and Carnarvonshire; he was a Deputy-Lieutenant for the last-named county, and High Sheriff in 1836. He was a most excellent magistrate, and died universally regretted.

My uncle, Sir Love Jones-Parry, who got my father's commission in the army, saw considerable service. He was a very witty man, and an excellent speaker. After he had retired from the service, he accidentally fell on a scythe which lay concealed in some grass; this necessitated the amputation of his leg, and the story is told that on one occasion he was asked by George IV. where he lost the limb. "On the field, your Majesty," was the reply.

Sir Love represented Carnarvonshire in Parliament for many years. He was considered so strong a candidate that he was selected to oppose Disraeli at Shrewsbury, and unfortunately (or rather, I should say fortunately) was beaten. I remember well his coming to Llwyn Onn after the contest, and my brother copying the state of the polls for him to send to all concerned.

There was a good story told by him of an old woman, who came up to him after an election, and assured him that her husband had worked very hard for him in the contest; she prayed him to do something for her son.

Sir Love asked what she wanted for him. "Well, indeed, Sir Love, if you could make him an ambassador or something of that kind, it would do nicely."

Sir Love always travelled with two spare legs, one of which he called his after-dinner leg, which was of cork, with swagger silk stocking and pump. He astonished the butler at a house at which he was to dine by refusing to be ushered into the drawing-room until he had put on his dining leg. It is said the late Sir John Jervis, sometime Attorney-General, caricatured Sir Love in *Punch*, as sitting with his wooden leg straight out, and saying to the shopman, "I'll trouble you to measure me for a pair of boots." This same wooden leg was a boon to us children, as we could always hear our uncle coming, and so get out of his way if in mischief.

My mother was a very active little woman, and had an excellent memory; she used to tell us many yarns about her father, and also stories about the Russian prisoners at Portsmouth drinking the oil out of the street-lamps, and leaving the town in darkness. She was the mother of sixteen children, of whom I was the youngest but two.

About this time, an uncle and aunt (Colonel and Mrs. Yale), who had no children, desired to adopt me. My father consented, and I was borne off to Plas yn Yale, situated in the very midst of Welsh Wales. No one spoke English in the household except my uncle, aunt, and my nurse Amy, a dear sweet soul.

What a grand solitude it was! No letters or papers unless we sent to Corwen for them; this only occurred if we went to church, or something was wanted for the household. We made our candles (I can well remember the process of making dips and rushlights), baked and brewed at home, and were very happy and contented.

My uncle was one of the very merriest men I ever met. He was full of all kinds of songs, and used to carol them out very often when the thunder-clouds were gathering at the other end of the table. When my aunt was frowning desperately he would chant out, "Lesbia hath a beaming eye," or when being severely scolded he would say, "Pray, Goody, please to moderate the rancour of your tongue."

I never was afraid of my uncle, and worshipped him with the same devotion as my dear old Admiral; there was something in bravery that even in my very infancy commanded my admiration.

Colonel Yale was indeed a hero; I have his services before me. It seems he was gazetted as an ensign in the 90th in 1805, and as lieutenant to the 48th in 1807; in this regiment he remained for the rest of his service.

In 1809, Colonel William Parry Yale[1] went out as captain in the 2nd Battalion 48th, and served in the advance-guard in the action of Oporto, and subsequently under Lieutenant-General Lord Hill in the battles of Talavera and Busaco, as well as in various skirmishes.

At Albuera the command of the battalion devolved on him, as all his seniors were either killed or wounded. He continued in command for some time after their return to England. He then joined the 1st Battalion in the Peninsula, and acted as field-officer at Pampeluna, Heights of Saire, on the Nivelle, and at Orthes.

In the action of Pampeluna he was severely wounded, and had his cap shot off at Busaco. He received the gold medal for Albuera, and the silver medal and clasps for Talavera, Busaco, Vittoria, Pyrenees, Nivelle, Nive, Orthes, Toulouse.

A letter signed "Fitzroy Somerset" says that Major Parry Yale's name had been submitted to his Majesty, who had been graciously pleased to desire that it should be placed on the list for nomination for the Royal

---

[1] He was originally Jones, and took the name of Yale on succeeding to Plas yn Yale, a property that had descended from ancient times, and from this branch of the family came the founder of the celebrated Yale College in America.

Hanoverian Guelphic Order. I do not know whether my uncle ever got it.

He often took me on my pony with him out shooting, and invariably gave me his last year's game licence, as I carried my little tin gun. On one occasion we met a tenant, when a little conversation took place apart, then the man came up to me and said, "May I ask if you have a licence, sir?" Of course I produced mine. The man touched his hat, saying, "All right, sir; I have to be particular, there are so many poachers about." My delight at being mistaken for a poacher was unbounded.

On the whole, I lived a happy life, and years after, when my dear uncle had lost his sight, I loved to read to him, and was overjoyed to see what a good, loving, devoted woman his wife had become: all harshness and irritability had vanished, and her brave husband was her idol and joy. My last recollection of him is my leading him about amongst the crowd of pleasure-seekers at Bath on the occasion of the Prince of Wales' marriage; we both wore medals, and I was proud to see the notice he attracted. He died in 1867, and was buried in the cemetery at Bath. God's acre there holds no better or braver man.

The time had now come for me to return home. Education must be thought of; so one fine day we drove off to Llwyn Onn, which property had been left to my father by my grandfather.

I think I was sent to school rather earlier than I should have been had it not been for the sake of the companionship of my brother. We were consigned to the care of Mr. Harrison, a Minor Canon of the cathedral at Chester, whose wife was kindness itself. Mr. Harrison, or "Old Billy" as we called him, certainly imported a fair amount of Classics into my youthful brains, and to him I attribute my love for them, small as my knowledge is.

We had nice friends in Chester, and were often asked

out. I fear I was a very proud little boy, for legend says I only took off my hat to the Bishop and Miss Ann Potts, a dear kind soul who showed us much hospitality.

The 83rd were quartered at this time at the Castle, and, as the Colonel's nephew was a day scholar and a friend of ours, we saw something of soldier life.

The Race week was our Saturnalia; my people always took lodgings for the week, and in spite of the protests of Billy we went each day to see the fun. All our amusements took tone from these events; we raced marbles named after favourite horses and had our own special colours. I am afraid to say how many coaches and four went out daily from Chester, and on May 29 it was a grand sight to see them go in procession all decorated with oak-branches.

Watchmen still existed, and turnspit dogs had not entirely disappeared in very isolated localities. Street cries were an abomination, especially "fine cockles and mussels!" and sedan chairs were common enough. May 29 each year was a day never to be forgotten. All the stage-coaches, and their name was legion, went out decorated with ribbons and oak-boughs. It was a very pretty and imposing sight. The drivers and guards of course wore scarlet and gold when carrying Royal Mails.

I forget how many years we were at Harrison's before my father carried out his intention of sending us to the Royal Naval School.

We started *viâ* Chester for Euston. I remember the solemnity of the leave-taking, a railway journey being a very serious matter in those days. What ceremony there was, what ringing of bells, and what caution taken lest any one should be left behind! As boys we carefully noted the name of the engine, and wrote home afterwards to dear mamma to say "a very good engine called Mazeppa took us quite safe; I hope when you come up you will have the same one, for I know it is a good one." We also noted the names of the stations, so as to be able to tell them at home to look out for favourite ones. On arrival at a distance of one mile from Euston, the engine was detached, and we were hauled in by ropes, lest the engine should become unmanageable, and go flying through London to the detriment of her Majesty's subjects.

The Royal Naval School then occupied Alfred House, Camberwell, and I am bound to say a more miserable existence could not well be imagined than a school-boy's at that seminary. The whole thing was over-handicapped for want of funds. There was not enough money to warm, feed, or instruct us.

The only pleasant memory of those days is the unswerving devotion to his duties of poor old Loyeau, our French master, whom we treated shamefully, but who nevertheless did his utmost for us. I do not think the poor old refugee could hate any one, but if he could he had much cause to loathe his cruel little persecutors.

It must be remembered that most of the boys' fathers had served against the French; indeed some boys had been born in French prisons. We consequently had been accustomed to hear Frenchmen cried down, and so were led to persecute some most good and worthy men.

A few years after, we went into our new building at Newcross, the foundation stone of which had been laid by Prince Albert. Here again want of funds was sorely felt.

My school days were not happy, for I was perpetually in hot water. I am certain I was not a stupid boy, for I could, between the bell sounding and class assembling, pick up enough of my lesson to save condign punishment; but I was hopelessly idle. No special interest was taken in those days by masters in their pupils. A class was a class and nothing more; if you learnt your lesson so much the better; if you did not, you only went to the bottom of the class, and punishments were rarely inflicted for idleness.

I have no pleasant memories connected with this period of my existence, but I must say that the object of the founders deserved and still deserves the support of the country. The number of orphans who were educated and fed gratis was never known to us, for it was a point of honour with the authorities never to disclose the names of those who were benefited.

If naval officers could only be induced to patronize the school, a successful future would dawn, and the object of our good Sailor King be fulfilled.

In after years I met our old head-master, Dr. Chambers, enjoying his holiday in Switzerland. On another occasion I met him at the Academy; we did the pictures together. There happened to be side by side two pictures, one of an old hound with her young family, the other a shipwrecked vessel, the stern only of which appeared out of the sands. I told the good old scholar that one was a "litter of puppies" and the other a "litora puppis." He had private hysterics, but on recovering he looked at me gravely and said, "Why did you not do better at school?"

Whilst I was still at the Royal Naval School—and I think doing better, for a nice master named Steele had taken an interest in me, a thing never before experienced by me—my father died. It was a sad time. I remember being asked if I would like to see him before the coffin was closed, and declining. I had such a dread of a dead body, and, though I have seen such scores since, the feeling has never left me.

I also remember that at the funeral the coffin was placed in the centre aisle, and in the chancel there was a table with a large silver dish on it, and all mourners and friends as they walked past put money into the dish; I think my brothers and I had to put bank-notes. The money went to the Vicar, and was, I suppose, a relic of the custom of payment for masses for the dead.

A great change in my prospects came with my father's death. I had been intended for the Artillery, my father being a personal friend of the Marquis of Anglesea, then Master-General of the Ordnance, through whose interest a nomination and subsequent commission became easy; but ways and means had to be considered, and it was eventually decided that I should try for an Indian cadetship. My father's cousin, Lord Dinorben, was appealed to, and a promise of a nomination secured.

I was removed from the R.N.S. and sent to Shooters Hill. A curious arrangement obtained here; the original proprietor of the school failed, and he became usher to the very man who had been his usher.

I hated the place; we were badly looked after, and used to go out at night to a public-house next door, and have toasted cheese and gin-and-water. No doubt Paul was a good crammer, for he turned out some good men, amongst others the late Sir John Cowell, who was there with me.

I had been for some time ailing, and fever set in; so I was removed to be under advice in London, as my eyes were much affected. I was attended by Doctor Ware, the oculist, the kindest man that ever lived, yet I dreaded his visits on account of the terrible pain he caused by dropping something into my eye. I had been very ill, my head was shaved, and in a limp and helpless state I set forth with my good sister for Jersey for change of air. What a lovely island, and what nice people, manners, and customs! As soon as I was convalescent I recommenced studies under a tutor, and there made the acquaintance of Clifford Mecham, of whom much more is to follow.

From Jersey I went to a private crammer in Gower Street, where I was as miserable as a boy could well be, though the kindness of both Mr. and Mrs. Howard was unbounded. I learnt little or nothing, and no pressure was put on me—doubtless by order, as I had scarcely recovered from my illness. I know no place where one can be so lonely as in London, and my leisure hours dragged on wearily between the squares and British Museum.

The Chartist riots were at this time threatened, and our biggest boys were enrolled as special constables. I went once to a meeting in John Street, and heard a man called Jones inveigh against everything and everybody. From Gower Street I went to Addiscombe for my examination. I can well remember my being put on in *Caesar* before an assistant-master. I wish Mark Twain could have a copy of my translation; the master said nothing, shut his eyes, and finally said wearily, "That will do." I knew my fate was sealed. I fancy I did equally badly in every other department. The mathematical paper contained questions that were Greek to me; so I was told to leave my name and address at the porter's lodge, and came away. I need scarcely say I was plucked.

My sister who had nursed me through my illness wrote again to Lord Dinorben, and he managed to effect an exchange for a direct appointment. Thus the idle boy got after all into the Honourable East India Company's service.

CHAPTER II

INDIA

THE excitement of getting my outfit was delightful, and on February 20, 1849, I got my commissions. I put it in the plural, because it was necessary in those days for me to have two. My Queen's commission was signed by the hero of Scinde, and countersigned by the great historian of the Peninsular War. My Company's commission was signed by Sir Henry Pottinger.

I was to reach India by the then somewhat new overland route, and I was put under the care of Captain Moresby, an officer of the Royal Navy, who had joined the P. and O. service. My first hours when we got out to sea were anything but pleasant, but the thought of being the actual possessor of a sword, gun, pistols, and uniform went far to comfort me. What a mite I must have been! Captain Moresby was most kind to me; I remember his bringing me a glass of brandy-and-water in one hand and a huge biscuit in the other. He made me drink the liquid, and then said, "Now, boy, go on eating that biscuit till it is finished; never mind being sick, you go on eating." His remedy was a good one; I soon got better.

What an imposing thing a P. and O. steamer was in those days, with sepoys in uniform, and a sentry always over the Captain's cabin, an excellent band, and no end of etiquette!

At Malta I landed with a lot of youngsters, and nearly had my head broken for trying to interfere with a Maltese who was beating his wife.

Before we reached Alexandria two cadets had quarrelled about some fair lady on board, and were going to fight a duel with their new swords; but Captain Moresby, hearing of it, threatened them with irons, and all blew over.

At Alexandria one mad young fellow nearly got into serious trouble. A bridal party was passing, and he jumped up on the donkey behind the bride and kissed her. Whenever anything untoward happened a cry of "*Ripon* ahoy!" brought instant assistance.

We proceeded up the Mahmoudieh Canal, and my modest eyes were somewhat shocked at the nudity of the children along the banks. We shipped on to another steamer at the junction with the Nile, and travelled far more comfortably but scarcely faster, as we were eternally running on sand-banks. We had a very fat passenger on board, and we made his life miserable by asking him every time we stuck to go to the stern to lighten the bows; this occurred several times during the night, much to the poor man's disgust.

Shepheard, the original proprietor of the now celebrated hotel, was on board, and he had some of the then newly invented gun-cotton. One day, whilst showing us that it did not act with a downward action, he exploded some on his hand and injured himself.

Of course at Cairo we did the usual sights, and then prepared to cross the desert in caravans. The purser on board the *Ripon* had told us beforehand to make up our parties, and I found I was put with a whole lot of girls and women. My *amour propre* was terribly hurt, for I felt that I was only put with them because I was so young and innocent. I had my revenge afterwards.

What a journey it was across the desert for delicate women and children to undertake! I can now remember with horror our being cramped up for so many hours, and the beastly dirt of the resting-places. We had a baby in our party, and I pitied the poor mother and infant so much that the maternal necessities of the situation were less difficult to bear. At last Suez came in sight, not before more than one mirage had raised false hopes.

We had on board Colonel Outram (afterwards the celebrated Sir James); he was hurrying out to try to rejoin before all our Punjaub troubles were over.

When we arrived at Aden, as it was dark, no passengers were allowed to land. Colonel Outram was the exception; but when the mail-boat came alongside, as soon as she had received her mails some half-dozen of us slipped on board. In vain the official in charge protested; a sharp rap over the knuckles of the man holding on by the rope made him let go, and off we drifted.

On landing we got at the hotel some villainous coffee for which we paid enormously, and then we sat down to play cards. The game was *vingt-et-un;* I shall never forget that game. I was a very unskilled player, and my luck was abominable. I lost all the money I had with me, and had not the courage to give up playing. Others had also lost their ready money, and paper I. O. U.'s were adopted. Oh, the horror of those moments! I did not know how I should ever redeem mine. I had a letter of credit on board for £100, but that was payable only at Madras. I was miserable. Luckily my deal came, and I had more than singular luck. I had redeemed my paper notes, and was about to try to retire, when I heard a voice behind me saying, "You young blackguards, what are you doing?—you're gambling." Some one ventured a "No, sir." "Yes, you are; look at those paper I. O. U.'s in the saucer." It was Colonel Outram. He was very angry, but eventually said, "I will not report you, on one condition—that you burn all those papers, and promise me never to gamble again." The papers were burnt, the promise made. "Now then, boys, come and have supper with me." He gave us as good a supper as the hotel afforded, and then sent us on board. I think I may say we all worshipped him, and I can add that to this day I have kept my promise.

Such was my first interview with the great and good Outram. I shall never see his like again.

Nothing eventful occurred during the rest of the voyage. I made the acquaintance of Sir F. Goldsmid (then Captain), which proved of service to me later on.

I am unable to fix the date of my arrival at Madras. The landing in the Massulah boats was immense fun; I felt a pang at parting with so many nice companions, and a sense of loneliness stole over me as I stepped over the ship's side.

Letters had been handed to me on board—one from my sister, who was married to a chaplain quartered at Vellore, begging me to come to them as soon as possible; also recommending me to accept the kind invitation of Major Maclean, who not only sent a *peon* (native orderly) to hand me his invitation, but gave him instructions to see me and my baggage safe to his house.

Another letter reached me which deserves special notice. It was from a Colonel Brown, who held some high appointment at Madras. It seems that he and his wife made a point of inviting all young cadets to accept their hospitality, and to look after them and see they got into no bad ways or evil hands. Their hospitality was unbounded, and they had a special bungalow in their compound (grounds) which was placed at the disposal of their guests. No hotels existed in those days, and many a friendless boy must have felt grateful for their kind protection.

It is not easy to give an idea of one's astonishment at being suddenly thrown in the midst of a new world. One thing I most fully remember, and that was my embarrassment at so frequently meeting native females in what seemed to me very scanty clothing. The Macleans had a large family of young children, and, as each had its own separate ayah, and I was not allowed to go out in the midday sun, I was eternally confronted with dusky houris carrying sweet pale-faced little mites. How devoted they were to them! I very nearly killed the youngest of these said mites. I was swinging her gently in the verandah when the swing came down. Luckily the child was deposited on a heap of cushions, and came to no grief. Major Maclean had noticed that the staple which held the swing was loose, and had told the head-servant to see to it—which he did by spitting on a bit of paper and putting it back : hence the catastrophe.

No words can express the kindness of these good people. They saw to everything for me. Setting out on a journey in those days was very different from what it is now. No railways or stages. I had to get a horse, baggage animals, tents, bullock-carts, and, last not least, servants. All these things were procured for me of the best quality, especially the servants, whose name was legion.

I got my route from the Quartermaster-General, and set out to do duty with the 52nd Madras Native Infantry, which was quartered at Vellore. It was a great leap to take from being a school-boy to being my own master with many souls dependent on me; but all had to go through the same experiences in those days. I was lucky I had only 200 miles to go; many had 1200.

On arrival at Vellore I was welcomed by my sister and her husband. My first duty was to call and report myself to the Brigadier, to the Colonel commanding, and then on all who were on my sister's visiting list.

I was extremely lucky in my regiment. The 52nd was a good one, officered by a set of well-educated gentlemen. I was more than lucky in my Adjutant, the one man in a regiment in whose hands one may truly say the fate and future of a youngster rests.

Coote was not only a good soldier, but pre-eminently a gentleman, and to him I owe a very deep debt of gratitude for precepts and example. I must mention one kindness, for it was a kindness of the true sort. Like many others, I fancied I had a grievance, and wrote to him in consequence. His answer was that of a friend, and he wound up by telling me, that, like a young bear, all my troubles were before me; they might or might not be serious, but in any circumstances I was never to ride out to meet them. That letter was written forty-eight years ago, but I have never forgotten it.

It was pleasant to see the way the officers identified themselves with their men. They used to take them out shooting when occasion admitted; cricket was as keenly encouraged as in an English county. Their men were obedient and loyal, and yet this excellent regiment was disbanded because the Bengal sepoys mutinied.

I have always thought the disbanding of four Madras regiments after the Mutiny the greatest blunder, and in the worst possible taste.

My sister's house was a good long way from the cantonment, which was inconvenient as regards attending drill. I was very happy there, but got a tremendous fright on one occasion. I was just going to bed, and had put out my candle, leaving only the small oil-lamp invariably left burning in India. In shuffling off my slippers I felt I was bitten on the toe, and I saw something wriggling into the corner of the room.

A cobra manilla immediately crossed my mind, and that meant death in a couple of hours. My first impulse was to lie down and die quietly without any fuss; my second was to tell my sister, so that no one might be accused of foul play. This I adopted. In great distress my sister came to me, and a most powerful dose of brandy was administered; then questions were asked, and finally some one suggested that the snake should be found. On looking in the corner a large centipede was discovered; so I had not to die so soon as I had expected. The beast was killed, and I suffered only from much brandy and a swelled toe.

By this time I had advanced sufficiently with my ordinary drill to warrant my being initiated in the mysteries of sword exercise; and as this instruction was to be imparted to us cadets at mid-day under the shelter of the Adjutant's roof, out of the broiling sun, it became necessary for me to attend drill three times a day. This was too much for me, living at so great a distance from cantonments; so I had most reluctantly to leave my sister and share a bungalow nearer my work.

I was fortunate enough to find a chum in my old Jersey school-companion Mecham. He was a nice quiet fellow, and we got on well together. He was given to flute-playing, and often sat out under the shade of the plantains discoursing sweet melody. One day I took a bath in a large well-shaped sort of tank from which our garden was daily watered. I lost my footing and went into about ten feet of water; the sides were so steep that I could not get a hold to save myself, and would certainly have been drowned had not Mecham in an interval of his music heard my cries and rescued me.

Our joint housekeeping was not of long duration, for Mecham was posted to some regiment up country; so I had to look out for another chum. I found one in another school-fellow of Shooters Hill renown.

Vellore had in former years three regiments stationed there: now it had only one, and two old mess-houses were in consequence vacant. We occupied one, and the large centre room which had been the mess-room now served us as a gallery for practising with pellet bows.

Few people would believe how expert we became with this singular and somewhat formidable weapon. Feats of almost incredible prowess were reported to have been done by two brothers whose names I have forgotten.

I am quite sure I must have been a very cheeky

youngster; one of my indiscretions is worth recording, as it brings into strong relief the forbearance of a good and gallant soldier.

Our Brigadier, a man of magnificent stature and build, was more than commonly kind to me, and his daughter made rather a pet of me. On the anniversary of my birthday I determined to give a big lunch, and I desired no one's presence more than the Brigadier's; accordingly I wrote and asked him to come and lunch. Only fancy a cadet inviting his Brigadier! I certainly meant no impertinence; but having at home mixed with all sorts and conditions of men, I saw no harm in, as I thought, showing my appreciation of the good man's kindness.

I got a note from the Brigade Major to say the Brigadier wanted to see me next day at twelve o'clock. I put on my uniform and went. When I arrived, the Brigade Major was in attendance. The giant rose up and came towards me, and looking down on me said, "You young vagabond, you have no business to be giving a lunch party to the cantonment, and still less business to ask your Brigadier to it. Do you hear? mind you don't do it again." I was speechless. Then putting his hand on my shoulder he said with a laugh, "You are a cheeky youngster; now go and talk to my daughter till lunch is ready." On the day of my lunch a dozen of champagne arrived with the Brigadier's compliments.

We were a very happy, friendly lot. Only once after a wine-party there arose a desperate quarrel which ended in a challenge. All was hushed up next day, and this was the last time I ever heard of a duel being proposed in serious earnest.

We used to go out shikaring, and no difference was ever made between us doing duty wallahs and the officers belonging to the regiment. All were equally kind, from the commanding officer downwards.

My health was anything but good at this time; I was seized constantly with a sort of violent colic. The doctor was very attentive, but his chief remedy for everything was "brown soap." He used to say, "You've fever, you have, and you'll be worse before you're better; take congee water, and use plenty of brown soap."

So delicate was my health at this time, that my retirement from the army was contemplated. Who knows what might have happened?—I might have become an archbishop like an old comrade of mine.

The time was drawing near for my departure; the long delayed *Gazette* at last appeared which sealed my fate. I was posted as a second lieutenant to the 1st Madras Fusiliers, a European regiment that had a glorious record. The 52nd officers paid me the compliment of asking me to apply to join them, and many friends strongly urged me not to accept the appointment, the reasons urged being that European regiments were fast and expensive. I would not listen to such arguments, for I felt in my inner mind that if I could not resist a certain amount of temptation I was not good for much.

What a break up it was!—some half-dozen cadets who had lived together like brothers scattered all over the great length and breadth of the Presidency, never to meet again. I often think, taking all things into consideration, what a good lot we were, for India in those days was very different from what it is now. All who then joined the Indian army were virtually banished from home for ten years. Marriage for a youngster was almost an impossibility: thus the custom of keeping a black mistress, or, as it was sometimes termed, "buying a native dictionary," was not only common, but often openly recommended by our superiors. Yet on the whole we boys were as a body fairly virtuous.

Now, let over-sensitive readers skip the next paragraph.

I do not mean for one moment to advocate the customs that existed in those days, but I do think the evil said to be produced by English officers *lowering* themselves by such acts was much exaggerated. The natives themselves were in no degree lowered; the habit broke no caste, offended no religious prejudice. On the contrary, it improved their social position in most cases; and it is very doubtful whether India would ever have been the great Empire it now is if some of our greatest men had not gained the affection of their coloured mistresses and thereby a knowledge of native affairs. The awful and sickening prostitution of young girls by the priests of the Hindoo temples for the sake of money is another thing.

It must not be supposed that we were all angels of light and virtue; we had our boyish escapades.

I well remember the Queen's birthday, 1850. I continued to drink the Queen's health long after it was necessary, and unfortunately considered that the glass used for such a toast would be polluted by being used for any other purpose henceforth. My mess-bill that month was excessive, and my headache next morning a caution!

With my appointment to the 1st Madras Fusiliers came also my instructions to join a detachment of cadets and recruits of my regiment under one of our officers on its arrival at Vellore. Our leave-takings were somewhat sad; I felt being severed from friends, and again being cast amongst strangers.

Before taking leave of Vellore I must mention a few very interesting characters I came across. First and foremost was Captain Wilson of the 52nd, whose career had been singularly 'eventful. He served with the Bengal Army during the disastrous Afghan campaign, and by reason of his intimate knowledge of Persian[1] volunteered to carry despatches to the relieving force. His disguise as a Persian horse-dealer was complete, and deceived all with whom he came in contact; but he could not deceive the brute creation. One night as he lay at a caravanserai, he was awakened by something pressing his throat, with two

[1] Captain Wilson had been *attaché* to his uncle, Sir John McNeil, at Teheran.

great glaring eyes staring at him. Of course he thought all was up, but to his joy found it to be only a poor Newfoundland dog, whose master doubtless had been killed in the Khyber Pass. The faithful animal no doubt had wandered for days seeking his late owner, and by instinct had discovered Wilson to be a European, and so clung to him. Wilson's difficulty henceforth was to avoid being identified as a European by the constant and affectionate presence of the dog.

Another singular character whose acquaintance I made, was an old trumpeter, whose name, if I remember rightly, was Slade. He had been trumpeter to Gillespie's Light Horse Battery of the 4th Dragoons at Arcot, and had sounded the assembly when the news of the mutiny at Vellore arrived. He said that Gillespie's guns burst open the fort gate. Slade had a mania for cutting sticks; he used to go out into the jungle in the cool season and cut hundreds, and then polish them up during the hot season. He never used the same stick two days running. I do not think he sold them, but I know he gave them away.

Amongst links with the past was the old sepoy in charge of the public bungalow; he had been orderly to Colonel Wellesley at Seringapatam, and was very proud of having been so. Some enthusiast hailing from north of the Tweed had taught the old fellow a Scotch song, which he would sing fairly intelligibly when in the humour.

The officers of those days were on much more friendly terms with their men than in later years, and I am bound to say that the officers of the 52nd were as intimate with their sepoys as the rules of the service would permit.

In due course of time the detachment of my regiment arrived at Vellore. I was introduced to my new commandant by Coote, who was good enough to give me an excellent character.

After two days' halt we commenced our journey. What a merry lot we were! I now made the acquaintance of Sladen of Ours, who was destined to become my lifelong friend. I remember as well as if it were yesterday, my feeling of dismay at finding him so much more proficient than myself in Hindustani. I rather prided myself on my colloquial knowledge, but I found him far and away my superior.

As I happened to be the senior of the party, the officer commanding made me a sort of Adjutant, and Sladen the Quartermaster and interpreter. Our duties were very light, as we had only about a dozen men to look after.

Nothing of particular interest occurred during the march. We were in medical charge of a half caste apothecary—not a very liberal kind of treatment where so many Europeans' lives were at stake; however, that could not be helped, we had to make the best of it. At one halting-place the infant of our commanding officer was taken ill. When some one was sent for the apothecary, it was found he was drunk. I had to put him under arrest, and on my reporting the circumstance to our commanding officer, his wife in despair asked me to see the child, as of course the apothecary could not.

How the inspiration seized me I know not, but I made up my mind it was teeth; so putting my finger in its mouth, I felt what I fancied was the germ of a tooth. I used a good amount of pressure, the child screamed, the mother seized her ill-used infant, giving me a look of anger; but the tooth was through, and the baby suffered no more, and I—, well, I became "Sir Oracle."

On arrival at Bangalore we made a short halt, in order that my friend the apothecary might be tried. I was principal witness; it was my first court-martial, and I was nervous. The prisoner tried to worry me, but Colonel Keyes of the 15th Hussars, the President, soon stopped that.

Many of the 15th Hussars were old friends of our commanding officer; amongst others, Nolan of Balaclava renown, and I remember even in those days his hobby was that cavalry could do anything against infantry if properly led.

In due time we reached Bellary, having hurried so as to enable us to be present at a ball to be given by the regiment to the Commander-in-Chief; thus my first introduction to my brother officers was at a great function. Everything was well done, and I felt proud of my surroundings.

A gentleman seeing me in the uniform of the Fusiliers came up and asked for an introduction to a very pretty girl. I told him I had only joined that very day and knew no one, but would ask one of our stewards to do the needful. The introduction was accomplished, the next day he proposed and was accepted; then continued his journey to Madras, came back to Bellary, and was married after a couple of days. Things were done quickly in those times.

As Sladen and I had shared the same tent on the march, so now we shared the same bungalow—an arrangement which tended greatly to my advantage.

Edward Bosc Sladen was no ordinary man. He was in my opinion certainly one of the most talented men I ever met; he almost attained the nature of a genius; and I believe his feeling of superiority over others often marred his success in life. He was so brilliant a classic that he told me Dr. Don, the celebrated head-master of Oswestry School, and Dr. Kennedy of Shrewsbury, both entreated his father not to accept a cadetship for him, as it would ruin his chances of becoming the most renowned classic of his day.

The very last time I ever called by appointment to see him was in Lowndes Square. He had not come in, and I was shown into his writing-room; there on his table lay an open Horace with a translation of one of the odes scarcely yet dry. This evidently was his relaxation, and this too more than forty years after he left school.

This is a good opportunity for relating a very amusing incident illustrating Sladen's scholarship. I forget at which school, Oswestry or Shrewsbury, it occurred; it does not matter. It seems the boys got rather tired of apple-puffs, which were served day after day. One boy, whom we will call Jenkins, was loud in his denunciation of the puffs, but it was noticed he ate them voraciously all the same. The thing became a joke, and Sladen did in Greek certain lines which the head-master rendered in English as follows:

"Jenkins ate three, then called the puffs no treat;
Had he liked puffs, what would the glutton eat?"

I wish I could give the original Greek: it must have been splendid, for the head-master most highly commended the lines, and the boys according to custom got a holiday. To me Sladen's scholarship was of inestimable value, for by this time I had learnt, I am glad to say, how fearfully uneducated and ignorant I was.

I determined to try to make up the lost ground, and Sladen cheerfully aided me in my plodding over Virgil, Ovid, and Horace. I also got an old volume of Cape's Mathematics, and used to do a certain number of what we called *sums* every day. As a goodly number of English Classics were to be had in Bellary, reading people not caring to burden themselves with trash, I filled up my time with such excellent companions.

Here let me say one word about the old Company's officer of that day. I can safely say I heard more good conversation in those days amongst soldiers than I have ever heard since. I heard my dear old Brigadier at Vellore cap quotation against quotation with the Bishop of Madras till my ears tingled with delight; of course

I thought the soldier won. Sir Mark Cubbon at Bangalore, so charmingly alluded to by Lady Canning, was a finished classic. I have heard Anstruther of the Artillery, Paddy Poole commanding the 5th Native Infantry, and Arnold of Ours keep a large mess-party spellbound by their classical lore when at Tonghoo.

I think we were by no means inferior to any class (bar the University men) in our general education, modern languages excepted; in those we were deficient. I did a little in the Hindustani whilst at Bellary, but never got beyond passing my second examination. Sladen, however, at once passed brilliantly as an interpreter.

A few words regarding my new regiment may now not inopportunely be introduced. I had, as may be remembered, been warned against joining on account of its fastness and extravagant habits. I found all this a complete falsehood. The officers, from the Colonel downwards, were quite as temperate as those of any regiment I have subsequently met. It is true that one or two of the old hands who had recently come from the temptations of Secunderabad thought plain water unwholesome, but that did not interfere with a strict performance of their duty on parade or elsewhere. The Adjutant was a good one, and consequently the men were as fairly drilled and disciplined as regiments serving in India usually were. There is no greater incentive to laxity than keeping a regiment too long on foreign service.

We were fairly worked, and no officer was allowed to go about cantonments except in uniform with sword. This in days of stocks and buttoned up frock-coats was trying, but no one complained. I never could see the hardship of making officers wear uniform, when the privates are compelled to do so. I think the way in which in this country officers pretend to despise their uniform is scandalous. The present uniform is, to my mind, as comfortable as a shooting suit. If it is too expensive for every-day wear, make it cheaper; but let it always be worn except when on leave, or on such occasions as arise, when flannels or any other costume is desirable.

We had plenty of drill, and a fair amount of field days. Our target practice, or, as we called it, "ball fire," was the most splendid farce imaginable. A target six feet by two was placed at one hundred yards, with a bull's-eye in the centre half a foot in diameter. If a man made a bull's-eye, he shouldered arms and marched home. If three bulls'-eyes were made, the company was excused further practice.

The stupidity of such a custom is self-evident as far as marksmanship was concerned; but it left a greater evil, for in this way many men seldom if ever fired their muskets at all, and, when they did, were so frightened at the kick, that they got to look on target practice as a curse. The ammunition was villainous; the bullets were undersized, and I believe frequently fell out on the ground. What a business the biting off the end of the cartridge-paper was! I have seen men's lips black and bleeding many times during heavy firing in action.

It was no very easy thing to steer clear of parties in those days. Society was divided pretty fairly into two groups: one set was termed "New lights," to whom all such things as balls, races, etc., were anathema; the other, "Worldies," who went in for frivolities. The "New lights" usually made the bid for the new-comers, and urged them to join prayer-meetings and such-like gatherings. It must be confessed that there were many temptations to ally oneself with this sect. I do not think I am unjust in saying that the chief road to staff appointments lay in that direction.

The existence of so marked a division is not to be wondered at in a country where life and death were so vividly before us—where often out of a merry party at breakfast one would be buried before noon next day.

I do not think there was much hypocrisy amongst these Psalm-singers; indeed I mixed much with them, and found them good and charitable in all things but one, and that was the rooted idea that those who did not think as they thought were doomed.

We had a good many Plymouth Brethren both in the regiment and amongst the civil population. They were headed by the Judge. The story goes that a funny old doctor, who had risen from being an apothecary to a high medical position, joined them; after a severe probation he was considered sufficiently elect to be allowed to preach. I do not remember his text, but the gist of his sermon was to prove that the reputed origin of the gods of the Hindoo mythology was absurd. He proceeded to prove his assertion scientifically, anatomically, and physiologically. As there were many women in the meeting, his discourse was not considered edifying, and he was told his preaching was not desirable. He left the sect in wrath, declaring that they did not appreciate the only man who had ever talked any sense from their pulpit.

I managed luckily to keep in, like the Vicar of Bray, I fear, with both sides, and, though I did not attend prayer-meetings, was not considered wholly beyond the pale.

Bellary is a beastly station; they say that there is only a sheet of brown-paper between it and the infernal regions, and that that has been nearly scorched through.

The cantonments are in the midst of an arid plain of black cotton soil. In the centre rises a rock something like the rock of Cashel, and on the top of the rock is a fortress, in which in my time there lived in "durance vile" a Nawab, or "Nabob" as the men called him, a state prisoner whose alleged offence was that of murdering a wife in our territory, but whose real offence lay in having a territory called Kurnool which we wanted.

At the bottom of the rock was another fortress which dominated the bazaar, and in which the main-guard was situated. It was the duty of the officer on main-guard to detach a sergeant's party each day to the upper fortress to take charge of the Nawab, and the officer had to visit the old sinner once a day and ascertain that he was alive and had no complaints. Oh, the fag of going up that rock! It meant a complete change of clothes on return to guard, as every rag on one's body was saturated with perspiration. On reaching the top we usually called out "Nawab," to which the old chap would answer. Then when inquiries were made as to any complaints, the answer sometimes would be anything but complimentary. The old fellow knew a good deal about the officers, and if he liked them would come out and behave civilly. He wore little or no clothing, and let his hair and beard grow untouched.

Sladen was a friend of his, and he often took a turn with him. On the ramparts one day our regiment was drilling on the plain below; the old fellow expressed approval, and Sladen asked him if he would like an army like that. The Nawab grunted an affirmative. "What would you do with it?" was the next question. The answer was, "Throw all heathens like you over the wall;" then he added, "No, I'd keep you, for you might be useful."

The Nawab had a great dislike to being made a show of. He seemed to know by instinct if a stranger was present (I think he had a peep-hole), and if he did not choose to come out nothing would persuade him. The civil magistrate in charge was the only official that could oblige him to show himself.

The story goes that on one occasion a lady friend of the magistrate was bent on seeing the old man. She and her host were conveyed up in a palanquin; on arrival the sergeant of the guard called as usual "Nabob." The old man grunted. The sergeant said, "Come out, Nabob." He replied that he was at his prayers. "You must come out, the big Sahib is here." Then Nabob appeared, but—

oh, horror!—stark naked! The scene can be more easily imagined than described.

I must mention our band and our young tigers. The band was quite unusually excellent. Our band-master was a very celebrated Hanoverian musician, his clarionet-playing being superb; his wife was a professional pianist: thus together they made delightful music.

The regimental badge was a tiger, with the motto "Spectemur agendo" under; consequently whenever practicable we had pet tigers. When I joined there were two dear little pets: they lived with David Brown, our Adjutant; they had to be got rid of when they became older and savage. We also had an antelope; it died of eating soda-water corks, which it picked up in the mess-tent. It never would touch anything that had been breathed on.

Time passed pleasantly, and I got a fair knowledge of my duties. Flogging was common in those days, but I never remember a man flogged except for a crime that fully deserved it, and the sentence was generally approved by his comrades. The men were very well looked after. I took the Bishop of Madras over my company's mess one day; he was much pleased, and said he would gladly strike a bargain never to have a better dinner if he never had a worse.

We were very sociable amongst ourselves, the married officers often asking us youngsters to dine. We were singularly fortunate in our officers' wives: they were charming.

The Adjutant's house used to be open to all for early tea and fruit after parade. This led to an intimacy and good-fellowship with the man, who might otherwise have been, as Sladen termed it, "an active bane." David Brown was a strict but most kind Adjutant, and, whilst every one respected him, no one feared him. He used to call me a cheeky youngster now and again.

We had a most wonderful drill-sergeant in Murphy. He lived solely to study the drill-book. In those days tight white trousers were the fashion, and report had it that Murphy used to put his on damp and let them dry on him. He could manage recruits better than any man living.

At this time urgent private affairs required that I should obtain leave for some months. I went to Major Hill, our senior Major, told him frankly my difficulty, and asked him to help me. He said at once, "You must go away, I will get you leave:" and no sooner had he said it than 'twas done. This was, I think, on a Friday, and on Monday I was off for three months to visit my sister and old friends at Vellore.

My baggage was sent off immediately, so as to have three clear days' start. Sladen accompanied me for eighteen miles of my journey, lending me one of his horses to ride. Then I found my own, which had been sent on, and the first day I did thirty-six miles. As soon as I arrived at a rest-house my servant got me my food, and then packed up and started for the next halting-place. I amused myself as best I could during the day. Books were too heavy to carry, so I took wools to finish a pair of slippers; these served to while away the long hours, and could easily be carried in my pocket.

I rode in a thick pilot coat which answered admirably. It kept me warm during the chilly mornings—for I generally started at 2 a.m.—and kept the heat out after sunrise. I did the journey between Bellary and Bangalore in an incredibly short time, considering that I kept my baggage in view. From Bangalore I travelled *dâk* (posted).

About two months of my leave had run when I got an official letter from the Adjutant to say I was to join the regiment on the line of march to Madras, as we had been ordered to join the expedition to Burmah, with which country war had been declared. It was joyful news to me for more reasons than one. A letter from Sladen informed me that he had sold all his furniture and mine by auction; so I was relieved on that point.

My endeavour to catch the regiment was a stern chase of anything but an agreeable nature. Cholera had broken out on the line of march, and at each bungalow at which I halted I was told by the sepoy in charge that many of our men had been buried there.

It was a sad and lonely ride. At last by making a forced march I overtook my comrades at about half-past eleven in the morning. I had barely had time to wash and have some food, when a message came that the Major wanted me. It appeared that he wished me to go round the hospital-tent with him. My name had been mentioned as having arrived, and, as all conversation turned on cholera at that time, the rumour got abroad that I had died of the scourge. This had a very depressing effect, and Major Hill thought the best way of dispelling the gloom was for me to show myself alive in the sick-tent.

Reader, I do not know if you have ever visited a hospital tent when full of cholera patients; it is a sad sight, especially when the sufferers are your own comrades. Some looked up at me piteously; others took no notice—they were already in the far-off land. To some few of my own company I spoke and bade them be of good cheer. Oh, how I longed for healing power!

That night a terrific storm of wind and rain swept over us. Tents went down on all sides, the hospital tent amongst others; many, no doubt, were suffocated before the wet folds of canvas could be raised from off them; but cholera disappeared from that moment, and we could enter Madras with a clean bill of health.

Some may be still living who remember this storm. I know I had to escort several ladies to my sister's bungalow at Poonamallee, which was close by, and at which they got shelter and dry clothes.

The regiment marched on to Madras; but to my intense disgust I was left behind in charge of invalids, and of the women and children who were to join the European depôt at that place.

What a grief it was to me! I followed the colours as far as I could, and then mournfully returned, bearing with me the last fond messages entrusted to me by officers who had taken farewell of their wives. "The girl I left behind me" is a pretty enough tune to march to, but the sight of wives and daughters left behind in the first hours of their sorrow is indeed a sad one. By some lucky circumstance other arrangements were made in reference to the invalids, etc., and I was directed to rejoin.

I now come to a scene which some might be tempted to leave out, but I prefer to tell things as they happened. On arrival at Madras, the regiment was encamped on the so-called island, a place in the centre of the town, surrounded by water, but connected with the mainland by two or more bridges.

Here we were divested of our accoutrements, and our muskets and bayonets taken from us. Now a soldier without arms and accoutrements is worse than a fish out of water. There was no possible way of keeping the men within bounds; if we had put picquets at the bridges, they would have waded to the town. Our Adjutant did all in his power: the roll was called every hour, prisoners were put in a tent, and sentries put over them armed with sticks. Did any one ever dream of a soldier hitting a comrade with a stick!

Well, of course nearly half the regiment were loafing about. They had thousands of rupees in the savings bank on leaving Bellary; it was almost all frittered away in Black Town. The chief amusement seemed to consist in hiring a palanquin coach and being driven about, sitting on the roof waving handkerchiefs tied on sticks, treating every one who would be treated.

On the morning appointed for our embarkation, as we marched to the beach we were joined by comrades from every hole and corner; and as a matter of fact we started with one man more than our roster, for a plucky fellow, of whom more hereafter, sooner than be left behind, ran away from hospital and came to the ship's side on a catamaran. Horace has indited an ode in honour of the man who first trusted his carcase in a fragile boat. He might have written more eloquently of the man who trusted himself on a catamaran in the Madras surf, with myriads of sharks ready to devour him.

No doubt much was said in reference to this event, but what was the head-quarter staff about? Why march us into Madras several days before embarkation? Why encamp us in such a place, and why take away the only emblems of discipline a soldier understands? I have since those days embarked thousands of men and horses. There never was any necessity to give up arms or accoutrements, neither were the men summoned to the beach until the moment for embarkation had arrived.

To my mind the staff at Madras was wholly inefficient, and I do not think they were over and above good anywhere. Bookworms and men with interest were the recipients of staff appointments, without reference to their other qualifications; so when a difficulty arose and technical knowledge was required, they were found wanting. I must except one department, and that was the Commissariat. No better organization exists than the Indian Commissariat, and after experience of Pegu and the Mutiny I still hold the same opinion.

In the Crimea the Commissariat got all the blame, but they scarcely deserved it. Their mistakes were the mistakes of a faulty system, which they did not originate, and by the storm of November 14 they were overwhelmed by misfortune.

CHAPTER III

RANGOON

On September 7 we embarked for Rangoon, in H.M.S. *Sphynx*, and the H. E. I. Company's s. *Mozuffer*, which towed the s.s. *Graham*.

If our voyage was lacking in incident, it certainly was not so in discomfort; even Mark Tapley himself might have been jolly without discredit. A troopship is never over and above comfortable, but a man-of-war improvised into a transport is the perfection of misery. We were crowded so that some sixteen officers had only a small place to wash and dress in. We slept on deck, and the mosquitoes as we neared land had a splendid time of it. Arnold Ward of Ours suggested that the last joined recruit should be tied naked in the rigging in order to draw them from us. Every one approved his suggestion, but strange to say it was not carried out. In addition to our other discomforts we were handicapped by having to tow the *Graham*, and her faulty steering not only gave rise to fearful swearing on the part of our captain and first lieutenant, but more than once the hawser broke, and we were delayed in mending it. We sighted the Andaman Islands—a spot so lonely that no one, I should fancy, would ever wish to see more of it than we did.

The approach to Rangoon is very tame and uninteresting, but the first glimpse of the town itself, with its magnificent pagoda and gilt *tee* glittering in the sunshine, is fine, and its background of forest is very beautiful.

The river too at the jetty is a magnificent outspread of water. We landed on the 14th, and formed up on the Bund, and then marched off towards the Great Pagoda, which is called Shoay Dagon. Our strength was forty officers and nine hundred and sixty rank-and-file—something like a regiment!

Our route lay along a broad flat road bordered on either side by innumerable small pagodas, more or less dilapidated. These were covered from top to bottom with masses of the most lovely maidenhair fern; whilst at intervals there arose topes of tall trees in the fullest foliage, having here and there on their branches some sort of crane or stork in the whitest plumage, looking like huge white blossoms. To me the scene was enchanting. I longed to fall out and gather ferns and flowers.

We were, I think, under canvas for the first few days until another regiment left for the front; then we occupied their huts. I was said to occupy the one that had been Wolseley's. I found written in chalk on the shutter some words in Burmese, which I found very useful.

After getting into ship-shape we began to have a look round. The results of our bombardment were strikingly evident, but the futility of our round shot was most plain. They merely went clean through the teak palisades of the stockades, leaving a tidy loophole for musketry for those inside. Wherever a shell had burst desolation was very apparent.

Bowen and I used to wander as far as was safe into the surrounding jungle, I in search of ferns and flowers, and dear old Bowen, as he said, "in search of dead Burmese, who might perchance have jewels about their persons." We found several, but no jewels, only an intolerable stench.

What a curious place Rangoon was in those days! So far as I can recollect there was only the one main road aforesaid running from the river to the foot of the pagoda. As you neared the pagoda you came across numerous

poonghie (priests) houses or monasteries, and behind
these were native houses forming the bazaar. This part
of the town was alive with soldiers and sailors of every
description, type, and nationality; then but a few yards
further on either side, jungle, forest, and absolute solitude
reigned.

The jungle had been cleared away to make room for
our huts, and a further strip had been cleared just sufficient for a regiment to parade. On this very ground
after the guards had been marched off, our Adjutant has
shot snipe. I don't know what an enterprising enemy
could have done, but the whole position seemed very unsafe, for we were entirely hemmed in, and there seemed to
be no outlying picquets.

One of our first duties was to try Private Smith afore-
mentioned by court-martial for deserting from hospital
and joining. There was a curious and somewhat romantic
history attached to this man. It seems that whilst at
Bellary he got weary of soldiering, and, seeing no other
way out of his life-long servitude, he loaded his musket
and fired a bullet through his hand, hoping thereby to
get his discharge. He was tried by court-martial, and
sentenced to a somewhat lengthy imprisonment. As no
European was allowed to undergo a long sentence except
in the military prison situated in a healthy spot on the
sea-side near Madras, our friend was sent down there.
It seems that, having served his time, he was sent to
hospital, and, finding his old regiment bound for active
service, bolted off and risked his life on a catamaran to
join us. The story went that he was refused admittance
on board the head-quarter vessel, so came to ours, where
he was hospitably received.

Well, I was on the court that sat and tried him at
Rangoon, and I remember we were reluctantly obliged to
find him guilty, but sentenced him to the very smallest
imprisonment in our power. The proceedings were re-

turned for revision, but we respectfully adhered to our former sentence. The proceedings were read out on parade with the additional words, "Confirmed, but not approved." Private Smith, I think, subsequently distinguished himself, and rose to be a sergeant.

My dear old Brigadier McNeill commanded our brigade, and was as usual more than kind to me, and I saw a good deal of him. Shortly after our arrival the 1st Bengal Fusiliers arrived. They were our twin regiment, we having left our left wing to form the nucleus of a Bengal European regiment after Plassey in 1757. We had not met for just one hundred years. Of course it was a fair and fitting occasion for an interchange of hospitalities.

The Bengal Fusiliers (now the Royal Munster Fusiliers) had a most celebrated batch of Moselle on tap, and, when it came to our turn to dine with them, the said wine was heavily punished, for they were a good hospitable lot. Towards the small hours it was said the two colonels and majors formed rallying square in the centre of the mess-room for mutual support against any enemy. One adjutant, a canny Scot who never lost his head, was seen holding on to the post of the verandah, shaking his fist at the moon, ejaculating, "How many times I've told you, all unauthorized lights out at eight o'clock," whilst the band-president politely told the band-master he "need not conduct standing on his head."

But how about myself? Well, it so happened I was on duty, so with me it was a case of *muzzle* instead of Moselle.

We had jolly times together; I wonder if the whole world ever produced two better or finer regiments. We stood at the General's inspection 1001 bayonets, and our average height was 5 ft. 8 in. Our men were bronzed and hardy. I think in justice that the Bengal Fusiliers were a smarter looking lot; they made their men clean shave, which gave them a younger and smarter appearance; they had, too, a goodly lot of medal men in their ranks, which always adds to the appearance as well as the credit of a regiment.[1] I have every reason to speak well of them, for their kindness was unbounded. When I met with a severe accident afterwards at Pegu, I got an invitation to go down to Rangoon as a mess-guest for change of air.

About this time cholera broke out, and caused a gloom to settle on the force. General Steele, our Divisional Commandant, encouraged sports to enliven and cheer up the men, and a theatre was also prospected by a stage-struck doctor attached to some Bengal regiment. I say *stage-struck*, for he evidently had had theatricals in his mind's eye, and had brought with him an endless assortment of properties. I unfortunately forget his name, though I well remember his undeniable talent and good-nature. Much opposition was raised to this theatre by those to whom everything connected with the stage was anathema. They did not formulate their objections in exactly that way, but declared that the building (a poonghie house) we had set our hearts on was too near a magazine, and would catch fire and endanger the whole place. It proved otherwise. But whilst we had, on the one hand, to combat those who denounced all such performances, we had on the other to encounter all kinds of difficulties in the shape of stage, scenery, dresses, etc. There was no costumier handy or stage-carpenter within hail, but our doctor-manager surmounted all obstacles with a courage that defied defeat. Luckily the fleet had canvas galore, and still more luckily we had Atkinson of the Bengal Engineers, who was a host in himself with pencil and brush.

Reader, have you ever seen *Curry and Rice?* If not, get it, and you will be well repaid your trouble. You

[1] The Bengal Fusiliers lost 412 men killed and wounded at Ferozshah and Sobraon out of 650, so naturally had many young soldiers in the ranks.

will see what a treasure we had in our principal scene-painter. Glover, of the 51st K. O. L. I., and I washed in sky, etc., and Glover filled in other parts, for he was a fair draughtsman, and then Atkinson finished off, leaving tableaux that were the admiration of all beholders. The first pieces selected by our manager were *The Wreck Ashore* and *Charles II.* I think, on the whole, they were good selections. I have not the plays before me, so must trust to memory for names. Glover took the part of Bella, and a more lovely heroine never trod the boards; he got up admirably. I, by reason of my height and beardlessness, was cast for Alice. I remember my dress was a crimson material called, I think, Persian, made by a regimental tailor; it had much white braid, taken from bandsmen's coats, sewn on the skirt, which was rather short. The bodice was black velvet, with no end of muslin about the sleeves; my neck and arms were bare; my wig was sandy tow, Bella's black. There was a little difficulty about our figures, but the doctor, who understood female anatomy, arranged that with tow and cotton-wool. Trafford of the 51st was my lover, much to my detriment, as will appear hereafter. Groom of Ours (afterwards killed at Lucknow) was Grampus, and our manager took the rôle of hero. We had a goodly number of rehearsals—indeed, more than usual for amateurs, for our manager really understood his business.

It was during our numerous rehearsals that I got an insight into the Bengal sepoys' style of doing "sentry-go." Whenever we went to rehearsal we found the guard, placed at the theatre to ensure safety from fire, lying perfectly devoid of uniform and accoutrements, the sentry lolling at his ease with only a ramrod in hand; he used to call out towards the expiration of his two hours' tour to the next for duty to put on his uniform and relieve him. Perhaps as it was only a theatre that had to be guarded, this *laissez aller* method was considered sufficient.

But to the play. Whilst at Bellary an order had been issued that infantry officers might wear moustaches. Oh, the joy! Alas! the chagrin of the cavalry; they would hardly speak to us for months after. Well, from the day of the promulgation of that order, my one cherished idea was to have a hirsute appendage to my upper lip.

At the time of my being cast for Alice a faint streak something like washed-out gingerbread had appeared, and it was not without terrible communings with myself that with a pang I resolved to sacrifice my incipient moustache to my sense of fitness as a performer. Reader, the reason of this digression on little hairy nothings will appear hereafter.

At last the fatal day arrived. The whole force was in a fever of expectation, the house was absolutely crammed, free list suspended, etc. Our band formed the orchestra, and struck up the overture to *Haidée* in which a lovely waltz is introduced. Bella, in her white muslin, was standing behind the slips, the stage was clear, the music too fascinating, we buckled to and commenced waltzing. Alas! the drop-scene was very thin, so we were clearly visible to the audience, who set up an immense cheer, which caused our manager to order an immediate retreat.

The curtain rose, and Bella's appearance was the signal for a burst of applause, with remarks friendly but certainly familiar from the Jack Tars in the gallery. My appearance was not so favourable; some brutal horse-artilleryman called out, "Gummy about the 'ocks." My dress, as I have said, was short, and I dare say my ankles were not as fine as sweet Trilby's, but he need not have called attention to the fact. Incident number one I remember was that Bella, after hearing the report of her lover's death, had to appear in the next scene pale and livid. We were all fearfully hot and perspiring, and, there being no dresser, had to valet ourselves. Our only powder was flour, and Bella, in her hurry to put on the flour to make herself look pale, dabbed it on, and was called on before she had time to tone it down, appearing consequently with a round white patch on her cheek, which caused intense merriment. It was only when I joined her that I saw the cause and managed to remove it.

Incident number two occurred during the attack on our house by Grampus. I had to seize a gun, load it, and fire at the villain. I unfortunately did the loading in correct military fashion, which was received with cheers, and, instead of firing in the air, I fired point-blank at Grampus, and very nearly blew his head off.

Incident number three was at the conclusion of an act, when I had to faint in my lover's (Trafford's) arms. I, of course, had my eyes shut, and was fainting most properly, but he, stupid fellow, never looked to see how we were standing, and the roller came on my bare shoulder and took the whole skin right off. There was a go! How on earth to stop the bleeding was the problem. But our inimitable doctor was not to be beaten; he burnt me with some vile stuff, and then put lots of flour on to hide the mark, and so we were able to bring the piece to a conclusion. *Charles II.* went even better, and our efforts were crowned with success. Of course our performance was repeated "by desire," and went off the next time without a hitch. It was always safe to run a piece twice, for the men on duty the first day would certainly come the second.

Now comes in a shaving, not saving, incident. I was sitting in my hut, having my semblance of a moustache taken off by a native barber, preparatory to assuming my petticoat rôle, when all of a sudden I fancied the man struck me a smart smack on the face. I jumped up to avenge the insult, when I found the poor barber leaning helplessly against the wall. Before I had time for further action, I heard a rumbling, and every one was rushing out. I followed suit, and found the magazine, which our theatre was supposed to threaten, had blown up, and our theatre was a dismal wreck in flames.

I can only account for the barber incident as follows: The first percussion had felt to me like a slap in the face as I was sitting, but it had hurled the barber, who was standing, against the wall; then came the rolling of the report which caused the whole community to turn out.

The sentry over the magazine was never heard of again. As usual, no one could account for the accident. However, our theatre was gone, and only by great exertions was the fire prevented from spreading.

The only satisfaction I had in this matter lay in being able to retort on our opponents by telling them their magazine burnt our theatre instead of our theatre blowing up their magazine.

With our theatre my chief occupation was gone also; I had time therefore to look about me and take stock of my surroundings. Of the military situation I knew but little, as indeed do most men in a campaign. I was aware that there were two divisions commanded in chief by General Godwin, C.B.; that we belonged to the Madras Division under General Steele, my old Bellary chief, with Neill of Ours as his Adjutant-General, and Travers as his A.D.C., and that our Brigadier was McNeill afore-mentioned. I forget all other commandants; as this is not a history of the war, I do not care to refresh my memory. Our duties were very light. I do not remember any working parties, and am quite sure there must have been plenty for them to do; but European soldiers were not worked in those days as they are now.

Strange to say, we found Mormons already settled in Rangoon when we arrived, but they were very different Mormons from those whom I visited in Salt Lake City in 1879. They seemed quiet, inoffensive people, and the chief attraction offered by their elders in order to gain members was the assurance that by faith miracles could

be effected. A story was current that one very faithful
neophyte, after a long probation, finding himself unable
to work any miracle, thrashed his worthy pastor for a
charlatan and humbug. I never heard that these Mormons
met with any success, and am quite sure their doctrines
were other than those of Brigham Young.

A word or two about the Burmese and Burmah may
not be out of place here. I have heard and read much
about the causes of the Second Burmese War which was
eminently unsatisfactory. To my mind the solution is
very simple. We wanted the country, and therefore
causes for a war were as thick as blackberries and close
to hand. But whilst I say this, I also say that the con-
quest of Pegu was an unmixed benefit to its inhabitants,
and that they felt it to be so was clearly proved by
subsequent events.

The country we were to conquer and occupy was and
is a mine of wealth, and I have never ceased to regret the
thousands of rupees spent in favoured Bengal on very
unremunerative improvements, whilst the same sum ex-
pended in Burmah would have realized a cent. per cent.
return.

Where on earth can you find a country more adapted
to river-traffic and railroads? I hear so many talk of the
ruby mines; I never hear them talk of the mines of
wealth that exist in the forests and in the rice-fields.
Yet the one is probably a chimera, the other is an
absolute fact; Burmah is now being looked on as the
granary of India. All eyes turn towards her in times
of threatened famine, and her productive powers might
easily be doubled. But how can I ever adequately in
words express my admiration of the quiet, peaceable,
merry people we were called on to mix with? What
they may be now after forty-four years of British rule I
cannot say, neither am I careful as to whether others
agree with me in the estimate I formed of them when

engaged in their subjection. I shall speak of them as I found them, and I only wish I could do more justice to them.

From the very outset they were friendly, and merely used pardonable shrewdness in waiting to see which way the wind blew before openly espousing our cause and flocking to us for protection. This was very manifest in the case of the refugees at Pegu. The cause of this friendliness is not far to seek. The Peguers were a conquered people, and were ruled by a tyrant in Ava. The beautiful pagodas that reared their slender points to heaven had been raised by their kings and ancestors; and although their religious prejudices had not been in any way offended by the conquering race, yet doubtless old associations made them cling to an honoured past, and now in their new conquerors they hoped at least to find less cruel task-masters than in the emissaries of the Court of Ava.

If any one thing struck me more than another it was the purity and picturesqueness of their religion. Their shrines and pagodas were handsome and well cared for, whilst their monasteries or poonghie houses were solid and ornamental. Their adorations were simple and heartfelt, so utterly differing from those of their co-religionists in China and Japan. Who could help admiring the brightness of the scene when thousands flocked up the main street to pray at the shrine of the great and good Gaudama on the terrace at the foot of the great Shoay Dagon Pagoda? The women were in picturesque bright dresses, the young girls with a spray of an orchid or some other pretty flower in their hair behind their ears. The elder ones carried the lotus, Gaudama's sacred flower, in their hands; their merry chatter always ceased when on sacred ground, and reverence was conspicuous everywhere.

Max Müller has said, I believe, that next to Christianity Buddhism is the religion most calculated to supply the wants of humanity. I hope so great a man has said so, for I think it well deserves such a high encomium. Alas, in the dogma of "Nirvana" (absorption) one loses individuality, and that is to most men a grave defect. But the manner in which in my time the priesthood conducted their office was beyond reproach. In no single instance during my whole stay in Burmah did I see or hear of any act that could in the slightest degree reflect on the character of these holy men. Often have I and others offered them money in return for some slight service; in no case was it ever accepted. I do not think they would sell any images, curios or books, though they would give them.

It is not my purpose to write more on this subject, but so long as memory lasts it will dwell with pleasure on the conduct and example of these men, who are not only the spiritual guides, but the school-masters, of the people. In my time every man, woman, and child in Burmah could read and write. Alas! I came back to Wales to find no school of any kind in my parish, and ignorance spread broadcast around.

But what am I to say about the Burmese men? Well, they were a good-humoured, sober set, but hopelessly idle. Of course our intercourse with them soon made them money-grabbers, and gave them an undue idea of their own importance. Yet I fancy they were good husbands and decidedly indulgent fathers. They were strict vegetarians, the taking of animal life being against their religion. Some few would eat eggs and drink milk, all would catch and eat fish. At the time I write of, a duck or a chicken could be bought for an empty beer-bottle, glass being so valuable to them. When money was given for any article it was generally used as an ornament for the children.

Marriage laws and customs were by no means lax in their sense of the obligations, though they may have appeared to be so to such splendid moralists as we are. Marriage was purely a matter of convenience with them. Of course we never dream of such a thing in sanctified Clapham or austere Belgravia. When a man wanted a wife he took stock of the daughters of Heth, and found his fate. He then went to the father and said, "How much?" The father named the sum, which went to him in trust as his daughter's dowry, and so the bargain was struck. If the young man was too poor to pay ready money down, an arrangement was made by which he remained in servitude as in patriarchal times until by service he had paid for his wife. They could separate by mutual consent, but if by reason of the man's fault then the dowry was forfeited; if by the wife's fault then the dowry was repaid.

Marriage was not a religious rite, though the poonghies generally put in an appearance at the marriage rejoicings to give an air of solemnity and respectability to the event. Adultery was almost unknown in my time, and I am glad to add that, speaking on the subject quite recently to a member of the Burmese Commission, I was told that it is almost unknown now; the only case he had come across was where a girl had left her husband for a white man.

The admiration of the Burmese women for Europeans was most noticeable; but, strange to say, their tastes were very different from that of the fair sex of other countries. They did not care for what we should call fine handsome men; they abhorred hair on the face in every form, so that our Grenadiers and Pioneers were out of it with them, whilst a fair beardless boy was in their eyes Adonis and Narcissus in one. They depicted their Devil as hairy, and would cast no sheep's eyes on a curled darling.

No one could avoid noticing the predilection of both sexes for tobacco. They smoked a curious kind of huge cigarette, the tobacco and some sort of pith being rolled up together in a kind of magnolia leaf, specially prepared by being dried on a hot stone or iron. The process of rolling was peculiar, it being generally done on a girl's thigh; their dress was formed in a manner to enable this process to be easily carried out. Not only did men, women, and children smoke, but infants unweaned also. I have scores of times seen a woman, when her baby loosened its hold of her breast, take her cigarette out of her mouth and put it into her baby's, who quietly smoked away until it went to sleep, when the mother took it back again.

I was told that the correct way of encouraging a lover was for the girl to make cigarettes for him. I believe, though no smoker myself, and not being on the look-out for a sweetheart, that modern girls do not hesitate to show their preference for eligible *partis* in the same way.

CHAPTER IV

PEGU

FROM September 14, the date of our landing, up to this time, we had enjoyed a forced state of inactivity; the time had now arrived for us to be up and doing.

The force under General Godwin, C.B., was composed of two divisions, one from Bengal, and the other from Madras. We naturally belonged to the latter, which for general purposes may be said to have been employed on the Pegu side of the country, whilst the Bengal troops were engaged up the Irrawaddy towards Prome.

The objective at this period seems to have been Pegu, which had already once been captured, June 1852, but for some unaccountable reason had been abandoned. On November 20th a force was detailed to recapture and this time occupy it.

The force detailed consisted of 300 Bengal Fusiliers under Colonel Tudor, 300 Madras Fusiliers under Major Hill, and 500 5th Madras Native Infantry under Major Shubrick. There was only a small detachment of Artillery, as transport was lacking, and the surrounding jungle but ill adapted to their use. Sappers under Lieut. Campbell, Bengal Engineers, and Lieut. Harris, Madras Sappers.

Unfortunately I did not accompany this expedition, so can only repeat the hearsay of my brother officers on their return.

It seems that considerable difficulty was experienced in getting the flotilla fleet and gunboats up to the place of landing, which was some miles lower down than the ghaut opposite the pagoda.

Amongst the very useful vessels which composed the flotilla, there was one which was commanded by a most worthy and somewhat eccentric old officer of the name of Digney. He was quite a character, and had adopted for his own special convenience a sort of dual identity. He was at pleasure either "the beast John" or "the intellectual Digney." Conversations were frequently heard being carried on between these individuals at night after all had turned in. The beast John always wanted an extra glass of grog, to which the intellectual Digney objected. "No, John, you've had enough, go to bed; the intellectual Digney says no, go to bed." The beast John pleaded for only one more, and always succeeded in gaining his point.

I mention this little incident more with a view to saying a word, a justly merited word, in favour of a service which I think scarcely got its just meed of praise for very valuable services rendered. Whilst cocked hats and brass spurs were everywhere lauded, these hard-working men and officers of the H. E. I. Company's marine service got little or no recognition of their services. Perhaps it may not displease them to find that one humble individual remembers them after a lapse of so many years.

To return to Pegu: the boats anchored for the night some miles below, and here it seems that the tarpaulins that covered the stores and ammunition caught fire, which was only extinguished by our officers and men at the risk of their lives and by intense exertion. The men had to be landed as a precautionary measure.

On the 21st at dawn amidst dense mist the troops were landed, and had to feel their way through almost impassable jungle. The rifles of the 5th Madras Native Infantry seem to have done yeoman service in this advance, and so closely were they pressed by the enemy, that men's heads were cut off by that fearful weapon, the Burmese dhar, before any indication of an enemy being near at hand was given.

Whilst approaching the pagoda, it seems that Privates McClory and Kelly found an old iron gun which the Burmese had been unable to take with them, and to this gun our men clung with a laudable pertinacity. Of the importance of this capture I shall speak again.

On arrival of the main body in front of the pagoda, a halt was made in order to allow the somewhat exhausted Bengal Fusiliers to regain breath, and then the attacking column was formed up and harangued by General Godwin, and the assault made with a rush under command of Major Hill. It is said Elliot and Daniell were first in.

In the rush up the steps of the pagoda Daniell got next to Commander Beauchamp Seymour, R.N., who was a volunteer acting as A.D.C. to General Godwin. The enemy fired a volley into the storming party; most of the bullets went over them; one, however, struck a rifle Seymour was carrying, and knocked it out of his hand.

The fact really was that a volley poured in previous to the rush had completely paralyzed the defenders, and so the stronghold was captured with the loss of one sergeant and fourteen men.

Our chief casualty lay in the death of Brigadier McNeill, of whom I have so frequently spoken. He died from apoplexy induced by sunstroke.

The value of this achievement must not be judged by the list of killed and wounded, but by the immense exertion made by the troops in a climate that almost defies description, and surrounded by obstacles which on seeing the place made me feel that such an attack in such a manner was almost foolhardy.

General Godwin this time intended to retain a strong-

THE SHWE-MA-DAU PAGODA

hold already twice taken, and of which the importance was accentuated by the determination of the Burmese to repossess it.

General Godwin and the troops returned in due course to Rangoon, leaving a garrison at Pegu of No. 1 and 10 companies of our men numbering 200, also 200 of the 5th M. N. I. under Captain Wyndham, a small detachment of Bengal Artillery under Lieutenant James, together with a few Sappers under Lieutenant Campbell, Bengal Engineers; the whole under command of Major Hill, with Lieutenant Dangerfield of Ours as Staff Officer. This small force must have set resolutely to work at once to clear around the pagoda, for, when I arrived a few days later on, considerable progress had been made.

As the Burmese never left the neighbourhood of the ancient capital of the district, gunboats were left to keep the river clear of the enemy's boats, and a river picquet established. On the 27th a very determined attack was made on the boats and river picquet by a considerable force of Burmese. But before entering into details of this serious affair, a description of Pegu and its surroundings will be of assistance to the reader.

The Shwe-ma-dau Pagoda, the key of the position, was built on an eminence either natural or artificial, and was of the usual pyramidical shape. Its foundation was on an upper terrace. The upper terrace had been surrounded by a low somewhat miserably constructed wall, which in many places had disappeared.

On this platform, the sides of which, as far as I can remember, were about 220 yards in length, there stood, abutting the foundation of the pagoda on all four sides, substantially-built wooden poonghie houses, which, following Burmese custom, were only closed at the sides by slight bamboo matting. Two of these poonghie houses became the dwellings of the officers of the garrison. On the terrace there were various other buildings of an even less substantial nature, which were used according to fitness as hospital and barracks.

In the centre of each face there was a wide entrance giving access to a long flight of steps which led to a platform, considerably lower than the upper one and with an area very much larger.

This lower platform also contained some buildings on the south face, and had small flights of steps corresponding with those up above, leading to the level plain on which stood the town of Pegu at the south-west angle. The town, if such it could be termed, consisted of huts made of bamboo and thatched with grass, and thus easily removable.

The pagoda and town lay in the centre of a plain (level except on the east where the ground rose slightly), and was enclosed by a huge walled parallelogram, each face being about a mile and a half long and fifty feet high. This wall was in a dilapidated condition in parts, but still served as a shelter of considerable importance to an attacking force against the pagoda, from which it was about 800 yards.

Almost everywhere the wall was covered with dense jungle, affording cover to the Burmese. On the north side there was but little cover between us and the outer wall. On the east some small pagodas ran right up to the lower flight of steps, and jungle had grown equally near, until a small belt had been cleared by our troops. On the south side the jungle was fairly close, and from a well, situated in this jungle, we obtained our only water.

From the west front, which became eventually the most important, the road, a substantial one, ran clear to the wall, which was here pierced by a large ghaut, and led to the river. Between the ghaut and the river there existed a swampy moat, 150 yards wide; this was crossed by a broad causeway, and then at a distance of 300 yards came the river, which at that part was not more than 100 yards wide, and fordable at certain periods.

Such was the position that Major Hill had to hold, and which, though strong in some respects, such as its commanding height, was yet most vulnerable by reason of its being dominated on the east by higher ground, and being certainly on two sides shut in by jungle—a fact more than usually favourable to the style of warfare adopted by our enemy. Beyond the outer wall, practically speaking, there was nothing but endless forest and jungle, though from the highest points of the pagoda to which we could climb, a few cultivated spots were visible.

But to return to November 27. Towards nightfall a very vigorous attack was made on three sides of the pagoda. At the same time the river picquet, consisting of thirty men of ours and a naigue (corporal) and twenty men of the 5th M. N. I., the whole commanded by Lieutenant Percival Ashley Brown of the Fusiliers, was also attacked. This picquet was strengthened by three gunboats under command of Lieut. Mason, R.N.

No sooner had the firing commenced around the pagoda, than Brown got the powder-barrels, sacks of provision, etc., together, and with some timber dragged from the river made a sort of breastwork, which prevented the Burmese from closing in on them; and from this breastwork at intervals, when the moon emerging from a cloud allowed them to see the enemy plainly, they made sorties. In this work and in saving the stores which caught fire, Private Clancey of the Fusiliers greatly distinguished himself.

But repelling the attacks on the stores was not the only difficulty that Lieutenant Brown had to contend with.

The Burmese, by means of trees, sunken canoes, etc. attempted to block the river, which at that time was shallow, and so prevent the boats from getting downstream. Brown, by his judicious arrangements, kept down the enemy's fire, until the sailors could remove the obstacles, and get off safely.

A curious feature connected with this gallant defence deserves to be noticed. The picquet was attacked from both sides of the river, the banks of which were very high above the water at this season of the year. One half of our men had to face the river-face, so as to keep down the fire of the enemy from the gunboats lying below. On their side the gunboats had to fire shot and shell over both banks as occasion required, and whenever the Middies called out "Starboard ready!" the whole picquet had to lie down flat on their faces, whilst the gunboats fired over them.

Lieutenant Mason, R.N., had his necktie shot off, and in the morning the awnings of the boats were found to be well riddled by bullets. Lieutenant Mason reported to the Admiralty that, if it had not been for the assistance rendered by the picquet, the gunboats would have run a great risk of being captured. The attacks on the picquet continued all night, and even after daybreak; in fact, until the picquet was strengthened from the pagoda.

Lieutenant Brown spoke in high terms of the conduct of the naigue and his comrades; he also recommended Private Clancey to the notice of his superiors, and he got promotion. Lieutenant Brown's gallant conduct was reported to the Governor-General, who specially thanked him for his services.

I now come to my own personal share in these interesting events, and I am greatly assisted in my work by letters which I wrote to relatives at the time, and which fortunately have been preserved.

On the night of December 1, about half-past nine, I was ordered to hold myself in readiness to proceed with a party of our regiment to Pegu, to start at 8 a.m. next morning. My stay at Pegu was to be of very short duration; indeed I was told that I was to return immediately after giving over charge of my convoy to Major Hill.

My party consisted of eighteen privates, no non-commissioned officer, so that on arriving at the beach I was obliged to appoint a steady man to act as corporal. Each man carried two days' cooked provisions in his haversack, and I had arrack for two days in a tin-can.

On arriving at the wharf I met Captain Shadwell, R.N., who said I was to take up two magazines for the use of the garrison, fifty dhoolie bearers, and three days' commissariat rations; the whole consisted of a convoy of four large country boats with one of H.M.S. *Fox's* gunboats as a guard.

I took the commissariat stores with me in my own boat with my eighteen men, and put the magazines in two other boats, and the bearers in the fourth. I was introduced to Mr. Smythe, the officer of the gunboat, and at noon we started. I had an awning of mats put over the boat that I occupied, to keep the sun off my men, and placed them "midship and forrard"; I occupied the poop myself, surrounded by my stores. All went smoothly.

In looking at my list of rations, I found mention of a keg of arrack containing two gallons, twenty-eight drams, which had not been handed over to me. I looked to see if it was there. I saw it was quite close to me; and fancying no one knew of its presence but myself, and not wishing to work my men, I did not put a sentry over it, but covered it with my boat-cloak.

At 4 p.m. the *Fox's* boat pulled alongside of mine, and Mr. Smythe asked me to come on board and have a cheroot with him. I went, giving charge of the stores to the corporal, who had been sitting on the poop with me.

I drew alongside of my boat at 5 p.m. and asked if all was right, and the corporal said, "Yes, sir."

At sunset I asked Smythe to put me on board my own boat as it was getting late. Finding our fellows rather merry, I looked for my keg of arrack. Alas! it was gone. I searched well, and then asked the corporal if he had issued the second dram from the tin-can; he said, "Yes." I then said, "Where is the small keg that was with these stores?" He answered he had not seen any, and added, "I have been sitting in this place, sir, ever since you left, and I don't think any one could have touched anything without my knowledge." I was so certain about it, that I ordered the boat to be searched, but to no purpose. By this time the liquor that had been stolen began to have its effects, and I heard high words passing in the bows. Presently those who were more sober tried to hush up the quarrel, which had commenced by one penitent telling another impenitent, "that it was a shame to take advantage of the officer's back being turned to steal liquor;" upon this another man shouted out, "Hold your tongue, you d—— blab, or I'll cut it out." Then the row grew worse and worse, until I heard blows falling like hail. Fancy my situation, in a country boat on a rapid river, at 9 p.m., and about fourteen drunken men; every move in the boat made it roll like a porpoise. I was in bodily fear of its being upset.

My first order was for the removal of all bayonets, which I had placed behind me. I then got every canteen and emptied it into the river, finding arrack in many. I then hailed the gunboat, and asked Smythe to give me some rope, and to remain within hail. Then I gave myself up to God's mercy, for I never was in such a fearful position in my life. The Burmese boatmen were paralyzed with fear. I almost wished to be drowned; the two or three sober men begged me to go on board the gunboat, as my life was not safe. I was not, however, quite so young as that. I dared not get a sailor on board, or they would have murdered him; moreover, Smythe very properly refused to run the risk. So I was obliged to let them fight it out, telling them at the same time that any man who did not keep quiet would be tied hand and foot, and put on board the ammunition boat. Still amidst all the madness of drink and rage there was a lurking sense of propriety which struck me much; it arose partly from discipline, and partly, I believe, because I was a favourite, for, whenever I spoke to any of them, they tried to answer respectfully, and they were all attention to a speech from a horrid drunken vagabond, made in praise of the *young* officer who was in command.

However, everything must have an end, and, after having given me as much of a fright as possible, they fell asleep, many of them having emptied their stomachs in an unpleasant manner.

Scarcely had slumber stolen over our crew, when I heard a splash, and found it was one of my blackguards in the water, who in a drunken roll had fallen overboard. The river was running like a sluice, and we had much difficulty in picking him up. Amidst his drunken hiccups he cried, "I can wim, nevermineme"—meaning, "I can swim, never mind me"—and we got him safely on board again.

Next morning it was anything but lively for them. They were parched with thirst, and I was reminded of Coleridge's lines, "Water, water everywhere, nor any drop to drink." I took no trouble about them, but had my food and soda-water on the poop, and let them take their river-water if they wanted it. At twelve o'clock they expected their grog, but I said, "No, no, you had all your grog yesterday, and you will not get any more from me; I shall report you to the Major when I arrive, and if he thinks fit you will have the drams I have stopped."

We landed at about two o'clock, and I marched my detachment up. I was much surprised on nearing the pagoda to find the working parties all armed; it looked very warlike. I reported my arrival to the Major, and he bade me get some dinner and then return.

I got my dinner, then went back to plead with the Major for permission to stay, for I saw that sharp work might be expected. He said, "Well, Parry, my orders are for you to return at once, but I dare say you would sooner stay, and, as I want every man I can get hold of, I will take the responsibility of keeping you." I need scarcely say I was delighted. I was then ordered to take my drunken rascals down to the river, and keep them well at work in unloading the boats; this was finished by sunset, and the stores sent up to the pagoda.

There was no firing that night, but I was anything but comfortable, as I had no bed with me. Next day the hospital provided me with everything, and I was as jolly as a sand-boy.

On Sunday the 5th we had no end of a busy day; we were employed cutting timber for a stockade to protect a large body of Peguers who had come in to seek protection the day before. It was a serious matter to find shelter for so many men, women, and children, about 2000, with 216 carts; but Campbell our engineer was a man who did not understand the word "difficulty." He placed them on the lower platform on the west side, and there laagered them in with their own bullock-carts, strengthening this position with a stout palisade.

I had now time to look around me, and my surprise and admiration were great at the amount of work that had been done in so short a time. Some may have thought that the small force had been left to guard a strong position. It had been strong once; but when General Godwin left it in Major Hill's charge, it was more than perilously weak. The terraces I have spoken of were so crumbled and beaten down that the Cathay Horse could at any time have ridden up on to the upper terrace. Grass and jungle grew to the very foot of each platform. Numerous solid pagodas lay on our east face at about 120 yards off, forming a shelter for the Burmese impervious to our shot. At various distances from us other pagodas lay, up which the enemy could climb, commanding with their muskets and matchlocks the platform on which we were housed. Add to this the rise of the ground on the east and south faces, and the high trees, then some idea of the way in which we were overlooked may be realized. Well, the first thing I noticed was that the immensely wide apertures at each face had been barricaded, leaving only embrasures sufficient for the guns; the grass had been cut to enable us to place sentries on the lower platforms, but so dense was the grass still left in places that only by the gleam of bayonets could the existence of a sentry be known to his comrades. The Burmese were most expert at jungle skirmishing, and, if they had made any determined attempt on us at this period, heaven only knows what might have been the result.

Our garrison consisted of:

      200 Madras Fusiliers (European),
      200 5th Madras Native Infantry,
       30 Bengal European Artillery,
       40 Madras Sappers.

Our armament was two 24-howitzers and some small guns which we had captured from the enemy. The whole under command of Major Hill of Ours, with Lieutenant Dangerfield as his staff officer.

The two companies, Nos. 1 and 10, of the 1st Madras Fusiliers were officered respectively by:

No. 1.	No. 10.
Captain Stephenson,	Captain Nicolay,
Lieut. Spurgin,	Lieut. Daniell,
,, P. A. Brown,	Second Lieut. Jones-Parry,
,, Menzies.	,, ,, Bowen.

The 5th Madras Native Infantry were commanded by Captains Wyndham and Brown, with Lieuts. Burns and

Maud Chadwick; Lieut. Campbell of Bengal was our Engineer; Lieut. James our Artillery commandant.

The Peguers were, as I have said, stockaded under protection of our guns on the second platform, and were very judiciously placed. Only about 250 of the men were able-bodied, and only fifty of these had matchlocks. These fifty were placed at intervals amongst the spearmen, and a leaven of the 5th Rifle Company were also infused to give them confidence. The old men, women, and children were placed under cover as far as possible in rear of the fighting line. The crumbling walls on the upper platform had been strengthened, and the gaps filled up with sandbags, barrels, etc.; the Commissariat supplied all the empty sacks that could be found, and then there was no help for it: sacks of flour and rice had to be used.

Towards evening four Burmese came in and besought protection; as they looked suspicious, Major Hill sent for the Peguer Chief, Moung Loung, and consulted him. He would not vouch for the honesty of these men, so they were escorted a certain distance into the jungle and told to bolt. This was a difficult point to solve, for we knew that the husbands of many of the women in our stockade were compelled to join the enemy and fight against us; these four might have been true men.

At about 5 p.m. two Peguers came in wounded, and said that a boat containing stores, bullocks, carts, etc., and guarded by a party of the 5th Native Infantry, had been attacked down the river, and that they feared the Burmese would capture it.

There was firing at night, only just enough to necessitate our reserve men lying down under the parapet with their muskets beside them.

At 10 p.m. the same night we heard somebody calling out, "5th regiment Sepoy, don't shoot," and we found it was two of the 5th Sepoys who had escaped from the boat. Their story was truly piteous: they said that their party, consisting of one native officer and twenty privates, had been attacked down the river, and that they had fired away all their ammunition in defending themselves; that the Jemadar had been killed, and unless we sent them assistance they could not expect to survive many hours. Sending assistance was utterly out of the question, as it would take an army to attack such a body of men in the night; so the Major contented himself with keeping a look-out for the direction of the firing, and detailed a strong party to go down to the river next morning under Captain Nicolay of Ours to try to recapture the boat.

We started at daybreak, Bowen leading the advance, Nicolay and myself with the main body, and Captain Brown of the 5th in the rear with fifty of his men. We got down to the river, and, finding no signs of the boat at the ghaut, proceeded up the river to the spot from which we had heard the sound of firing.

Whilst marching along, a guide who had been sent with us touched me on the shoulder and pointed to the bank of the river, leading the way himself. I followed, bending down, and saw a large cargo-boat stuck in the river, with the Burmese busy unloading it. I immediately gave the alarm to Nicolay, and then hurried on to the advance guard to warn them to halt. I came up with them, and found that Bowen had already halted them behind a bank within shot of the boat, and was waiting for the reserve to come up. Whilst speaking to Bowen, Sergeant Finlayson said to me, "Sit down, sir, or they will see your red jacket." I did so, and, while settling myself, I saw a Burman on the opposite bank hail his comrades in the boat and point to us.

We were just in time; another minute and every sepoy would have been butchered. On rushed our men under Bowen, perhaps thirty of them, and let fly a withering volley into the boat. To see the way in which the crew jumped into the water and scuttled on the other side was

F

absurd; they were taken quite by surprise, and were actually carrying the sepoys on shore when we fired.

It was piteous to see the position the sepoys were placed in, poor fellows, half dead with fright and hunger, naked and tied back to back, struggling in the water up to their chins, and with a current running seventeen knots an hour. One who had been carried into the jungle made his escape and came rushing back, and, from the fact of his being black and naked, our fellows took him for a Burman and shot him; luckily the ball hit him in the thigh, so that he was not killed, and he soon got better. The first impulse of every one was to dash into the water, and cut our poor sepoys loose. One fine fellow, named Callaghan, jumped in, clothes, belts, and all, carrying with him sixty rounds of ammunition; he found the weight too great, so returned, threw off his pouch-box, and then went in again with his pocket-knife between his teeth, and cut the sepoys loose.

After having released our sepoys, viz. fourteen saved, we found the Jemadar and two privates dead in the boat. Three were missing. We put our Taliens (Friendlies) in the boat, and they began towing it down the river to our wharf to unload, for the Burmese had not had time to take anything except the arms and accoutrements of the sepoys.

Whilst we were doing this, however, a shell from the pagoda came whizzing over our heads, and burst so near us that it was necessary to lie down on our faces. We were surprised at the shell coming, but fancied our gunners at the pagoda, having seen the smoke of our musketry, or else the Burmese running on the other side of the river, had fired at them.

Bowen and I came back very leisurely, burning everything we could lay hands upon, until we arrived at the wharf, where we found Nicolay getting the commissariat carts, bullocks, etc. out of the boat. He sent Bowen on with the sick and wounded, and told me to keep a sharp look-out around. Scarcely had I left him, when I saw a man in a red jacket amongst the houses that we had set on fire on the bank of the river, and, thinking it must be one of our men amusing himself burning, was sending to call him in; but to my surprise I saw two Burmese with him, and the sergeant said, "Sir, they are down upon us." I lost no time in telling Nicolay, and asked for a party of twenty men to extend across the bank to keep these fellows from outflanking us.

I placed my men in extended order, their left on the river, and their right on the bridge. I had a beautiful ravine in front of me, at the end of which they had to pass to try and outflank me, and many a pretty shot we had at the vagabonds. Their shot came pelting over us; but from the position I occupied, and from the hurried way in which they fired, none had any effect. However, soon their numbers increased so much that I found my force too small, and had to rush back to Nicolay for reinforcements, which he gave me in the shape of twenty riflemen of the 5th M. N. Infantry, who were of great use.

I held my own until Nicolay ordered me to fall back. On reaching the ghaut I found that Nicolay had emptied the boat and sent off the stores to the pagoda. As I passed I noted one bullock-cart alone left behind; it contained salt, and I got a Quixotic idea into my head that in a siege salt was indispensable, so I attempted to get the bullocks to move off. To my disgust I discovered the linch-pin was gone. Whilst stooping down to try and find it, I was suddenly whipped up round the waist and carried off just as an Irishman does a small pig. When I recovered myself on being set down, I found that Private McClory of my company, seeing I was on the point of being surrounded, rushed forward and rescued me in this somewhat undignified manner. He most truly saved my life, and subsequently got promoted.

It seems that the bugles from the pagoda had been sounding the retreat vigorously, for from the upper terraces of the pagoda itself they had seen the swarms of the enemy which were coming down on us from their stronghold, the White Pagoda, some three miles off. This also accounted for the shells that had burst over us.

My party were told to hold the ghaut for a while, and then we retreated in an orderly manner to the pagoda, where we received the warm congratulations of our comrades on our own safety, and on the successful rescue of our poor sepoys of the 5th M. N. Infantry.

In a despatch to General Godwin, Major Hill spoke very highly of this affair.

We had scarcely got in and were having our well-earned breakfast, when there was a violent cry of "Turn out!" Then came the peculiar yell that the Burmese make when they intend attacking in earnest.

It seems that the force that had annoyed us at the river had followed close on our rear, and, hoping to catch us unprepared, had commenced a most desperate attack on the Peguers' stockade at the south-west angle.

When sentries know that they hold their lives in their own hands, they keep a pretty sharp look-out. Ours at once gave the alarm, and we were prepared at all points; and it was necessary, for they fired on us from all sides, and from every point of vantage. Had we been all as big as the pagoda, we should have caught it; as it was, but little harm was done.

From this time we were surrounded, and there was no cessation of hostilities. Indeed, we were much happier under fire than without it, for any lull in musketry-fire betokened some worse devilry.

There could be no doubt that the enemy intended to remain, for they occupied the rising ground on the east and south faces in large numbers. It became necessary to take extra precautions. The men were getting exhausted from the incessant work of improving our position by day and watching the enemy by night; so the Major divided the force into three divisions; each division took three hours on duty and six off.

Our duties were to keep eternal watch over our respective foes, and, in case of necessity, call up the reserve. I need scarcely say every man slept fully accoutred. Each face was under the immediate superintendence of its captain, who visited us constantly during the night. The Major was thus able to act as supervisor of the whole, and he certainly was ubiquitous, always on the move round the upper platform or the Peguers' stockade.

We had also a very sensible custom of having in the earliest dawn some hot gruel with a dram of arrack in it for the picquets coming off duty and those going on. This did not interfere with our daily allowance, but was an extra dram given by the Major in consequence of increased duties.

Our position, in consequence of the higher elevation of our enemy, was very unsafe. Traverses, therefore, were erected where experience showed the shot fell most frequently.

Our mess in which we lived and fed was established in one of the afore-mentioned poonghie houses, namely, the one facing east, and was unusually unsafe. As a matter of fact, Lieutenant P. A. Brown received a severe contusion from a jingal ball; a Peguer was killed, and several of our servants were wounded, in the mess-house.

It was not unusual to find a pith helmet with a bullet-hole in it, and more than once a similar untoward event occurred to a pillow. I remember on one occasion the Major went his rounds, and on returning found a bullet had gone through his pillow just where his head would have been; this, however, was in the poonghie house situated on the south front. And our mess-house was even more exposed. Of course it was necessary to improve our protection, which was done chiefly by our own servants. Whilst on the subject of the mess-house, I must mention our mess. We were never hard up for food, though of course it was the usual salt ration; so the common joke amongst us was that the end of all things would be that Menzies would get the scurvy. Hence pickles were at a premium, and, as we had only one bottle in the mess, the President used to give every one his bit of pickle; there was no handing round the bottle and "help yourself": they were far too precious.

I also remember the universal cheeriness that existed. I do not know what others felt, but certainly no one showed any signs of undue anxiety, though at this time the Major, in consequence of the short supply of ammunition, had been obliged to send messengers in to General Godwin to ask for a further consignment.

Of course (as later in the Crimea) we had our shaves; they were constant and narrow. One day whilst I was steadying my telescope against a solitary palm-tree, in order to reconnoitre the position of some sharpshooters on one of the small pagodas before mentioned, the field suddenly became completely obscured, and on looking I found a bullet had struck the tree just where the end of the telescope rested, forcing the sap out which covered the glass. I need scarcely say I made tracks. We never could make out whether these lucky shots were the result of good shooting or merely accident; if good shooting, then there must have been other firearms than matchlocks. The men soon became very careless, and it was a hopeless task to try to make them cautious. One, Private McKinley, was for ever exposing himself; he was repeatedly cautioned, but always answered that the bullet was not yet made that would kill him. However, one day just on leaving the mess he was hit, and, strange to say, he stooped down and picked up a bullet, saying, "This done it." However, it was not that bullet, for the one that killed him was not extracted till after his death: it was embedded in the knee-joint, and McKinley died from lockjaw.

I must here say a word or two about our artillery under Lieutenant James. They were excellent, but alas! how few, only thirty, and this to serve their own two howitzers, and assist the guns on the other faces. It was necessary to instruct our men. The custom of teaching gun-drill to Europeans had not then been introduced.

I do not know what the officers commanding other faces did; indeed, it was remarkable that, though all within a few yards of each other, we seldom knew what others were doing, and this because all attacks were made simultaneously on all faces, though of course with greater vigour on one particular one. I know myself I did not care a button what others were doing in a fight; I only thought of my own work, and that was enough for me.

This complete ignorance and indeed indifference of the men as to others reminds me of a story, which, though it sounds incredible, I can easily believe. It is said that at the battle of Trafalgar news came down to the lower tier guns that Nelson had been wounded; there was a general pause of consternation, when an almost naked captain of a gun shouted out, " Who the —— is Nelson? —get on with your loading." I do not think anything would have disconcerted us when we were well in for a good fight.

But to return to our guns. A party of our No. 10 men were told off or volunteered for artillery practice. Our gun was the one captured by McClory and Kelly, a bulldog-looking thing with a touch-hole as large as a church-door.

We had an excellent instructor in one Bombardier Sale, as grand an old soldier as ever wore a belt. He had, strange to say, served under his great namesake in the defence of Jelalabad, and also in most of the Punjaub battles, and was just the man we wanted. He had, I think, three ribbons, which in those days, when medals were not given till won, was a record score.

The men who volunteered were, as far as I can remember, Liptrot, Vincent, G. Moore, Weir, Saunders, Dunsheath, and Denis Kelly. They soon learnt their work, and took no end of pride in their gun; but it was a marvel that we were not all blown up into mid air, for their sole idea seemed to be to cram it up to the very muzzle with any and everything that they could lay hands on.

But alas! when thus loaded, they were seized by an uncontrollable desire to fire the gun. No matter in season or out of season, off it would go with a deafening boom. To check this inordinate firing where ammunition was running short was a matter of great importance, and I may add of no little difficulty, as the following story will prove:—Daniell, who was on duty on our face one night, had scarcely turned his back to visit his sentries, when boom went the gun; he rushed back telling them not to fire, that there was no enemy near; the noise they heard was caused by our sheep, which had broken loose and were skurrying into the jungle. After this, Daniell, in order to prevent further waste of ammunition, sat on the gun. Just then the Major came round, and asked him why he was sitting in front of an open embrasure, through which a bullet might come at any moment. Daniell explained that he was sitting there to prevent the gun from being fired off unnecessarily—an explanation which amused the Major greatly.

I am afraid they were encouraged in firing by old Sale, for they overheard a conversation that passed between him and me. I said one day that I hoped we should not run short of ammunition. "Lord bless your soul, sir, there ain't no fear of that; as long as we've buttons to fire there ain't no need for bullets; and as to guns, why pebbles and brickbats is as good here as they were at Jelalabad."

One word here on the old campaigner. He is sometimes a bore when you yourself have been under fire, and know all about it; but with new levies he is invaluable, and I would myself never let a regiment go on active service without drafting into it some old hands who had been under fire, provided the regiment had none of their own.

The howitzers under Lieutenant James and his men were invaluable in all cases of attack. They covered chiefly the west face, and never were brought to our assistance, to the best of my recollection.

I must here mention an incident that has not appeared as yet in any published form. At the north-east angle of the position there existed a large solitary clump of bamboos; the ground between it and us had been cleared of grass, but the clump was occupied by a party of Burmese. These were very troublesome, even going so far as to make it the point from which they sallied forth one night with ladders to try to escalade us. It was no use firing shot or shell into the clump, for bullets only stuck in the bamboos, and balls went through them, leaving perhaps a loophole for the enemy's matchlocks.

Now the brilliant idea suggested itself to Bowen and myself to burn this clump. Accordingly we quietly collected all the dry shavings, grass, etc. that we could carry, and, taking advantage of a lull in the enemy's fire, and also of the Major and others being at dinner, we sallied forth, first having warned the men of No. 1 and No. 10, who met each other at that angle, to cover our advance and retreat with an awful fire in case of necessity. We took very few seconds to reach our clump, and luckily found it unoccupied, but we found also the secret of the safety of the nightly occupants. They had made a lovely shelter-pit, in which they could lie with perfect security. We put down our combustibles, and with a match set the pit alight. No sooner did the smoke curl up than it was seen by the enemy, who commenced a furious fire on us; this was answered by our men, and in an instant there was a general turn-out. We only got in just in time to be confronted by the Major, who threatened us with court-martial and sudden death. However, we were let off with a fearful reprimand for our folly in calling down fire on our comrades, and so the matter ended; but the enemy never occupied that clump again: they knew it was sufficiently near for a sortie at any moment.

I think the next incident that may arrest the attention of the reader was a terrific night attack on the Peguers. These poor creatures seem to have been the special object of the hatred of the Burmese. The attack commenced about 11 p.m., and continued with great activity for two hours, when they were beaten off.

I have said we were much happier when under fire than in stillness, and sometimes we were safer. An illustration of this occurred on the north face. A sentry complained to Lieutenant Spurgin that he had the most exposed post every day and night since the investment commenced, and thought it only fair some one else should have it. The thing was only reasonable, so Spurgin relieved him and placed him in a securer spot. The night was dark, and the enemy particularly quiet. About midnight this same sentry thought he heard and saw some one trying to creep up to the wall, so he craned his body over as far as he could to gain a better view. The next sentry, ignorant of what was taking place, saw a body moving against the wall, fancied it a Burman creeping up, and fired, shooting the poor fellow clean through the back. He gave one awful shriek, and was dead. It was a pure accident, but it showed how keen our sentries were and had to be, for the enemy had more than once crept up to our walls, and thrown lighted torches in to try to burn us out.

I have already mentioned the impromptu nature of

our defences. It soon became lamentable to see the rice pouring out of a hole made by a bullet; but there was no remedy. Day by day as sacks were emptied of rice and biscuit, they were filled with earth to replace others full of food.

The mention of biscuit reminds me that any one visiting our mess at meal-times would have taken us for woodpeckers tapping, or perhaps for chairmen of public bodies calling attention to the chair. Neither would be correct. We were simply tapping the weevils out of our biscuits; of course bread there was none!

How Noah came to leave so much biscuit in the ark is a mystery, but certainly ours could have come from nowhere else, and had had the advantage of lying in some store-house at Madras for centuries.

A great difficulty arose about water. There was only one well, situated outside the pagoda on the south side. The Burmese evidently knew the position well, and kept up a smart fire on it, so that our water-carriers were often wounded. Campbell during the night made an excellent covered way to the well, and henceforth all was safe.

Although I do not enter each day's work or attack in detail, it must not be supposed that we were free from fire; on one day only do I remember a total cessation, and that was only a prelude to a very desperate attempt to overpower us.

It was somewhat alarming to hear their *reveillée* every morning. Gongs were beaten and horns sounded; commencing at the north and extending in a semi-circle to the south-west, the ground occupied by their forces must have extended for miles. No estimate has made their numbers under 6000; pretty fair odds, I think.

The officers on duty during their three hours' watch sat down beside the gun, with the gunners at the central gate of their respective faces, moving about now and then to see all sentries were on the alert. About mid-day, when going my round, I was struck in the side either by a jingal ball or a fragment of brick from the parapet. It took the wind out of me, and I was carried under the wall. Dr. Cholmeley came and examined me, and pronounced no harm done. I was awfully disappointed; I expected him to say at least "mortally wounded." It is curious how often a severe wound is painless, whilst a trivial one is painful enough. I suppose it is a mere matter of nerves.

On the morning of the 11th we heard firing down by the river front. There could be no doubt that it proceeded from British guns. We were all anxiety, and many of the bolder ones got up on the shoulders of the pagoda with telescopes to get a better view of what was going on. We were absolutely certain that relief was at hand, for not only were the guns British, but we could distinctly see rockets, which could only be those of the Royal Navy.

Presently there was heavy musketry firing opposite the ghaut, just where the landing-jetty stood. By this time my hopes of relief had become a certainty, and I consequently went and put on the only clean shirt I had, and did a bit more washing than usual, in order to present a becoming appearance to our rescuers. Alas! towards mid-day the firing became fainter and fainter, until at last it ceased altogether. It was all up: a junction evidently could not be effected; so I quietly put on my dirty shirt again, determining to keep my clean one for a more suitable occasion. It is useless to say we were not disappointed, but we had the consolation that our condition would be known at head-quarters, and that relief was only a matter of a few days.

I may as well mention here that we subsequently learnt that the Commodore, finding that the sepoy boat had been attacked as described and had afterwards been burnt, sent a strong force of boats and blue-jackets under Commander Shadwell, R.N., to proceed to Pegu and re-open communication. It will be remembered that Lieutenant Mason, R.N., had been ordered to return after the attack on the picquet and boats on November 29, as Major Hill considered his force too small to protect a picquet at so great a distance from his main body. Well, Shadwell came up and tried to land, but found the river bank strongly stockaded; he was received by a murderous fire, and in a few seconds lost four killed and twenty-eight wounded, three of them mortally. His coxswain was shot dead by his side. Commander Shadwell therefore most wisely decided to retire; no one in his senses would have attempted in the circumstances to force the ghaut, and march up a mile and a half to the pagoda.

It seems that whilst this little diversion was being carried on, Major Hill's letter to General Godwin for more ammunition had safely reached head-quarters. The messenger who carried the letter described the situation, and the difficulty he had in making his way through the cordon that surrounded us. The General therefore decided to despatch two hundred of the Madras Fusiliers, under Captain Renaud, with a strong force of armed gunboats to convoy ammunition and also to strengthen the garrison. The naval force was under Commander Rowley Lambert, R.N.

It so happened that Shadwell in returning met this force, and of course reported his failure, and the nature of the Burmese defences on the river face. A council of war was held, and it was determined to return to Rangoon and report the tide of events. This step met with approval, and General Godwin determined to effect the relief in person with about 1500 men, whilst a land column under Colonel Sturt made its way along the right bank to effect a junction and cause a diversion.

The question of the necessity for the return of Renaud and Lambert was canvassed at the time, as with Shadwell's contingent it was considered strong; but, it must be remembered, only two courses were open to them—either at all risks to force the Burmese defences on the river face and run the gauntlet to the pagoda, with but little chance of convoying any ammunition; or else to land the Europeans lower down and turn the enemy's works. When the impenetrableness of the jungle is taken into consideration, this latter seems quite impossible.

But to return to our own force. I do not think the withdrawal of the gunboats affected our spirits much. I am sure not many of us knew how short ammunition was running. That night, strange to say, was the only night of perfect cessation of firing. We thought that the enemy had had a good fright on the river bank, but their stillness always portended mischief, and at early dawn they came on in earnest, this time on the south-east corner. With their usual yell they were right on us. This time my dear company shared the brunt with the 5th M. N. I. and the Peguers down below. We were ready for them, and a blaze of musketry illumined the whole face. So determined was the attack that the reserve was for the first time called out, and the Peguers strongly reinforced.

The Peguers fought like demons, and were well supported by a gun which was brought to bear on the south-east angle. We fired chiefly into *yells*, for the fog was too dense to allow of our seeing our foe. It was not until they had felt the cold steel of the sword-bayonets of the rifles of the 5th M. N. I. that they lost heart and retired.

When daylight allowed us to count the cost, it was found that very many Peguers were wounded by spears and dhars; half-a-dozen dead Burmese were found just outside the stockade, which the enemy had not been able to carry away: amongst them one was recognized as a chief, whom the Peguers hung. The loss they sustained in this attack must have been considerable, for canister was poured in upon them whenever by their shouts we discovered their whereabouts.

We on our side did not come off scot free. Chadwick of the Rifles, who had already been once wounded, had a narrow escape of having his head cut off, as he was peering over the stockade. Many Peguers were wounded by spears and dhars, and numerous hand-to-hand contests took place. The Peguers behaved splendidly, as did the Rifles of the 5th M. N. I.

I think it was on the night of the 13th that we heard two guns down the river, and James, our Artillery officer, reported seeing a rocket fired up into the air. This was considered to be a signal, and James was ordered to answer it. The night of the 13th passed quietly.

On the morning of the 14th we were all anxiety; it was not, however, till about eleven that we heard firing on our east face. It grew nearer and nearer; I was too intent in listening for the advance to think of my clean shirt. Presently we heard a cheer, then saw our men's red coats, and in a few more seconds Elliot of Ours was in through the embrasure of our No. 10 Company battery. General Godwin had given the post of honour to our men. So ended our troubles for a time.

General Godwin in meeting Major Hill on the upper terrace said, "I had given you up till ten minutes ago." The fact was that the Burmese would not surrender their positions until driven out, and had General Godwin attempted the relief in any other direction than that indicated in Major Hill's letter, his loss would have been very great: as it was it only amounted to three killed and nine wounded.

The rush of our relieving force on to the upper platform was immense, and I confess to feeling intense disgust at our little force being converted into a dense crowd.

Amongst General Godwin's force was Armstrong's Sikhs, a splendid body of men. The first impulse that seized the new-comers was to climb the pagoda, and watch the retreating army. I was with a mob of all regiments looking on, when a body of the enemy, from a mound behind the clump of bamboos before-mentioned, fired a volley into the dense crowd, wounding three, one of them a Sikh who was standing close beside me and had the tip of his nose taken off. The blood poured down his moustache and beard, and the thing was so ridiculous that we could not help laughing, whilst his comrades chaffed him. He was a splendidly handsome man, and his vanity no doubt was affected; he got into a towering passion, and was led off by his comrades to have his nose dressed. Later in the day two columns were sent out, and soon cleared the north and west faces of any Burmese that were still lurking about.

We had now nearly two thousand souls on the upper terrace, and, in order to prevent confusion in case of an alarm, Major Hill asked permission to employ only the old garrison for the night work. How I blessed him! Well, we did "sentry-go" as usual. A few shots were fired, but our sentries did not answer them. My turn for duty came round at 3 a.m. I went to my post and kept awake fairly well till about five, when I lay down beside the gun, telling the corporal to be sure to wake me if any one came round. Of course the Major came, and I suppose the corporal did not hear him, or failed to wake me; anyway the Major caught me, and the first words I heard were, "You were asleep, sir." I could say nothing. He took me aside, and told me he ought to try me by court-martial, and shoot me for being asleep on my post in face of an enemy, etc., and having piled up the enormity of my offence, he let me go. I did feel guilty, and blackguarded the corporal to my heart's content on my return.

I have now brought our operations down to the relief, and propose to say a few words in reference to the fruits of our defence.

Of course the most important result was the sheltering so many Peguers. This acted in two ways; it showed not only our willingness and ability to protect those who sought our protection, but it gave them a good idea of what a stubborn lot we are to conquer. No doubt the incidents of the defence would be carried far and wide, and so reach the ears of the Burmese, fighting for the King of Ava. It also showed the ready way in which all engaged, though they had never been under fire before, came to be as steady as rocks. It was lucky that our commandant had seen service in this very country, and so knew the manners and customs of the enemy.

The actual loss we sustained was trifling: two officers wounded, and forty-five privates killed and wounded, irrespective of camp followers, servants, and Peguers. The smallness of our loss is only to be accounted for by the fact that Campbell's traverses were well situated, and that we never had more than one-third of our men exposed at a time. Those actually on duty knew to a nicety the best shelter places, and the others lay down under the breastworks.

Our mess-house was always unsafe, and I never could quite make out whether the shots that dropped into it were the result of good shooting or accident. No doubt the enemy knew that such a building was occupied by Europeans, and consequently directed a fire against it. On the whole I am inclined to think they must have had a few weapons of precision, though most of them were armed with matchlocks.

This section may be concluded by quoting the words of General Godwin. In his despatch to the Governor-General, he says: "I know few moments more gratifying to me than when I met Major Hill of the 1st Madras Fusiliers on the pagoda."

CHAPTER V

PEGU—SECOND DEFENCE

I NOW come to the subsequent events at Pegu, and am again assisted by letters written at the time on the spot.

General Godwin relieved us on the 14th; after that event, for the next few days, we of the old garrison had rest. I was particularly benefited by the relief, for my servant came up with my baggage, and I had plenty of clean shirts. I occupied my leisure moments with Bowen in prowling about the positions occupied by our late enemies. I got a pretty good idea of their strength. Amongst other things I found that most of their earthworks were strengthened by the literal sowing of small and larger bamboo skewers. I use this name as being more applicable than any other I can think of. This mode of defence was thoroughly Burmese, and very effective, as Major Renaud found to his cost, and as I also found to a smaller extent in my researches.

The plan was to cut bamboos into certain lengths, say ten inches, then split them up into any number of skewers, sharpen the ends to almost needle-points, dip them in poison, and then throw them into the soft earth sticking upright. Passers by knew what that meant better even than treading with bare feet on the business end of a tin-tack. We found many long trenches filled in with earth, evidently graves.

On the 17th, the General with all the relieving force set off after the enemy towards the north. A detachment of my regiment under Captain Renaud, with Lieutenants

Raikes, Daniell, Menzies, Wing, and myself, accompanied it. Our march was in a northerly direction, and about four miles off we came, at a place called Kullie, across very extensive entrenchments, behind which a large body of the enemy were posted; these were the men who had harassed us at Pegu. I wish I could here make out as stirring a narrative as General Godwin in his despatch; what really occurred was, that owing to delay in the attack the enemy had time to bolt, and we found the entrenchment empty. We halted here, to my mind quite unnecessarily, and then went on to Sephanghoon, which we found occupied by an old woman and a broken-down bullock cart.

From Sephanghoon, where we had slept, we proceeded to Mausaganoo. We arrived about twelve o'clock, and sat down quietly to lunch. I remember we had some marmalade, and the flies at Mausaganoo had never tasted real Dundee. The joyful news spread like wild-fire, and soon there were more flies than marmalade. Mausaganoo was but a poor place—a few huts and some poonghie houses; it was situated on the edge of a vast plain covered with grass, and surrounded by a belt of jungle.

General Steele commanded our Division, and Neill of Ours was his A.-A.-General. Now it so happened that Neill had a new Minie rifle, which he wanted to try, so he went with two or three others to have a shot at some videttes of Cathay Horse, which had been seen moving about the edge of the jungle. I saw Neill moving down, and, fancying something might be going on, I followed, and, being known to him, was not ordered away. Well, he got near a wooden bridge, and there loaded, and with the fullest sight up let fly at these Cathay Horsemen; the first shot made them bob, at the second they bolted. Just then down came a staff officer in band-box get up, to know who the d——l had been firing, and, if it had not been that Neill himself was a big gun, we should have got into a fine scrape. But this was not all. Travers, A.D.C. to General Steele, galloped out towards these Cathay Horsemen to reconnoitre, and got some distance towards the belt of jungle where were the two horsemen at whom Neill had fired, when a considerable body of horsemen appeared in support of their comrades, and then the whole belt of jungle seemed alive with men. Travers rode quietly back. I do not remember all the subsequent manœuvres of our troops described by General Godwin!

I remember a large poonghie house full of every kind of image of Gaudama in silver, bronze, and alabaster being looted. I never took one, and made it a rule both in Burmah and the Crimea never to take anything from a church, temple, or sanctuary.

We marched back to Pegu, and, so far as I know, no one was killed, wounded, or even frightened. We used to call it the battle of Musshiboo; I call it the battle of "Much ado about nothing."

On December 20, General Godwin embarked for Rangoon. He left us Renaud's force of two hundred of Ours as a reinforcement, and some guns, but not a single gunner. He also left orders that we were to re-establish our rear picquet, stockading it. He left Commander Tarleton, R.N., and three gunboats, and finally, *as per usual*, left the whole of the large force, which he himself describes as having seen at Kullie and Mausaganoo, within a few miles of us!

All was now activity in the work of erecting a stockade on the river bank. This was a very different business from the work of finding shelter for the Peguers under cover of our guns on the platform.

The river was, as I have said, a mile and a half from the pagoda. The immense Bund covered with jungle intervened between us and it; the only place where this Bund was pierced was at the ghaut through which we had retreated, followed by the enemy, after rescuing the sepoys of the 5th. Our sappers had been taken away, and consequently our reinforcement was in reality less than the two hundred men spoken of, for we had to supply the place of sappers, and give our men to serve as gunners.

Luckily our improvised gunners under the superintendence of trained artillerists proved very efficient.

At this time, too, the 5th M. N. I. were replaced by a similar number of the 19th M. N. I., under Captain Young; good men, but of course not acquainted with the ins and outs of the place, or up to the ways of the Burmese. Our so-called reinforcements were employed as river guard and as working parties.

I must not forget my own extra work, which consisted in building, with the aid of my servant, a lean-to next the mess-house, which seemed luxurious to me after the crowded state of the mess-house since the new arrivals.

A word may now be said about this river picquet. Thick jungle grew up to within a few yards of the jetty between the river and the Bund, on both right and left; the river, about a hundred yards wide, lay in front, the banks being extremely steep; in our rear was a somewhat open space to the bridge that crossed the old moat; then came the Bund with the ghaut, and then the plain which extended right up to the foot of the pagoda, the high grass on which had now been burnt, so as to give a clear view of the Bund. The only thing that was in our favour was, that on arriving at the river to make the necessary preparations, and mark out the lines of the stockade, we found that the Burmese had stockaded strongly in the vicinity, and we were able to use their timbers for ours.

My letters are full of the amount of work to be done, and that on January 4 a few shots were fired at the picquet, and spies said the enemy were coming down on us in force.

On the 5th I went up the pagoda to have a look round,

and saw a lot of the enemy busy stockading themselves in, on the north. Several shots were fired into the picquet. Dangerfield later on discovered a body making along the Bund for our stockade, and sent into them a rocket and a dose of canister, which, as he expressed it, caused them to "do attitudes in the air."

January 6.—Got up at 5 a.m. to prepare for river guard, which was relieved daily, in order to keep the road open. We took two days' supplies with us, in case of being hemmed in. On account of the fog we did not start till eight o'clock. Spurgin of Ours commanded fifty of our men, with a party of the 19th. The Major told us that if any opposition should be made at the ghaut, he would flank us right and left with a mortar and twenty-four-pound howitzer.

I was sent out in front with skirmishers, but found the ghaut clear, so we arrived safely, and, after having had the dangerous points indicated, the old guard marched off. The enemy fired a few shots at the old guard as it passed the ghaut from the jungle on the north.

The work of stockading was instantly commenced, and was no trifling job. We had to nail boards on to the stout uprights as quickly as possible, in order to hide our men, until we could strengthen the work from inside.

Our men were constantly being fired at whilst working, and our main body had to act as a covering party. At eleven o'clock one of our men was struck by a jingal ball, right through the calf of the leg—a horrid wound; we gave him some brandy-and-water, and put him in the ditch out of danger. Two other men were hit from the fire on the other side of the river—contusions only.

Our position was now somewhat critical, for, owing to the enemy's having taken up a position on the right bank, opposite our weakest face, we were in reality hemmed in on three sides; but still we managed to keep down their fire pretty well. Spurgin removed all our sentries from the east face, as the shot across the river caught them in rear.

The enemy at this time took possession of an old indigo factory, a brick building of considerable strength, situated exactly opposite to us across the river on our west face. We fired a six-pounder into it, but with little effect. I see by my notes that at this time we had to send up for a pocket-case and bandages. Old Sale took it to the apothecary, and in coming back over the bridge was hit by a bullet; he merely said, "Oh, God!" and fell. I was sitting in our hut looking at the bridge, and saw him fall, and helped to carry him to our little hospital. He merely sighed, and was gone. Poor old fellow!—he was a grand soldier, had three medals, and, as I have already mentioned, had served with General Sale all through the celebrated Jelalabad siege. We always called him General Sale. His death caused a depression and an immense amount of anger; our artillerymen, whom Sale had taught, wanted to fire every gun at the brutes to avenge his death.

We had lost pretty heavily that day in proportion to our numbers. Firing ceased at sunset. Like children, whenever they were quiet they were in mischief, and we fancied they were entrenching themselves. However, the pagoda people knew their position, for they had fired at them all day.

The night was one of intense watchfulness. Next day, instead of being relieved as usual, we were kept down as a working party. However, we made the river face much stronger.

We discovered as soon as the sun rose that a party of the enemy was working on the old wall near the ghaut, evidently intending to cut off our communication with the pagoda. A couple of rounds of canister made them leave off.

On the 6th I find this entry: "I hardly know how to

begin to-day's work; I have had no sleep, and it seems like a continuation of yesterday. Fancy, I have been here a month and four days, and have never had my clothes all off at the same time for one single night, and now with the enemy round us, I think it will be another month before I have a chance."

At twelve we were allowed to march off to the pagoda, leaving Captain Nicolay on duty. I was again sent on duty immediately I arrived, so I had forty-eight hours of it without taking my boots off.

Next morning the river guard arrived, bringing with them one man wounded, and poor Nicolay dangerously so. It seems that he was standing outside the hut, when a bullet struck him in the neck; he fainted on the spot, when he recovered consciousness he begged to be taken to the pagoda. I saw him arrive, and was present when the bullet was extracted. It went in on the left side of the throat, and passed out at the right side just above the collar-bone. The old guard was very heavily fired on from the Bund on its way up. I do not quite remember when Tarleton with his boats retired, but it must have been about this time.

Mention has been made several times of the Royal Navy boats retiring; the reader may depend upon it they never retire unless absolutely compelled to do so. And in every case this occurred. Gunboats in those days were very different from what they are now. There were no steam-launches, and no cover for the men. Consequently at the jetty these boats lay as it were in a deep ditch, commanded from above on both sides, and quite unable to answer effectually the fire poured down on them. Again, as in the case of Lieutenant Mason, the Burmese could bar their retreat by a boom, or by sinking trees or canoes. Anyway the boats had to go, and so the necessity for our picquet was in a great measure removed, and the Major decided to give up the river picquet a second time. Even if we held it, we had no means of ascertaining that the river bank was not strongly stockaded lower down, so as to prevent gunboats coming up. I was delighted at the idea of giving it up, for I thought it a most unsafe place to hold, commanded as it was by that indigo factory on the west, and by the high Bund on the north-east.

News was brought in next day that the enemy intended to attack the picquet and pagoda in force at night, so that there was an additional motive for relinquishing the place.

A party of one hundred of Ours, one hundred and fifty of the 19th M. N. I., one hundred Peguers, and all our coolies went at 4 a.m. on the 8th to relieve the picquet. Captain Stephenson, who was on river guard, had orders to have all his guns, ammunition, and stores ready by daybreak. We on the pagoda were on the *qui vive* in case the passage of the ghaut should be disputed. All, however, was quiet, and the whole party arrived safe and sound at 7.30 a.m., bringing everything with them without a shot being fired.

Up to 11 a.m. there were no signs of any enemy near the picquet. Great surprise was felt, and mischief apprehended, but, on going up the pagoda, we found an immense cloud of dust to the north in the direction of our old friend Mausaganoo. It was difficult to account for this move; the enemy had retired exactly at the same time as we did from the river. Our surmise was that General Steele's column threatened their flank, but the real reason was want of rice.

We now sent out reconnoitring parties, and found how strongly they had entrenched themselves to the north. The Bund was literally bristling with those horrid bamboo spikes, and an assault there would have been difficult. I forgot to mention that Renaud in coming to our first relief had been badly staked, and the wound took a long time to heal.

Our spies went six miles down the river, and found a very strong stockade at a place called Jeedee; the enemy before leaving had burnt it; boats could not have passed it without difficulty.

On the 9th January poor Nicolay died. They held a *post-mortem*, and found that the ball had cut the jugular vein and carotid artery, besides injuring the spine. On fainting in the intense cold, the blood had coagulated on both those places, and so had stopped hemorrhage. Cholmeley certified that he died from shock to the nervous system. We buried him on the north front of the pagoda. He had a great many trinkets, amongst others lovely miniatures of his children; these were of course sent to his widow. Other things were sold; I bought a silver tea-spoon in memory of my captain of the east face. There was a bottle of gin sold, and one of our men bid up to thirty-four shillings for it, but the Major would not allow it to go, lest the man should get drunk. Anything to eat or drink went at fabulous prices.

We had time now to look around and see the positions the enemy had occupied. On the 10th I went down to the river with one hundred and forty coolies, with orders to cross the river (which I did on a coolie's shoulders), and destroy the indigo factory and pull down all poonghie houses I came across, and float the timber down to strengthen our stockade, which we again occupied. I had a covering party in case of attack. The indigo factory was very strong, and we blew up a great portion. I found near it a long newly-made grave and the scalp of a Burman.

Burning jungle was difficult work, as, although it looked withered, the sap was still in full vigour; no wonder our clump on the north-east front did not burn.

During the night there was again much firing from the pagoda. A band of Burmese tried to get in; one threw a lighted torch on to the roof of one of our buildings. A sentry bayoneted one, but he got off. This was the last time we were under fire.

On the 13th a large convoy came up, bringing provisions and treasure.

During the second investment a large number of real Burmese came in and asked for protection—about 1000; they had been kept as prisoners at Sephanghoon, and escaped at our advance. These men and their families were located south of our river picquet, but, as soon as firing commenced, they bolted bag and baggage up to the pagoda. Cholera broke out, and as many as sixteen a day died of it. Luckily it did not attack our men.

Whilst on river picquet with Spurgin, and going rounds one bright moonlight night, I slipped off the raised footpath, and fell, cutting my trousers and hurting my knee. I was so bad that Spurgin sent me up next day in a dhoolie. On arrival Cholmeley found I had cracked my knee-cap; it was a wonder it did not sever. I had to be put in splints, and my leg supported in a sling to a bamboo put across my bed. It was a nasty accident, but I soon got over it.

Nothing of any importance occurred during the remainder of our stay at Pegu. Our times were very pleasant. We used to go out often after jungle fowl. They were very wary, and difficult to shoot; they never rise, but run like rabbits from clump to clump.

David Brown, our Adjutant, was lucky one day when I was out with him; he fired at a hen just on the edge of a clump, and, on going to pick her up, found he had killed three. Our grub was lovely, with all the various contributions of our sportsmen put into a stew with our rations. I guess I had an appetite in those days!

One word before I leave Pegu for ever. In looking back, after some experience in warfare, I cannot help thinking that the original garrison was left somewhat short in the matter of guns, artillerymen, and ammunition.

Major Hill very modestly said that, had the enemy attacked us vigorously during the first few days of our occupation, our position would have been critical; I think he might have said *alarming*. Luckily their delay gave us time to put the place in some sort of order.

We had a most excellent engineer in Campbell, and the Madras Sappers under Harris worked as they always had done and ever will do. This corps has a world-wide reputation.

Our losses were, as I have said, wonderfully small, owing to wise precautions, but still they amounted to 10 per cent. of our force, and at the river picquet the percentage was even more in proportion to the small numbers that were engaged. The smallness of loss is more striking, when it is considered that the working parties were exposed to heavy fire before our stockade was fairly finished.

Major Hill got the command of the Gwalior Contingent as a mark of the Governor-General's appreciation of his services. The force generally got the special thanks of the Governor-General in Council and Commander-in-Chief of the Forces, and also got a medal and clasp for Pegu, as did every one, even those who never saw Pegu or heard a shot fired.

Only four officers of the original garrison are alive, viz. Lieut.-General Sir John Spurgin, K.C.B., C.S.I.; Colonel E. S. Daniell; Colonel P. A. Brown; and the writer of this narrative. Long may we live, say I.

Losses during the campaign: Killed—Captain T. F. Nicolay; Captain A. A. Geils. Wounded—Lieutenant E. L. Grant (severely); Lieutenant P. A. Brown. Died—Major Hawes; Captain W. Brown; Captain C. W. Tulloch; Captain A. Ward; Surgeon Anderson; Second Lieutenant Bryce; Second Lieutenant Bowen; Second Lieutenant Wing. One hundred and eighteen noncommissioned officers, drummers, rank and file killed or died.

CHAPTER VI

OUR JOLLY MARCH

ABOUT this time General Steele was making his way towards Shoaygheen, and our garrison was ordered to convoy supplies to meet him somewhere. A detachment was told off under command of Spurgin of Ours, and I am bound to say I have never ceased to congratulate myself on my good luck in being detailed for this duty.

Our party consisted of Lieutenant Spurgin, Lieutenant Bowen, Dr. Cholmeley, and myself. We had the jolliest and most exciting time. We were told to go to Shoaygheen, and it was a case of "go, and thou goest," but how we arrived in safety is a marvel. We got no route, in the proper acceptation of the word, for no one could give us any; we had to traverse a "terra incognita." No road really existed; jungle tracks there certainly were; beyond that, nothing. Our commanding officer had no interpreter; so to Providence and Spurgin's good sense we were indebted for our ultimate success.

The convoy chiefly consisted of barrels of gunpowder and commissariat stores, drawn in native carts by bullocks. Our tents were carried by elephants.

Well, off we started. Every soldier knows what it is to serve under a thoroughly capable and congenial superior, and, as we had both qualities combined in ours, we were indeed a happy lot; but our jollity was increased by the many amusing incidents that occurred.

As I have said, road there was none, so we had to send an officer and small escort to feel our way each day; and when several tracks converged there was a fearful parley amongst our guides, carried on in Burmese, until the right one was decided on. The officer then made a preconcerted mark at the spot where the roads diverged, and proceeded on. Now try to realize a wholly unknown country as flat as Holland, with no distinguishing marks, covered either with forests of gigantic trees or high pampas grass, abounding in tigers and elephants, and a possibility, not to say a probability, of a body of hostile Dacoits; and you have a pretty good idea of our surroundings.

I unfortunately had to realize all this in a very marked manner, for one day when I was with the advanced party at an awkward divergence of paths, I either neglected to make my mark sufficiently evident, or else the main body did not notice it. Be that as it may, I trudged on until I came to a place where the guides told me that there was good water. There I remained, but no main body arrived. I waited and waited in hopeless anxiety. At last a scout turned up, and the main body quickly followed. Spurgin good-naturedly admitted that they had overlooked my mark, and so had wandered miles out of their way.

In a country like Burmah we naturally came across rivers, and had to ford them as best we could. The usual method was for some of our men to strip and wade over, and then to return and carry our commanding officer and others over. On one occasion a fish mistook Spurgin's impromptu charger for some specially desirable bit of bait, and bit him, thereby causing him to jib and nearly capsize the commanding officer into deep water.

As to our convoy, heaven only knows how it was got across! I can only remember that bullock-carts were lightened to the utmost, and then by almost superhuman exertions were dragged across, the elephants assisting in a marvellous manner by pushing with their foreheads from behind. The sagacity of these dear creatures was here fully realized. There was a baby elephant with us, and the way in which the mother taught the little thing to assist was not only pretty but marvellous.

Our humorous moments were occasionally varied by others of intense anxiety. While encamping in one place, we were startled by the sound of what appeared rapid musketry. Spurgin was at a loss to understand the cause, for no Europeans were supposed to be anywhere near, and the Burmese could scarcely be fighting amongst themselves. The firing, however, approached nearer and nearer, when to our dismay we found that the neighbouring jungle was on fire, and that the musket-like reports came from the joints of the huge bamboos, which exploded with considerable force as the fire converted the sap and moisture into steam.

We were in a cruel dilemma, for our convoy consisted chiefly of gunpowder, and to be enveloped in flames meant complete destruction. Spurgin immediately placed the ammunition in as safe a position as possible by laagering up, and then gave orders for all grass and undergrowth around to be cleared. But the sepoys, possibly on account of some caste prejudice, declined to work; however, a threat from Spurgin to shoot the first man who refused brought them to their senses, and our camp and convoy were saved. It was a near shave, and I should not care to run many such risks.

Another peril we had to contend with was that of gigantic trees falling across our route. In a country so densely wooded and with such an intensely hot climate, either from spontaneous combustion or other causes, trees became burnt and charred round the stems to such an extent that a mere breath of wind or the tramp of men's feet in passing was sufficient to bring them down with a crash. On such occasions, and they were frequent, there was a cry of "Look out for yourselves!" which was promptly obeyed, and discipline was in abeyance for the moment. I remember coming across an old fallen tree, which had caused a temporary stoppage of our convoy by blocking the way. I counted a dozen different kinds of orchids on the branches, many of which were then in bloom.

It was a glorious country for a botanist. One day I found what to me was a new fern. I gave it to Spurgin, who sent it through his father to the Royal Botanical Gardens (Regent's Park, I think), and it was pronounced to be either new or rare. I see it commonly enough now.

"Travellers ne'er did lie, though fools at home condemn them." So says Shakespeare. I am therefore emboldened to relate a truly wonderful and well-remembered event. One morning, on coming out of the jungle just as dawn began to break, we came on to an immense plain, when, to our astonishment, the whole earth for miles seemed to rise into the air; in a few minutes the vision developed itself into a mass of myriads of pelicans, storks, and other wild birds—truly an astounding sight. In Egypt huge masses of birds are often seen, but nothing compared with those we now came across.

We had yet other causes for anxiety. One early morning, when passing through a deep gorge, we were startled by a brisk rustle in the jungle to our right, and immediately a magnificent antlered stag bounded over our heads, evidently escaping from some beast of prey, possibly from the tiger whose footprint we had just found in our path, and who by the way had relieved one of our bullock-carts of its driver the day before. When subsequently we were encamped at Shoaygheen, we had so many bullocks taken by tigers, that we had to place loaded sentries over the Commissariat yard.

At last we got to Shoaygheen, and encamped on what seemed to be a most suitable and healthly eminence, but to our horror we soon perceived a very ancient and loathsome smell. On searching round, a sergeant brought us a mass of human hair, and we discovered we were in close proximity to a Burmese burial-ground. It was a case of "up sticks," and off we went to another less picturesque but more wholesome encampment.

At Shoaygheen we fell in with red tape and officialism, and a dear jolly little march was henceforth no more than a pleasant memory. I venture to think that, if in those days we had had dailies and specials, some notice would have been taken of our performance.

Our next move was along the left bank of the river to Tonghoo. I do not remember anything striking occurring during this march, but on arrival we found that Major Neill of Ours, who was Assistant-Adjutant-General to General Steele's Division, had met with a terrible accident, which necessitated his return to England. This circumstance affected me personally, as will be seen further on.

CHAPTER VII

TONGHOO

TONGHOO strongly resembled Pegu in most of its features. The pagoda, much smaller, stood on an eminence in the centre of a vast plain, surrounded at a considerable distance by the same sort of wall and embankment. The river, which is much wider than that at Pegu, runs on the east face at a distance from the Bund, and was approached by a ghaut as at Pegu. A very wide moat ran along the east and south faces. I never explored the others.

On our arrival we found the people already settled, and the bazaars were fairly full; the Commissariat had no trouble in buying rice and grain. I noticed that, although so similar in many respects, the foliage of the jungle was far less tropical-looking than that around Pegu. The poonghie houses were surrounded very generally with trees; amongst which figured the Ferrea, very graceful and bearing a lovely blossom, and concerning which the legend exists that Gaudama, at his next and last appearance, will be found lying sleeping under this tree. Hence the custom of planting it around their temples and monasteries, in hopes their particular tree will be the one selected. There were fewer palms, but any amount of that largest and most graceful of all grasses, the bamboo.

Our first duty was the housing of our men, and learning the different positions of importance.

Major Hill had been appointed to the command of the Gwalior Contingent, and Colonel Apthorpe (afterwards Sir East Apthorpe) reigned in his stead. Our new Colonel was a very excellent soldier in every sense of the word, and had seen much service under Sir de Lacy Evans in Spain. We got on very well with him, and the regiment was proud of him. We were not so fortunate in our Brigadier. For some reason we never got on well with him. This was the more strange, as both Major Hill and Colonel Apthorpe were most zealous and efficient officers, and our regiment had given satisfaction hitherto with all under whom it had been called on to serve.

One feature was very noticeable in our new cantonment. The houses were all built on piles at a considerable height from the ground, and the main roads were at least two feet above the surrounding plain. When the rains came on we understood all about this, for we could easily have fished through the interstices of our floors, and the revels held by the frogs at night were simply distracting. As usual I chummed with Sladen, and we occupied a small poonghie house situated on the main road leading to the pagoda.

We officers were soon the centre of attraction for the pleasure-seeking populace of both sexes. Our toilets, which were of necessity partially performed in the open air, brought crowds, who squatted on the ground in the most orderly manner, smoking their cigarettes, and commenting on the unusual procedures of soap-and-water. Seton of Ours was the cynosure of all beholders; not only was he fair and beardless, but he had two false front teeth which he could displace with his tongue at pleasure, and he used to sit on the wooden steps of his poonghie house, and show these teeth on the tip of his tongue and then put them back again. At first the women fled in dismay, thinking him a wizard, but they soon came to look on it as a joke, and would sit quietly for no end of a time to see the wonderful trick performed. This I need scarcely remind the reader was long before *King Solomon's Mines* was thought of. I wonder if the author ever heard of this incident.

The inhabitants were intensely friendly, and would always welcome us and invite us to sit in the verandah of their shops, and offer us cigarettes. They were a merry, peaceable, idle, play-loving race. Their chief game was football, in which an open cane-work ball, very elastic, was used; the play consisted in standing in a circle and keeping the ball off the ground with their feet. It was marvellous the dexterity with which they kicked the ball up. I think they were great gamblers, but of this I am not sure.

The jungle around Tonghoo was extremely beautiful. One tree, called, I think, the *Butea frondosa*, when in blossom looked like one mass of fire; indeed, it required but little imagination at times to believe the whole jungle in places was burning.

But whilst surrounded by beauty and good-tempered inhabitants, we had our troubles. One considerable source of alarm arose from the number of mad dogs, and consequent hydrophobia. Several of our men died of it; one of my men in particular, whose case I well remember. He asked to fall out on morning parade. When we were dismissed I asked to see him. He told me he had felt ill, and had gone to the canteen to see if a dram would do him good, but could not touch it. By twelve the symptoms had set in seriously; he died next day. It seems a mad dog had run right through the guard-room at night, and had bitten this man whilst he lay asleep.

In a country so intersected with great rivers and endless streams, it seemed strange that hydrophobia should be rife. I can only account for it by the fact that the native dogs, as in Constantinople, were a perfect pest, and officers and men used to destroy them; I have a note that at Pegu we destroyed eleven in one day. Of course many were only wounded, and perhaps from the heat of the sun they went mad and bit others, thereby spreading the disease. Our men and officers began also to suffer from dysentery.

At this time the archbishop of the district died, a very good and holy man. The ceremonies connected with the final disposition of his body were curious and interesting. First of all, a magnificent poonghie house was erected, as if by magic, for him to lie in state in. Then he was put in a wooden coffin and covered completely with liquid honey; for a whole year he remained in this honeyed state, and was visited by thousands. I do not know if these actually saw him, but they walked round the catafalque that held the coffin. The walls of this new erection were covered with pictures quaintly drawn. Our men and officers were constantly depicted, with faces very white, very brilliant coats, and fully equipped. Their devil was frequently introduced, but always as black and very hairy. After the old gentleman had been in honey for a year, the liquid was drawn off. (I decline to believe in the reported use it was put to.) And at this juncture the neighbouring villages sent each a highly ornamental car, on which in turn the body in its coffin was placed. Then commenced a sort of pull-devil, pull-baker game. The villagers of the car in which the body rested manned the ropes in front, and began a sort of chant, extolling the virtues of the deceased, and claiming the honour of having his body amongst them for cremation. The Tonghooites on their side pulled behind, shouting that nothing should deprive them of their saint. This process was carried on till all the village cars had been used in turn, then the grand Tonghoo car came, on which the coffin was placed, and all present gave a hand in dragging the ponderous edifice to an open glade in the jungle. Here a funeral pyre had been erected, in the midst of which were several barrels of gunpowder. The wood had been saturated with oil, and inflammable matter freely introduced. Long rattan guides were fastened from surrounding trees to the pyre, and to these rope-like guides rockets had been tied on runners. As soon as the old gentleman had been securely placed on the pyre, and the car removed, these rockets were fired at the pyre. Several missed their aim. At last one set the pyre ablaze; it burnt furiously until the gunpowder was reached, and then, amidst suppressed exclamations, the body was blown into thin air. The crowd was so immense, that we men and officers were ordered to go with side-arms, but no attempt at disturbance occurred.

To return to the Burmese: they are naturally a peace-loving race; it is only the Dacoits that give any trouble. I have heard words pass often in the bazaar, generally between women. I never but once saw a regular fight, and it was a curious sight. Our main-guard was just opposite the market-place. One day when on guard I heard a commotion outside, and our men laughing. I went out, and found two women vociferating and using menaces against each other. A ring was formed round them by the bystanders, who enjoyed the scene most thoroughly, laughing loudly at each sally. At last the two women became furious. They looked like demons, and when the last insult had been hurled, they both whipped off the only garment that they had, smacked their bodies, and went for each other literally *tooth* and *nail*. I now saw that the climax had been reached, and ordered the sergeant to interfere. The crowd assisted quite cheerfully, and the two combatants were separated. This was the only real quarrel I ever saw. I was told it would have ended fatally if they had not been separated.

The mothers seemed fond of their children, and a child's cry was seldom heard. Our men evidently took an immense liking to these people.

It is strange to see how soon the British soldier forms his estimate of his surroundings; to note how he will fraternize with one regiment and not with another; how he foregathers with Sikhs and Ghoorkhas, and not with

Hindoos. The liking of our men for these people took a very usual form. I had been in temporary charge of a company, when one day the sergeant told me a private wanted to see me. He was ushered in, and I asked his wishes. He told me he wanted fifty rupees " to buy one of them Burmese women." Of course I was properly shocked, and told him that by the Governor-General's proclamation there was to be no buying or selling; that he had better spend his money in some wiser manner. In a fortnight he came back and said he had thought over it, and would still like to have the money to buy a *time-piece*. Of course the money in the savings bank was his, and I could not refuse it further; but I wondered where time-pieces were to be bought in Tonghoo. The sergeant told me next day that he had married the girl after Burmese fashion, which in those days did not count for much.

At this time sickness became very prevalent, and I fell amongst the victims. I was very bad with dysentery; indeed so bad that Anderson, our doctor, got permission for me to be moved into the head-quarter poonghie house, in which he himself lived, as being nearer to him, and more airy and healthy. Sladen was bad at the same time, and three others. I am afraid to say the number of leeches I had on; it seemed to me that every day a new dozen was ordered. Poor things, they had no chance; out of the dozen about two got something, the rest went empty away. I do not think now a pin's-point could be put where there is not the mark of a leech-bite; such was their remedy in those days. Anderson was more than good and gentle with me; he was an immensely powerful man. I remember at Pegu his lifting single-handed a gun that no artilleryman could move with two. He was, besides, a delightfully clever man, and a great lover of Shakespeare, and I have now many extracts in my common-place book that he gave me. Poor Anderson, he got dysentery and died from over-leeching himself.

My new quarters were certainly much healthier; I think about six of us occupied the house. As there was only one flight of steps up to the floor, which was raised on piles some sixteen feet, I had a lean-to erected at the rear of my room, and a private flight of steps, up which the dressers and my servants could come without disturbing the other occupants. I lay in a critical state for weeks, if not months, when a curious accident occurred. I was sitting in my back-room, making myself some tea one afternoon. The kettle was on a brazier filled with charcoal; I had just filled the teapot, when by some mischance I upset the teapot right on my lap. I had only thin pyjamas on. To throw the tea-leaves off was the work of an instant, then I called my servant; by this time I had nearly fainted. I was carried to my bed, and the doctor was sent for. But before he arrived my servant had suggested putting *ink* on with a feather. I was in such agony that I did not care what he did, and I fancied he knew what was best to be done, so raised no objection. When the doctor came he found me painted as black as ink could make me. It was impossible to suppress a laugh, it was too ridiculous. However, he soon did me up in oil and cotton-wool, and by means of a strong opiate I slept through the night. Strange to say, whether it was counter irritation or not, the dysentery disappeared from that day, and I had only the scald to get over. It took a long time, for where the tea-leaves had rested on my thigh the wound was very deep. The dressing was very painful, but I got used to it, and in due course of time was sufficiently well to go out every day for air and exercise in a dhoolie. This was indeed a sad time, for now that I could get about to talk to my comrades I found out what gaps had been made by death in our little band. Anderson I knew had gone, but not poor dear Bowen. What a loss he was to me! He was one of those charming manly fellows that one makes a hero of. Then

Bryce and Wing were no more. As to men, it is impossible to say how many succumbed. Funerals were conducted without pomp or ceremony, in order to decrease the depressing effect.

Add to this, an uneasy feeling showed itself in the mind of our Brigadier. In consequence of reports of a threatened descent by the Burmese, sentries were doubled and loaded at sunset. This extra work in such drenching tropical rain told greatly on the men. No one can have an idea of what rain is until he has gone through a Burmese monsoon. We often could not see a sentry a few yards off the mess-house.

This leads me to an incident that may perhaps arrest the attention of the reader.

As already stated, Sladen and I on first arrival occupied a small poonghie house in the main street leading to the pagoda. Behind there was a long strip of garden, which was covered with fruit-trees growing in the very wildest disorder,—a perfect jungle.

One day when I was prowling about, I heard the sound of clack-clack going on towards the bottom of this garden. I followed the sound, and, from behind a bush that concealed me, I saw two Burmese girls sitting in the verandah, weaving those silk cloths which the women delight in, and which form their only garment. Presently I made my way towards them; the instant they saw me they beat a hurried retreat into the house. I went up to it, and called for fire, about the only word in Burmese I knew. After calling more than once, an old lady, evidently much frightened, brought me a piece of live charcoal in a pair of pincers. I made a salaam, and gave her all the cheroots I had in my case.

Next day I went again, using the same device, and after a few days, seeing that I meant no harm, confidence was restored, and the girls continued their weaving in my presence. I used to take a note-book with me, and by pointing to certain objects made them understand that I wanted to know the name in Burmese. In this way I commenced a vocabulary. We soon got on friendly terms, and then by the aid of an interpreter I gave an order for a silk cloth, drawing the pattern of the plaid with some crushed brick mixed with water, on a sheet of white paper, with a bit of twig beaten soft at the end as a brush. I have the silk in my possession now.

I found that the old lady was the sister of the poonghie in whose house we were living, and that on the death of her husband she had come to live near for the sake of his protection; they were evidently people of good birth and education. I never knew the names of these girls. The one who usually took the lead in all matters, and whom therefore I supposed to be the elder, was of a much more refined type than the general run of Burmese. This one I shall call Maima, which is really the generic for all females. The other was a plump rosy girl of the usual Burmese type, whom I shall call Fatima, because she was so fat. On ordering the cloth I gave an advance of five rupees, in order to enable them to buy the silk. About this time, as I have said, I got ill, and moved my quarters, wholly forgetting all about Maima and my silk.

One afternoon, when I had come in from my daily airing in the dhoolie, I heard a voice calling out "Tukeen, Tukeen!" (my lord, my lord!) outside my back entrance; I went to see who it was, and found Maima. I scarcely recognized her, she was so altered from illness. I bade her come in, which she did, squatting on the floor; she then produced a handkerchief from her girdle, and placed five rupees on the floor in front of me. I sent for an interpreter, and found, as I had surmised, she had come to return me the money I had advanced. Her story was as follows:—Shortly after I had left the poonghie house the Engineers had come and told them the site of the house was required for Government purposes, and without giving them any compensation had turned them out; they had tried in vain to find me to intercede for them, so had been compelled to go into a miserable hovel in an unhealthy part of the town, where fever had overtaken them. The old mother had had the fever slightly, but Maima and her sister badly; weeks had passed, and their sufferings had been very great. One day, whilst in the bazaar, the old lady, seeing me pass in my dhoolie, had set a watch to find where I was carried, and thus found out my quarters; then Maima came to restore the five rupees, as their looms had been pawned to buy food, and there was no chance of the cloth being made.

I was much touched by the girl's honesty, and most interested in their case. I bade her keep the money, and get back her looms, and promised to call next day and bring them assistance. I gave her the bread, tea, sugar, etc., that I had by me, and sent a servant with her to see where she lived. That evening, when the doctor called to see me, I told him the story; he said that probably a little port wine was the best medicine for them, but that if in seeing them next day I found them bad, he would call and see them.

I may here mention that on all occasions officers, especially medical ones, were only too glad to conciliate the natives by little kindnesses. Our men, too, liked them, and never cheated them, or tried to beat them down in their prices.

Well, next day I went to see my friends; they were living in a miserable hut in a swampy place. I can hardly describe the looks of Fatima; she had shrunk from a jolly chubby-faced girl to be like a wizened old monkey, all cheekbone and eyes. The old mother was fairly well. I gave them the port wine with explicit instructions as to its use, and left a goodly supply of arrowroot, etc. I then told the mother to look out for another house, and gave an order for a second cloth, leaving a further deposit of five rupees.

Occasionally I visited them in their new house, and was well pleased to find a rapid improvement in their looks. They were industrious, and soon got their heads above water. It was nice to see the simple way in which they tried to show their gratitude for any kindness. They knew I was fond of flowers, and I seldom went to the house without their having some new specimen to show me, and their anxiety to make me understand and pronounce the name was amusing. Maima came, I think, twice to my house to deliver the silks when finished.

Here I must leave the subject and get on with other matter. As I said, there was an uneasiness as to the movements of the Burmese army, which by this time had assumed the nature of isolated bands of Dacoits.

Our Brigadier held a council of war, at which officers commanding regiments and heads of departments were present. The story goes that Colonel Anstruther, the hero of Chinese captivity, when asked his advice, gave it more forcibly than politely. He was a marvellous man, and the stories told of him would fill a book.

He was perhaps best known by the wonderful caricatures he drew in charcoal on the walls of the racquet-court at Madras. I hope they are still preserved.

The Assistant Commissioner, Mr. O'Riley, had by this time arrived, and, with Major Allen, was about to fix the boundary of the province we had annexed. A company of my regiment under Captain Geils and Lieutenant Grant, together with a detachment of the 5th M. N. Infantry, some Sappers, and a few Irregular Horse were ordered as an escort. No special danger that I am aware of was felt in respect to this movement. The force was to leave on January 24. I had not been detailed for it, not being attached to Geils' company.

A strange thing occurred on the evening of the 23rd. It was an awful downpour; such a day as no reasonable person would be out in. Just as it grew dark I heard the usual "Tukeen, Tukeen!" It was Maima; she was drenched, as she had no umbrella. How she had passed the sentries, heaven only knows. She was very mysterious, and though speaking volubly did so in an undertone. I could not understand a word she said, and wanted to send for an interpreter; she understood, and at once objected to my doing so. Finally, finding she could not make me understand, she signified by signs her wish for paper and pencil, and then wrote a word in Burmese, which of course was incomprehensible to me. No sooner had she written and given it to me than she disappeared before I could stop her, or try to take measures for her safety. Here then was a mystery, a very considerable one, and no means of unravelling it. I spent much time in pondering over the whole thing, for I was certain, from the girl's manner, that her mission was of importance. Next day I thought the matter over, and determined to take the bit of paper to Sladen, who had already made great progress in the study of the Burmese language, and ask him the meaning of these mysterious words, without telling him any of the surrounding circumstances. I knew that, if he could not interpret them, he had some one near who could. However, Sladen found no difficulty in reading the words, and said they merely meant "Don't go."

I must here again hark back a bit to an event that stirred all Tonghoo, male and female, to the very innermost recesses of their hearts.

Madame Meyer, the wife of our bandmaster, unexpectedly arrived. A most stringent order had been given against any women accompanying the force; but this, I suppose, was considered to apply only to those connected with the force; and Madame Meyer, being a German subject, managed to smuggle herself on board some ship, and so eventually arrived safely at her destination. She was of a purely German type, very fair, plump, with a profusion of golden brown hair. What could man want more? I have tried to describe the *levées* of Burmese that attended our morning toilet; they were nothing compared with those who assembled and waited with the greatest decorum until Madame should appear in the verandah, radiant with smiles and clad in spotless white. All Tonghoo, male and female, then gave a suppressed murmur of admiration. They had never seen a purely white woman before; the women simply adored her, whilst the men worshipped her from afar.

Now to my story. On the very morning of the departure of Geils' detachment, Madame Meyer was much exercised in her mind, and revealed the cause to her friend, Seton of Ours, who having been educated in Germany could converse with her in her own language. She told him that her husband had had a dream. "Nothing wonderful in that," was Seton's remark. But she explained that there was a great deal in it, for her husband had the power of foresight in his dreams, and his recent dream was one of ill omen. The dream, as told to several of us youngsters by Seton, was briefly as follows: "Taylor of Ours had come to Meyer, and asked him to compose a new funeral march, as Captain Geils had been killed."

I must mention that Taylor was on leave, I think at Singapore; at all events hundreds of miles away. Somehow, everybody seemed to take this dream seriously. I confess it took hold of me, and was in my mind connected mysteriously with Maima's words.

The force was still within easy hail; should I tell the Colonel of Maima's visit, of my fears of treachery, and urge the utmost precaution on the part of Captain Geils? I dismissed the idea, being in reality afraid to say that this Burmese girl had been to my quarters.

The force had only got to a place called Kaleen, about seventeen miles off, when they were attacked in ambuscade, and the news came back that Grant of Ours was wounded, together with some of our men. Most of us now believed that Meyer's dream had been sufficiently fulfilled, and were consequently comforted; not so Meyer himself—he was still uneasy.

On the receipt of the news of Grant's wound, Lieutenant P. A. Brown of Ours, with Dr. Boutfleur, were sent out on an elephant with three of our own men as an escort. I wonder if any one in this world ever heard of two officers being sent out seventeen miles on an elephant into dense jungle, probably full of hostile Burmese, with only three men as a guard. The thing seemed to me incredible, but so it was. Fortunately they arrived in safety, but only to learn that the force had again been attacked, and that Geils was severely wounded.

The Brigadier now sent a very efficiently-constituted force under Colonel Poole of the 5th M. N. I. to support Geils; but opposition had ceased, and Colonel Poole brought his force back again into Tonghoo..

Captain Geils had indeed been severely wounded; a matchlock ball had hit him in the shoulder, and the bullet, imbedded beneath the clavicle, could not be extracted. Grant's wound, though severe, was not dangerous.

On hearing the account of the way in which the enemy had laid a trap for the force, I could not fail to feel certain that Maima had got wind of the plot devised by the Burmese soldiers, who were no friends of the peaceful inhabitants of Tonghoo, and, fearing that I might be ordered on this duty, had warned me not to go. I found out afterwards that my surmise was absolutely correct, and the girl, by trying to save my life, hoped to pay any kindness that had been shown to her and her belongings.

Now to the sequel of Meyer's dream. Poor Geils lingered on week after week, life quietly ebbing away, for some of the cloth of his tunic had been carried in with the bullet and caused sloughing. He was one of the occupants of our poonghie house, and I saw him many times a day. His patience was very touching, and to watch him become thinner and thinner each day was most painful. The doctors were greatly alarmed at his condition. Just then Taylor rejoined from leave. Geils and Taylor were sworn allies; so after a consultation the doctors told Taylor that the only hope of saving life lay in taking the arm out of the socket, and begged Taylor to convey this decision to poor Geils. The result was that he consented to the operation. It was performed. Geils rallied only for a second, and then passed away.

Colonel Poole had arrived by this time with his force, and, as a portion of the 5th M. N. I. had accompanied Geils, a message was sent to say that as a mark of respect the whole regiment, with their band, wished to join in the funeral procession. Then it was that some one (whether Taylor or not I cannot say) went to Meyer and said as there were two bands they were to play alternately, and asked that as the 5th knew no other funeral march than that from *Saul*, our band should play some other appropriate tune. I think he arranged a German hymn-tune for the occasion.

Such then was the realization of our bandmaster's dream. Facts are always stranger than fiction. These facts are, as far as I am aware, absolutely correctly stated in this matter.

Was ever man more lucky than I in the matter of friends? Somehow or other so many took a kindly interest in me, and no one more than Arthur Moberly, our Engineer officer in charge. He used occasionally to dine at our mess, and there our acquaintance commenced.

One day he came to me, and told me that Government wanted to ascertain whether an old road known as the King's Road, between Tonghoo and Pegu, still existed, and that an officer was required to accompany a force, and survey and report on it. Would I care to undertake the work? I told him I should like it above all things, but my knowledge of surveying was most limited; to which he replied that he would soon put me in the way of picking it up. Accordingly he lent me books and instruments, gave me Sappers as chain-men, and supervised my work day by day. When he thought me sufficiently instructed, he told the Brigadier, who ordered him to examine me and report the result. I need scarcely say I passed, and was appointed in Brigade Orders to accompany a force to proceed overland from Tonghoo to Pegu. Hitherto we had always come round by Shweghine, and then by boat up the Sitang river.

The party detailed as my escort comprised, I think, fifty of our men and fifty of the 5th M. N. I., under command of Lieutenant Wetherall, a most charming companion and first-rate officer. Strange to say, although Wetherall was my senior in army rank, the command of the whole party was given to me. A party of Sappers with necessary tools accompanied the force, together with commissariat stores, elephants, etc. I do not think we had any bullock-carts, as the existence of any road was more than problematical. A doctor accompanied us whose name I forget.

On the appointed morning we started. Of course our first march was easy enough. Wetherall started at early dawn, and I followed as soon as there was light enough to see the needle of the instrument. I had a perambulator in order to measure the distances. My own personal escort consisted of four Sappers and two coolies to wheel the perambulator and carry instruments.

We got on capitally for two marches; then the road became intricate, and in places closed up with jungle, which Wetherall had to clear before his men and animals could pass. The value of our elephants on such occasions became singularly apparent; they crashed through when

I

feasible, tearing up small trees and breaking branches with their trunks. Nothing could surpass the wild beauty of these spots. I longed to remain and collect specimens of ferns, orchids, etc.

In places the traces of the King's Road were very distinct; the sides had been faced with brickwork to the height of as much as two feet, evidently to raise the road above the floods in the monsoon. These parts were covered with mosses and maidenhair fern, making it almost sacrilege to tread over them.

Many interesting incidents occurred. My orders were to buy and pay liberally for anything I required, and in every way possible to conciliate the natives. At the second or third halt we came to a village where no white man had ever set foot. The whole population bolted *en masse*. Presently the old women crept cautiously near, and squatted down to observe our movements; then the young women and children joined, and finally the men formed up at a most respectful distance in the rear. Peaceful overtures were made to them through the interpreter, and then the women advanced and mixed with us. A few fowls seemed their only possessions, and so poor were they that I was told they subsisted on the seed of the bamboo, which is like very inferior oats. Though the Burmese will not take life for food, they do not mind selling to others for such a purpose; so we bought fowls and eggs, and paid handsomely for them.

Confidence was now restored, and an old woman came up to me as I stood with my shirt-sleeves rolled up, and took my hand; before I could stop her, she put out her tongue and licked a good portion above the wrist. I found out that she merely wanted to ascertain whether the colour was natural or effected by some pigment.

We showed them watches, which they readily understood to be connected with the sun. The instruments they did not understand, and in connection with them a laughable incident occurred. For some scientific reason which I cannot explain, all objects on which the telescope is directed are reversed. I let an old woman of an inquiring mind look through the glass at a group of girls standing by. As soon as she saw they appeared standing on their heads, she gave a scream and shouted out something, on which all the girls squatted down, and afterwards nothing would induce them to stand up whilst the instrument was in use. Percussion-caps were a mystery: we allowed several to be fired, also a round or two of ammunition at the butt of the tree near at hand. The effect was satisfactory. Strange to say, after this villagers were never afraid of us; no doubt news of the object of our march and the friendly nature of our bearing was transmitted from village to village. Occasionally we came across rivers, but had no trouble in getting over; our elephants carrying the men in cases where wading was deemed undesirable. We met with the spoor of large game wherever there was water.

On one occasion I had got the theodolite fixed, and was taking a bearing, when a huge rock-snake came with a rush across the road. I gave a jump, over went the instrument, and away went my people. I found out, however, that it was a very harmless beast; so my fright was unnecessary.

Encamping on the bank of a lovely river one afternoon, the doctor and I went in to bathe. All went serenely till I heard a cry, and looking round I found the doctor struggling in deep water. I saw him go down, and come up again wildly throwing about his arms. I can remember my thoughts and feelings at that moment, though over forty years ago, just as vividly as if it was only yesterday. I could barely swim myself, and I turned over in my mind whether I ought to try to save him at the risk of my own life or not. In a second all the pros and cons passed through my brain, and I determined to make an effort.

I got to him as he rose again, and he clutched me in a frantic manner, and down we both went. My thoughts were not so much of myself as of the party, for I gave myself up. Luckily the elephants came down at that moment to water, and, seeing our situation, the mahout put one in, and the sagacious beast dragged us out. I was very exhausted, but the doctor was much worse: it was some time before he came round. He never said "Thank you" to me, but he was a man of few words.

Wetherall, unless delayed by having to cut his way through jungle, always had his camp pitched and breakfast ready before I came in, and then we had the whole day to ourselves. He was a most pleasant companion.

At one halting-place, somewhat late at night, I was roused by a voice outside my tent. I got up in a second and seized my pistol: I had no revolver in those days. On going to the door I found a woman, kneeling in a most supplicating manner. I roused my interpreter, and demanded her business. She told her story in a plaintive trembling fashion as follows:—She had lost all her children one by one of a curious complaint; the last one was now fast fading away, and, hearing that I was a great astrologer and medicine man, she had come to entreat me to save her child. Luckily I had already given orders for a halt, as the men had been overworked. I told her to come early next morning, and I would take a doctor with me and see what could be done.

As directed she came, and conducted us to her house. There we found the husband, a sickly-looking mortal, in charge of a little invalid. The doctor examined the child, and pronounced the disease consumption, but of a type and at a stage when by care it could be arrested. He took much interest in the case, and prescribed at once. That evening we saw the child again, and already it seemed better. So anxious was I for the cure of the little one, and so sure did I feel that if a cure could be effected it would redound to our credit, that I offered the woman a dhoolie for the child and free rations for herself and husband, if she would accompany us to Pegu, so as to let the sufferer have further treatment. The interpreter fully explained my offer and the advantages. The poor woman silently looked to her husband for some sign of assent. He held his head down over the little one, but said nothing. Then she took my hand and led me outside, until we came to a bushy shrub, on the branches of which hung strips of scarlet and white paper. She pointed to it, and then said she could not come; all her little ones lay buried there, and if they left there would be no one to put up charms to keep the Nāts from injuring them. If their last was to be taken, God's will be done, but she could not leave those who had already gone. She thanked me with tears in her eyes, and kissed my hand, and so we parted.

Next morning, when on my way surveying, I came across the husband and wife, she bearing her little one well wrapped up. They bowed to the ground when they saw me, and stood watching me until a bend in the jungle hid me from their sight. I would have given much to have saved that child.

I reached Pegu in safety, and reported my arrival to Rogers, the Engineer-in-charge, and to head-quarters at Rangoon. I got orders to remain at Pegu till my report was ready. Wetherall and the party were to rejoin at Tonghoo, *viâ* Shweghine. Rogers very kindly gave me house-room, and lent me all that was necessary for plotting out my survey. Reader, that survey was truly a *magnum opus*. I commenced on too large a scale, and, as the distance traversed was 149 miles, it required acres of paper. Sheet on sheet had to be joined; and when completed it looked like one of those monster petitions that are ordered to lie on the table of the House. Terror must have seized the Chief Engineer when he saw it, and no doubt it was ordered to lie in the corner. However, a report accompanied it, together with a route in which the distances, all information concerning villages, water, wells, etc., with the names, were written in English and Burmese. This, I fancy, satisfied them, and they paid me handsomely for the work.

Rogers made an application for my services, as he required assistance. This was not granted, and I was ordered to rejoin *viâ* Shweghine. I rode this time, and had no other adventure than a good fright from a solitary elephant, whose presence was observed afar off by my Burmese groom.

From Shweghine I went by boat, such a wearisome journey. I took a six-pound jar of black-currant jam and a tin of biscuits with me. I loathed jam by the time I arrived. I halted whenever the boatmen pleased, and got eggs and chickens, sometimes ducks; my servant was a good cook.

On reaching Tonghoo I was attached to the Sappers under Lieutenant Shortland. My work was levelling and superintending the clearing of ground beyond the outer wall on the river face, for a new cantonment. I lived with Moberly, but Shortland was my immediate commanding officer.

Here, then, when the rains set in, I again got dysentery, and Bond, who was in medical charge of Artillery and Sappers, decided on sending me home.

One word about poor Bond. He was a charming man, thoroughly beloved. He came to a sad end. He had recently married, and was, I think, in charge at Martaban. One night on returning from a dinner-party, he wanted to take a pill, and unfortunately, instead of lighting a candle, he groped in the dark, and in error took a strychnine pill he had made up to poison wild dogs. He realized at once his mistake, and sent for the apothecary. A stomach-pump was instantly used, but

alas! he was dead in a few hours, leaving his young wife
disconsolate.

As soon as a convoy was ready, I was shipped on board.
No one can tell what I felt at leaving Tonghoo: all my
hopes seemed dashed to the ground. I had just got my
foot on the first rung of the ladder, and I was driven
away by sickness. To me, being attached to the Sappers
was the height of my ambition, for the Madras Sappers
had a world-wide reputation, and to be under such good
fellows as Moberly and Shortland more than bliss. So
with a heavy heart, and indeed a feeling almost of despair,
I watched the great pagoda fade from my sight.

My route again was from Shweghine to Pegu. How I
managed I know not; I know I could not have ridden,
so suppose I must have been carried. At Rangoon I
went before a medical board, and so grave was the nature
of Bond's certificate that I was ordered to Europe for
three years.

Scarcely had I smelt salt-water than I began to improve, and before I reached Calcutta I felt in excellent
health. My homeward journey was uneventful until we
re-embarked at Alexandria. We took on board several
sick and wounded from the Crimea, amongst others
Burgoyne of the Guards, severely wounded at the Alma,
and Prince Ernest of Leiningen, who had contracted fever
whilst serving on the Danube with Omar Pasha. I had
met the Prince on board the *Hastings* at Rangoon; but
as the sailors called him "Mr. Prince," I fancied his sur-
name was Prince, and had no idea he was a swell.

We came in for that awful storm of November 14, and
a pretty state we were in when we reached Malta—not
a single boat left. Strange to say, some ortolans in a
crate on deck survived, but we lost valuable horses, a
present from the Khedive to the Queen.

A curious incident brought this storm vividly to my
recollection some years after. While staying with my

friend Lloyd Philipps of Penty Park, some of us were walking from church one Sunday, when the wind was blowing freshly from the sea. The conversation naturally turned on storms, and I said I had been out in a terrible one. General Bolton, who was of the party, said he too had been out in a fearful one. I was not going to let his storm be worse than mine, so I piled up the agonies; so did he, until we had no more agonies to add. Then I asked him when and where his storm occurred, and then we found that we were talking of this very same Balaclava storm—that we had been on board the same ship, but in the lapse of time had forgotten each other. Lloyd Philipps was much amused at our anxiety to prove our respective storm the fiercer.

On board our ship I shared a cabin with a most worthy old Major, who had not seen his native land for years. He always made me turn out first; but the last morning he got up first in order to see all he could of the old country as early as possible. We were well in smooth water, when the cabin-door opened, and I was seized in the fervid embrace of a very robust female. On perceiving her mistake, she beat a hasty retreat. It seems it was the Major's wife, who had come out on the pilot-boat, and had been directed to the Major's cabin by the steward, and in the blindness of love (you know love is blind) had mistaken me for the Major. I only hope he did not get it hotter than I did, for I felt bruised for some time after.

Can any one tell me whether Southampton nursery-maids are noted for their beauty? It might only have been fancy, after having been surrounded by dusky houris for so many years; anyway I thought all those who assembled on the quay to witness our arrival more beautiful than any promised to the faithful by Mahomet.

CHAPTER VIII

LONDON TO CONSTANTINOPLE

LONDON in those days was very different from what it is now. There were few Clubs, and to any one not overburdened with money hotels were practically barred.

I lodged in Jermyn Street, and used to put on my dressing-table exactly what I could afford to spend during the day; if by good luck I spent less than that amount, the balance went to credit of the next day. I dined anywhere, and soon found out where I could get most for my money, "with the use of the cruets!"

I remember Simpson's at Billingsgate was very good, but the distance was an objection. In the Strand I found an ample variety of good eating-houses.

As to the evenings, I went often to the pit of the theatres, where, if you went tolerably early, you got a very good place. Music-halls were not much in vogue, but I was often at Evans' in Covent Garden, and got many a civil bow from Paddy Green. I have seen many celebrities there, and had Dickens and Thackeray pointed out to me.

One Herr van Joel was a great character; he imitated, as he termed it, "the trosh, the naghtingale, and the plackpord," and sold cigars. It was considered a great honour to lend him a walking-stick on which to perform a solo.

One day a gentleman announced as Mr. Bathurst came on and sang 'The Miller of the Dee' splendidly. I fancied I recognized him as an old school-fellow, and asked the waiter his real name. The man evidently pretended ignorance; so I told him to give my card, and found I was right, and Bathurst and I had a quiet supper together after his turn was over.

The singing at Evans' deserves more than a passing word. It was excellent: and Paddy Green used to boast that he supplied the Abbey and St. Paul's with trained choristers.

Casinos were more popular then than now, and I used to go to several; the Argyll Rooms chiefly. The band was very good and the company orderly. In the gallery, to which admittance was, I think, sixpence extra, you would meet most of the young *élite* of London. One very well known character was an *habituée*. She was called the Diamond Duchess, of course owing to her jewellery—a quiet unobtrusive woman. Some years after I met an old school-fellow, who told me he had been summoned from Chester to prove the will of the Diamond Duchess, and that by it numerous charities were benefited. These Rooms were to my mind most unnecessarily and unjustly done away with.

I remember dining about this time at a friend's house where some very distinguished men were guests, amongst others a celebrated London stipendiary. When we were putting on our coats to go, he very kindly asked me if he could give me a lift in his brougham. Asked where I was bound for, I said, "The Haymarket; won't you come too?"

"Oh!" he replied, "I dare not show my nose there."

"Why?"

"Because they know me too well; I have had so many of them before me."

With the characteristic impudence of youth I exclaimed: "What a shame!"

"Yes, my boy, I often think so myself; but I did not make the laws, I am only there to administer them." Then he added very gravely: "I am old and may never see it—you are young and may; but mark my words, if they continue to persecute those poor creatures in the way they do, refusing them even shelter, they will soon make London an abomination worse than the cities of the plain."

I have never forgotten those words; the reader will judge of their prophetic value.

There were other casinos and some music-halls of doubtful character; but, on the whole, the amusements for my class of young men were much more shady than those of the present day; the streets were safer, and by no means presented the scandals we now see.

However, London had not any attractions for me. I felt miserably lonely, and was glad to accept an invitation which released me from a distasteful life.

Before leaving, as I now felt perfectly well, I called at the India House and War Office, and volunteered for any service that was open to me.

My time after this was passed chiefly in Cheltenham, where I was made an honorary member of a most comfortable Club at the 'Plough.' Invitations to dinner and dances poured in, and with the weekly ball at the Assembly Rooms my evenings were anything but dull.

The winter of 1854-1855 was very severe. I was staying in South Wales, and I remember woodcock being half starved; I used often to see them roding over warm springs in sheltered places. I took to skating, and did my nose a serious injury. I find by my diary that I bottled for my future father-in-law about thirty dozen of port, some of which I am still drinking. It is prime.

After a pleasant visit to South Wales I joined my mother in Paris. Whilst enjoying the sights of the gay city, I got a letter from Mr. Melville of the India House, announcing my appointment as A.D.C. to Colonel Williams. As an A.D.C.-ship is an appointment of a private nature I was puzzled. I could only imagine that, the Crimean War being at its height, there was a paucity of officers of H.M.'s army available for such a post.

This letter necessitated my immediate presence at the India House, and there, to my misfortune, I met Colonel Neill of my own regiment, who greeted me cordially and inquired my mission. I told him. He shook his head and said, "Don't accept it. Colonel Williams is only a Frontier Commissioner, and you will see no service with him. Come and join the Turkish Contingent. I am promised a command, and will look after you." And so it came to pass that I declined the A.D.C.-ship, and missed the glorious defence of Kars.

No difficulties were thrown in the way of my joining the Contingent, and, after a certain amount of delay, an order to proceed to Constantinople *viâ* Trieste was sent to me with a special Foreign Office passport.

I joined my travelling companions (all of the Indian Army) at the British Hotel, where we dined, and sat smoking till it was time for our train.

A curious incident occurred here: an American gentleman asked to be allowed to join our party, and, on ascertaining that we were bound for the Crimea, he left the room and presently returned with a goodly packet of tobacco. He handed us each a portion, and said he hoped it would solace us in the trenches. He said it was a sample of the best ever manufactured in Virginia. I remember it was of a light colour and very good.

Nothing very particular occurred during our journey. When in Austria, I met an Austrian cavalry officer travelling to Vienna on court-martial duty, and found he belonged to a regiment of which a cousin of mine was Colonel. He was very polite and assisted us greatly, but alas! at Vienna itself I got into difficulties.

We were not on the very best terms with the Austrians at that time, on account of our sympathy with Garibaldi.

Unfortunately, I had a lot of red flannel shirts; these, added to a sword and revolver, were more than the custom house could stand, and I was detained. Of course I became indignant, and so made matters worse, when, to my joy, my recently-found friend came to my assistance and I was released. We remained at Vienna for some days, as our Austrian Lloyd's would not arrive till later at Trieste.

Lord John Russell was in Vienna then at a conference. and, as one of our party was connected with him, we availed ourselves of his permission to make use of his commissioner, who rendered us much service.

Here I heard the old Strauss, and danced to his music. We did theatres and opera. One night, on returning from the opera, we were having supper in the *salle-à-manger* when an Austrian gentleman and his wife entered. We were the sole occupants. The gentleman after a while asked to join our party, in order, as he explained, to improve his English before starting for England. We cordially acceded, and asked him to bring the lady. We were a merry party, and, before leaving, he told us he was a meerschaum-pipe manufacturer, and was proceding to England with a large assortment on exhibition. Lord John Russell and others had already visited his manufactory; he asked us also to come, which we promised to do on the morrow.

After showing us his exhibit he presented us each with a pipe, saying "They are not expensive, but they are of the best quality." It was strange that one gentleman in London should have given us tobacco, and another in Vienna pipes wherewith to smoke it. Some customs in the hotel at Vienna were curious, but, as our commissioner said, "no one notices it." The casinos and public thoroughfares were singularly orderly.

I saw *The Barber of Seville* well done at the Opera House, and heard Borghi Mamo for the first time: she became celebrated afterwards.

Our journey to Trieste was uneventful, save for the surprise at going by train over the Styrian Alps—a feat in engineering which was then considered marvellous. At Trieste a warm bath after such a long journey was delicious, but it nearly cost me very dear. The housemaid showed me the bath-room, and filled the bath, pointing out the handles that regulated the degree of heat and cold. She then retired and I undressed, but finding the water too warm desired to add some cold. The handles were marked F. and C., so, like an idiot, I turned on the one marked C., forgetting I was in Italy, and that therefore C. stood for Calde, when to my horror I was enveloped in steam. I could not even see the tap; the room was one dense mass of vapour. I had nothing to do but to open the door and scream for the woman, who luckily was close by. She saw the dilemma I was in and turned off the steam; I hope the state of the atmosphere served me as a veil.

We now embarked on one of the Austrian Lloyd's steamers; a more miserable attempt at a passenger steamer I never saw. Of course we were crowded, as indeed were all other lines at this time. In our cabin we had one washhand-stand for six.

On starting we ran into a brig, and that delayed us. The food was execrable, but "sweet are the uses of adversity": I learned on board to like raw ham, olives, and oil in various forms.

We picked up at one halting-place—Lissa, I think—an immense number of Turks going on a pilgrimage to Mecca. They brought an amount of live stock on their persons that rendered any intercourse with them impossible. I was, however, tempted to go forward by the piteous little cries of a baby. I interviewed the mother, a pretty young Italian, and told her the baby only cried because it was in pain, being swathed up in the country fashion, and never having been cared for during the first few days when the mother was prostrate with seasickness. By protesting that I was a Hakim (doctor), I persuaded her to undo the bandages; then by aid of a nice finger biscuit the sweet little mite soon became quiet, and I think had a good time of it. The incident reminded me of my former experience *en route* to Bellary.

Our engines broke down, and that delayed us again. At Athens we did the sights. I was struck with the heavy scent that filled the whole air, and was told it came from the trees, of which the flowers perfumed the air, and from which the bees got the Hymettus honey.

A stout lady was pointed out to me as Byron's Maid of Athens.

The regiment quartered at Athens was chafing at not being sent on to the front.

At Smyrna my comrades and I took various routes. I had a private introduction, so went to deliver it. Of course I bought a drum of figs as a present for our cabin, in which we were four. On my return I saw a comrade come on deck, so I tackled him and said, with some amount of delight, that I had bought a drum of figs *pro bono publico*. "Oh," he said, "what a pity! I bought one too." Another cabin companion came and informed us he had a treat for us, and produced his drum. Then, alas! came the fourth, proudly carrying his drum under his arm. Yes, dear reader, four drums of figs in a cabin holding four men with scarcely room for two. I don't know what my companions did; I gave my drum to the girl with the baby.

Few sights are more lovely than the passage up the Dardanelles to the Golden Horn. We did it in the most brilliant sunshine. How I long to dwell on all we saw! A book might well be written on that short passage alone. At last we passed into the Golden Horn, and anchored off Galata.

Now, as I have said, the food on board was awfully bad, and anything but plentiful; the only thing one really could enjoy was a cup of coffee early in the morning with an English ship's biscuit. Just as we neared our destination, the steward came to me with a bill amounting to £3 4s. 2d., a considerable item of which was for our morning coffee, which we had not ordered, and naturally fancied was included in our passage-money. I objected and appealed to the purser, who, with many shrugs of his shoulder, referred me to the captain, by whom I was again referred to the purser. We were all equally furious at the extortion, and I stoutly declared I would not pay. I was politely told by the purser that I could not land without my passport, and the passport would not be delivered to me until I had settled my account. By a piece of luck I happened to have a second passport; I ran down to my cabin and put it in my pocket without saying a word. My baggage was all on board; I had it put in a caïque, and was getting in, when the purser shouted out, "It is no use your going, you will be sent back." I took no notice, but landed, showed my passport, got my luggage through, and heard no more of the Austrian Lloyd's steamer, my coffee, or my bill.

It was no easy thing to find accommodation in those days in Pera. Misseries, the Grand Hotel, was crammed. Most of our party got housed in the Hôtel de Bezance, which overlooked a cemetery made more than desolate by howling dogs that congregated at night to try to rob graves; but we were fairly comfortable, and our early days were spent in sight-seeing.

One of my pleasantest haunts was the Sweet Waters of Europe—a lovely garden, through the tamarind trees of which a little brook flowed in dancing ripples until it lost itself in the waters of the Golden Horn. Here the band, a good one under Donizetti's brother, discoursed all sorts of music, and here the belles of the Bosphorus thronged, attended by their janizaries, who bristled with swords, pistols, and daggers. The ladies sat placidly down on the grass, and after producing little boxes containing combs, cosmetiques, etc., lowered their yashmaks and leisurely proceeded to improve nature. I noticed, the prettier they were, the lower the yashmak fell, and the more touching-up the eyebrows and eyelashes required. The male attendants glared at all giaours who dared to look on.

One day a group particularly attracted my attention. The careless way in which the girls uncovered their faces was quite refreshing and excited my wonder, until I looked round and saw a splendid specimen of humanity, in Staff uniform, standing with folded arms, quietly looking on. I think it was a case of mutual admiration. That same Staff officer eventually became my Chief.

Pera was crowded. Wherever you went you met English officers in every variety of uniform, and the *table d'hôte* at Misseries was a brilliant sight. Eighty usually sat down to dinner, and amongst them no end of notables. I remember Slade Pacha and Beatson of Irregular Horse celebrity with a host of others. Whyte Melville particularly attracted my attention by his look and manner; subsequently I became better acquainted with him.

So crowded were the principal hotels, that General Vivian gave orders that officers were to place their names conspicuously on their doors, so that orderlies might know where to deliver official letters, etc.

We had a Captain Wilde Brown, who was very particular that the Wilde should never be omitted by any one when addressing him; accordingly he put on his door " Captain *Wilde* Brown" in large type. A very amusing man named Gammell occupied the next room, and he put up in equally large type, "Tame Gammell." It nearly led to a grave breach of the peace.

We had a fine time at the commencement of our service. No men had arrived, so there was nothing to do. We knew absolutely nothing of our various appointments. The heads of departments were of course known. Neill and Colonel Hunter were to have infantry brigades, and

Mayne had been promised the appointment of Brigade-Major to the latter; beyond this all was vague. Most of us set to work diligently to learn Turkish, and so the days moved swiftly by.

There were not many amusements. The French had established a good *café chantant*, whilst at the Opera they were playing *Nabuco*.

An order existed that no one was to go out after dark without a lantern; so it was usual for pedestrians to carry a long concertina-shaped Chinese paper lantern, with a small bit of candle in it. These were not unfrequently suspended to a pole, and carried hanging over the bearer's back. A very favourite amusement of some of the Britishers was to arm themselves with the thinnest, most pliable cane, and, as we returned from the opera, if the opportunity offered, by a swift slash of the cane without making any noise to cut the paper in half, letting the lower part fall to the ground, and so leave the bearer in darkness. The astonished Turk or Greek seldom understood how the darkness was caused, and whilst he was looking at his lantern, and trying to find the bottom part, the mischievous party could easily get away.

On the penny steamboats, plying between Pera and the various villages on the Bosphorus, they gave us flimsy bits of printed paper that served for tickets. These were demanded not only on leaving, but constantly, very officiously, during the few minutes' voyage; we in revenge used to roll them up into pills, and when the men demanded it a paper pill was delivered. It took such an age to unroll and decipher the reading on it, that the men soon dropped asking for tickets, except when necessary.

We had the greatest difficulty in getting servants. Twelve pounds a month was the wage usually asked by some cut-throat Greek or Italian.

By my diary it appears that on May 5, thirty-five

officers were ordered to Beyukdere, a lovely spot on the Bosphorus. In the midst of hanging gardens overlooking the sea was situated the Russian Embassy, which had been selected as the residence of General Vivian and the head-quarters. My old friend Glover, of whom I spoke in connection with our Rangoon theatricals, was on Vivian's staff as an A.D.C.

I find also about this time I got three things: a servant, a horse, and a touch of the old complaint that caused me to leave Burmah. I was bad.

From this time on I am luckily assisted by my diary, and find that on May 12, Colonel Crewe, the Adjutant-General, sent for me, and asked me to go with General Smith to assist in selecting a site for the camp, as some 10,000 men were on their way to be placed under our command.

Here I may not inappropriately say a word concerning ourselves. We were, I think, the first body of English officers who had ever been officially commissioned by the Sultan to command his troops. True, there had been many English officers who had volunteered to serve with Turks, and who had distinguished themselves; there had been renegades who had accepted service under the Sultan, and who had renounced their original faith. But we were the first body of Christians supplied with a distinct Turkish commission, in order to command, and even supersede, all Turkish officers serving with us.

I have my Turkish commission now, with the royal sign manual, which looks for all the world like a complicated spider, spotted over with gold-leaf. I am told it gave me the rank of Caimakan and Bey, which former would enable me to take command over any Turkish officer likely to be with our force, and the latter would enable me to order supplies from civil authorities, if necessary. I do not vouch for the accuracy of this assertion, but merely tell it as it was told to me.

That the service we entered was considered a somewhat risky one, was proved by the rates of insurance demanded of some of the married men of the force. The war risks were not higher than usual; but the possibility of the Turks turning restive at our taking command over their heads, was made much of.

But to return to my appointment under General Smith. It was the first indication of any desire to make use of my services in a special line, and to what good luck I was indebted for it I know not.

General Smith was a most charming companion. We had a very heavy day's work, being in the saddle for ten hours, and in my delicate state of health it told on me. But I would not give in, although I see, by my diary, I nearly fainted when I got back to my hotel.

I continued to serve under General Smith for some time, and I think I must have got on well with him, for I note he offered me an A.D.C.-ship.

Shortly after this I was ordered to conduct Generals Vivian and Michel, the Chief of the Staff, over the ground we had selected for the three camps, namely, two Infantry and one Cavalry. Only Generals Michel and Neill accompanied me. It was a ticklish job, for I had many miles to travel; the country was covered with low Spanish chestnut growth, so I had no special land-marks. I knew if I failed it would be disastrous. Luck favoured me, and I escorted them safely round all three encamping grounds, showing them the water supplies, etc. On reaching the Embassy, General Michel thanked me and said, "You were a little hazy sometimes, but you got us round all right." Michel was not a man of many praises, so I was delighted.

My next job was to confer with contractors about the drainage of the Embassy at Beyukdere, and also to visit the source of supply of water for Beyukdere from the aqueduct, three miles off. What my special qualifications were for these duties I know not, but I felt I was fast assuming the position of a "general utility man," and that it would lead to something. The only drawback was that it interfered with any study of Turkish. I made my report about drains and water personally to General Vivian, and got orders to remain over-night at Pera, as the General expected important letters which would require a special messenger to the British Embassy at Therapia. Next day I went to the Embassy at Therapia to interview Lord Napier, and lunched at the Embassy: Lady Napier was charming. I received orders for headquarters to occupy the Russian Embassy.

"May 31. Went out with Brigadier Hunter, who offered me his A.D.C.-ship. Met General Vivian, who thanked me for the trouble I had taken about the water-supply and drainage at the Embassy."

Entries continue of different work I had on hand. Amongst other things I find I was introduced to Colonel E. Wetherall, and in him recognized the handsome Staff officer of the Sweet Waters of Europe. After a lengthened interview with him I was ordered out to camp.

Up to this time, as my work lay in and about Beyukdere, I had joined a party in hiring a house which we called the Agapemone. We chummed together, and had a pretty decent mess. I call to mind that General Neill and Brigadier Hunter, Major Mayne, Captain Hearne and myself were of the party; I think two others also, but I forget their names.

Whilst living at the Agapemone, Mayne got his appointment to a cavalry brigade, which gave great satisfaction; he had been originally Brigade-Major to Brigadier Hunter. Mayne was a first-rate officer.

Just on the eve of my leaving the Agapemone for camp, my servant disappeared, and one William Thompson, A.B., no doubt a deserter from some ship, reigned in his stead.

I seem to have been busy now in surveying. Colonel

Wetherall wanted me to superintend erecting huts: this work I could not conscientiously undertake.

Major Elkington now appeared on the scene as an Assistant-Quartermaster-General, and I got orders from him to take the first batch of tents and pitch them, as men were to arrive immediately.

A *levée* was held by General Vivian; all officers attended. I remember being struck by the curious mixture of uniforms; some selected for utility; others of a very fanciful description. Our Contingent uniform had not then been settled.

At this time the First Division, under General Cunynghame, seems to have been in camp, for I find I am ordered to apply to him for three hundred Turks, with entrenching tools, to make and mend the roads from Beyukdere to the various camps. I also find that I selected my camping-grounds for three detachments at intervals, remaining with the centre one myself, and that Colonel Wetherall inspected and approved my disposition.

Here an incident occurred to which I attribute my subsequent appointment on the Staff.

The cholera broke out in my centre detachment. I had seen much cholera in India, so took what I considered the necessary precautions. I shifted my ground, made the men cut heather to put under the sick men to keep them off the damp ground, and forbad all fruit coming into camp. I gave them from my private store a supply of arrowroot, coffee, etc. I may here state that I had with me only my interpreter, a youth from Smyrna, who was a complete polyglot; a young medico raw from Birmingham; and Mr. William Thompson, A.B., afore-mentioned.

I had however a Yusbashi (or captain), a Soudanese as black as jet, who was my special friend and true ally. Our friendship commenced over some tobacco, the arrival of which from England I had so much bewailed. I had paid duty on it at Southampton, and in writing to Grindlay and Co. for a certain bullock-trunk, had specially directed them not to send out a particular one which contained only tobacco and Burmese curios, etc. They sent the very trunk I did not want, and with it the tobacco, causing me to use naughty swear-words. However, I had reason to bless that tobacco eventually.

It was the very finest from Cairo, a brand recommended to me by Mecca Burton. Well, the first day of my interview with my Yusbashi, I of course, following the custom of the country, offered him a chibouk and baccy. He did his level best with it, praising it, and saying it reminded him of his dear Cairo. His visits became so frequent as to be rather a nuisance; however, he was such a grand soldier that I did not discourage him. He had seen no end of service, and, when he took off his fez to scratch his head, I noticed endless cruel scars, which he told me he had got in skirmishes with Arabs and others.

Well, when cholera broke out, I found the Turkish remedy was to send for the barber (who in those days was as of yore with us the blood-letter), and bleed the patient—in other words, finish him off. I knew this was all wrong, but before taking any steps I consulted my medico, and got him to send me in an official document saying bleeding was fatal under the circumstances.

Armed with this I summoned the three native officers and determined to bluff largely. I told them through my somewhat terrified interpreter (his terror did me service, for they thought he was terrified at me, not at my threat) that I had served in India many years with Mussulmans, and knew their religious prejudices as well as they did. I also knew what cholera was, and that bleeding was madness; that my medical adviser (whom I described as a man of great learning) endorsed my views; and finally told them that if any barber dared to bleed another Turk, I would shoot him. My life might thereby be forfeited, but I intended to carry out my threat.

Reader, this of course seems very childish nonsense; it had, however, its desired effect, thanks to my dear black Yusbashi. All were silent; at last the swarthy soldier spoke and said, "No doubt the English officer was right; he too saw no use in bleeding, and they would forbid it in future." I suppose they did, for I did not shoot any one, and cholera soon disappeared.

That same evening General Vivian came and inspected my arrangements. I told him what measures I had adopted (*except the threat of shooting*). He was pleased to express his approbation, and from his manner I think my fortunes were secured.

My troubles with these road-makers were anything but light; they were good and obedient, but lazy and absolutely inefficient. They scratched some earth, and then carried it in little bags over their shoulders. Spades, picks, and wheelbarrows were unknown to them. In order to get them to use them I established sports every day after work was over, giving tobacco and small coins as prizes to those who wheeled a barrow fastest, or drove a pick furthest into the ground. They soon got to understand the implements, and willingly adopted them.

An order came one evening for me to get an apology for a road scooped on the side of a steep hill, ready for a battery to pass by twelve o'clock. It seemed impossible, but I had learnt to reject that word from my vocabulary, so set to work to place fascines down in the narrowest parts, covering them with as much earth as I could in the time procure to keep them safe. In due time the battery appeared. I met the officer and told him my perplexity. He halted and surveyed the ground with me. "All right," he said; "I will rush it at a hand-gallop, and the guns will be over before their weight is felt."

I may mention that the Turkish artillery handed over to us was very superior, I think by far the best arm of our service; and the English officers appointed were first-rate men.

Off they set; all got over but the last, and by some mischance that went over. I forget what damage was done, but I think not much, as I have no record of casualties. It was said afterwards that an English officer flipped one of the horses in the eye with his whip and caused it to swerve, and thus the accident occurred.

I showed General Vivian that same evening the place where the gun went over. No blame was attached to me.

My next entry records that Neill was to have a Division, and that Colonel Abbott offered me an appointment in the Irregular Cavalry, which I declined. It may be noticed that I have frequently made mention of good appointments being offered to and refused by me. This did not arise from any over-rating of my value, or dislike to the nature of the appointments, and certainly not to those who paid me the compliment of offering them; but I think it was because Neill told me not to be in a hurry about tying myself. He may have had some appointment of his own in his mind's eye, or else knew that I was to get something good: be that as it may, after the cholera episode I was gazetted as Deputy-Assistant-Quartermaster-General, and so came under the permanent orders of my good friend Wetherall.

On July 16 I joined head-quarters in my new capacity. I confess I did feel somewhat proud of being in the department which in war time is the eyes and ears of the army. I am quite sure I never thought I deserved such luck, and yet I cannot say I had not worked up to it, for I should tire the reader if I entered from my diary the number of odd jobs I was set to do. I can assure the reader I got my Staff uniform with no little glee.

On the 17th there was a grand review of the whole force, before the Duke of Newcastle and the Seraskier.

I had bought a horse, a very fine stallion, from Brigadier

Fitzgerald, and with a new charger and new uniform I thought to cut a splendid figure before the crowd of spectators.

A telegram came to say that the Duke had been detained, and would not be present for another hour. The order was given to pile arms and stand easy. In a second a huge white cloud arose above the force; it was the smoke of 10,000 cigarettes which had been instantly rolled up and lighted.

When the Duke appeared I had to ride in front of the brilliant staff to show the way. Just as I got to the right of the line my beastly horse threw up his head and hit me an awful blow on my nose, so that my splendid appearance resolved itself into a profusion of blood which I could not staunch. Pride must have a fall.

Next entry is to the effect that Brigadier Fitzgerald's rascal of a groom had already sold the horse above-mentioned without permission to some one else. I had no end of trouble in the matter, but I stuck to my horse.

Then comes the entry, "Major Luther Vaughan brought on the strength of the office an officer with a splendid reputation, who had seen much service in the Punjaub."

"Sunday being an off-day, I went to see Lewis of the Buffs, who distinguished himself at the Redan, in hospital at Scutari. Met West of Ours there acting as Paymaster. I was introduced to Florence Nightingale, who gave me a cholera-belt."

By this time the Second Division, under General Neill, was fully organized and encamped.

I remember a characteristic incident connected with the good Scotchman. The first Sunday after he assumed command, a question arose about having Divine Service. Some suggested that it might wound the prejudices of the Turks. Neill's answer was, "Nonsense! the Turks are not afraid of saying their prayers before us: why should we be afraid to say ours before them?" Parade was accordingly held, Major C. A. B. Gordon, the Assistant-Adjutant-General, acting as chaplain.

As may be imagined, the wily Turk and peculating Greek lost no time in reaping a fine harvest out of us, and many were the extortions I had to set my face against. I find I had an interview with Lord Stratford de Redcliffe about the claims of a Madame Vitalis. I forget her claim, but I remember distinctly what a bear the "great Elchi" was. I did not esteem him the more for being overbearing to a youngster who dared not retort. On another occasion I met him out riding, and he was anything but civil. We had an idea that he did not like the Contingent; but of this more hereafter.

These claims remind me of a capital story of Wetherall. He, and indeed all the chiefs, were very kind in asking me to dine. One day after being on a committee on boots for the force, I dined with the Colonel. We had an excellent dinner, and to my surprise champagne.

My host asked me more than once if I liked the champagne. I readily assented. He asked, "What did you do on committee to-day?"

I answered: "We passed 5000 pairs, and rejected 10,000."

"I'm glad you like the champagne, and glad you rejected the bad boots. The contractor sent me three dozen of that champagne last night; I could not well insult him by returning it; all the same, I'm glad you rejected his beastly boots."

The Colonel had a wonderful servant called George, a veritable Guardsman. I asked how he came to have him. The Colonel laughed and said, "George only exists at curious intervals; lately he was supposed to be a prisoner in the hands of the Russians; now he is supposed to have been drowned in the Bosphorus. He turns up again at the proper time." But I must get on.

Orders for embarkation arrived; our destination was

said to be Balaclava. This, however, was countermanded, and Kertch substituted.

Embarkation was no easy job at Beyukdere. The village lay in one long line of houses along the steep hill fronting the Bosphorus; only the esplanade intervened between the houses and the sea. There was only one entrance available for the troops; and to get Cavalry, Artillery, and Infantry in by this one route required much careful planning and still more exact timing. Jetties were constructed by the Engineers, and large flat-bottomed boats collected. So well did Colonel Wetherall work out the plans, that no hitch occurred, except once, when a commanding officer in his zeal to be in time arrived too soon, and so blocked the road against the regiment that should have embarked before him.

A memorandum was given to me by the Colonel, telling me the jetty each division was to embark from and the minute they should be there. All went like clockwork where orders were obeyed. In galloping to hurry up some detachment, my horse slipped and fell on its side, crushing my ankle against my steel scabbard. I was terribly sprained, but kept going as long as I could; then I had to have my boot cut off and my ankle bandaged. This was my only personal mishap during my service. The horses on one raft broke loose and swam ashore again, and one officer's charger was killed in hoisting on board.

I next have an entry of an outbreak in the Bashi Bazouks under General Beatson, which my friend General Smith was sent to suppress. "At this time we lost a very good officer in Major Archer Burton, who was buried at Therapia, I think. On September 8, Sevastopol was taken. A review for our Ambassador and Seraskier went off well. Seven hours in the saddle. Splendid illumination at night. By this time I had engaged my fourth servant, a lad named Percy, an American, who had been a cabin-boy on board the Cunard line. He turned out a trump."

I have no further entries of importance. I constantly met Whyte Melville when embarking the Cavalry. He was subsequently sent on a mission to buy horses at Bucharest, where I fancy he conceived the plot for *The Interpreter*. At last all were off but the head-quarters, and with them I set off for Kertch.

All these events cover but a small space of paper, but in justice to the officers of the Contingent, their unparalleled exertions should be recorded. Troops did not commence arriving till the middle of May, and yet before September 1 a body of some 15,000 men of all arms were clothed, drilled, and equipped in a manner that would do credit to any army in the world.

The English Commandants gave all words of command in Turkish, and had by their zeal gained the confidence and respect of those Turkish officers whom they had come to supersede. A soldier only can appreciate the mortification felt by an officer on finding his regiment taken from him and given to another, under whom he is bound to serve.

A word too respecting the head-quarter Staff. We were in a strange country, dealing with perfect strangers. The head-quarter Staff had not only to organize and dispose of this large force, but to equip, clothe, and furnish them with every possible necessary, from silk to tie up arteries, to shot, shell, and all tools necessary for defensive works. I gladly bear testimony to the assistance we received from all other departments, especially the Turkish Naval authorities under Slade Pasha; but I cannot resist asking for a meed of credit for General Vivian, General Michel, and their respective staffs.

CHAPTER IX

THE CRIMEA

ON arriving off Fort Paul, General Vivian ordered me to remain on board until every biscuit, every ounce of forage, and all firewood had been landed. All the troops had arrived safely, and were either under canvas or housed in the town. The brigade at Fort Paul was under canvas.

It was late before I could leave our ship, and on landing I went immediately to Major Elkington, the Assistant-Quartermaster-General of the First Division, to get orders and food. I was as usual hospitably welcomed, and shared such viands as the situation afforded. When it came to turning-in time, Elkington said: "There is only one bed, and you are not going to have that, but we will make you as comfortable as we can." A number of tent-sacks were produced for me to lie on; one, I noticed, was put on one side. When I had settled myself down Elkington said: "You'd better get into this sack, for the rats are awful; and would eat you up as soon as look at you." I was tied up in a sack; my saddle put over my head, and a cloth over that, so that I could breathe, and thus I passed my first night in the Crimea, rats running races over me all night.

Next morning I rode into Kertch, and found my Chief had taken care of me, and quartered me with my friend Hearne in a nice little villa next to the head-quarter offices.

The Bay of Kertch is simply magnificent, quite equal to that of Naples. Kertch itself reminded me of Athens and Bath—two very different places, yet Kertch had the contour of the former, whilst the buildings somewhat resembled those of the latter.

The chief objects of interest were the Museum, sadly plundered by the French; and the tomb of Mithridates, which stood just above the Museum, on a high projection of the central mass of hills.

The town was neat and clean, but the place was straggling, and, though capable of almost any amount of defensive works, when we arrived it was but miserably fortified.

As I rode along the shore from Fort Paul to the town I noticed the skeletons of the ships that had been run ashore to escape falling into our hands at the time of the capture. These were of inestimable value to us subsequently.

My first duties were to make a plan of the place, and to put up in English the names of the various streets. I have the plan of the town now before me, and well remember Gentleman Street, and Upper Gentleman Street, together with Pentecost Street. I do not think that the houses in Gentleman Street were better than in any other.

Writing of maps and plans reminds me that a very strict order was published against sending home information concerning our position and outpost. The order was rendered necessary by reason of a letter from the Secretary of State for War, reporting that London newspapers contained full particulars given by a Kertch correspondent. Would any one believe there could exist such idiots in the force as to send such details home?

In our little villa next to the head-quarter office, we had each a room, and one room with a good stove in common. The place had a court-yard and out-houses, which seemed like farm-buildings.

Hearne said he heard next to his room noises for which he could not account. Some weeks after our arrival my servant Percy, to my surprise, produced eggs for breakfast. I asked where they came from, and then learnt that he had purchased them from the old woman of the house. I did not till then know of her existence, but subsequently found that an old blind man, his wife, and a younger woman with two children were secreted in the back settlements: hence the noises alluded to. I visited them frequently, and found that in a room next to Hearne's, blocked out entirely from daylight, the younger woman and children lived. A solitary oil-lamp placed under an icon dispelled the gloom. The household gods and goods were all stored up in heaps in the corners. I do not know whether any one else knew of the existence of this family. We took great care of all the property, and when I was ordered to Yenikali I gave the old woman my cooking-stove, which had been such a white elephant.

The whole force was now well in working order, and we were enabled to form a just estimate of the efficiency of the various arms. The Artillery were, I think, the best arm. The Cavalry were so well armed with repeating carbines, that they would, if called on, have proved a dangerous foe. The Infantry, amongst which were many of Omar Pasha's regiments, were a sturdy lot. The Militia regiments seemed to me the most serviceable.

I cannot say I thought the Turkish officers bad. Our officers commanding regiments constantly told me how keen the Turkish Commandants were about drill. They would play by the hour at doing manœuvres with wooden blocks. Some of their formations and manœuvres were retained by us as being very practical. I cannot, however, speak with any confidence on this point, as being on the Staff I had little to do with drill.

All must, I am sure, agree with me as to the behaviour of the force. I only remember one case bearing the faintest approach to a disturbance, and that was caused by the Provost-Marshal, Captain Guernsey, most unnecessarily drawing his revolver and wounding a Turkish soldier. It seems that there was a row in the bazaar between some of our men and some of the riff-raff that followed the force. Guernsey assumed it to be an *émeute*, and fired; luckily the Turks took the thing quietly. Guernsey was dismissed the force. I think he was mixed up subsequently with the premature publication of Gladstone's Ionian despatches.

Before leaving the subject of the men, I must mention their surprise at receiving their pay into their own hands. They actually asked what they were to do with it!—and when told they might spend it as they liked, the grin on their faces would have shamed a Cheshire cat. Poor fellows, hitherto their pay had gone into their officers' pockets.

Only one word more on this subject. After the force had been broken up, and we were no more to these men than any civilian in Pera, I never met one of our old comrades that did not salute; and one day when at a public bath, a comrade (whether an officer or private I know not) came up and gave the bathman strict injunctions to treat me with special attention, as I was a friend of his. The attention was bestowed, and consisted of hotter water and a longer process of massage than usual.

I will now return to our position at Kertch. The disposition of the force was as follows:—Half of the First Division was under General Cunynghame, C.B., at Kertch, with a Brigade at Fort Paul. The Cavalry also were in Kertch. The Second Division, under General Neill, was at Yenikali. We had also a portion of the 71st Regiment and a body of French infantry in the town, together with a squadron of our 10th Hussars.

My diary enables me to fill in accurately some of the leading events of this period.

Winter was the enemy we most dreaded; we knew full

L

well we should be frozen in, and consequently no provisions or supplies of any kind would reach us by sea.

Our only other danger was by attack from Simpheropol —a contingency to be guarded against, as Cossacks were eternally prowling about watching our movements, and ready to warn the troops collected at Simpheropol the minute they found that our watchfulness was relaxed. Patrols were constantly sent out.

My particular duties lay on the beach with working parties, unloading and storing all sorts of provisions as they were landed from the boats. I used to visit each ship before signing the discharge papers, and was thus enabled very often to cajole the captains into selling me a bit of ham or a pot of jam, I need scarcely say at ruinous prices. I have an entry of butter and jam sent to Neill and Carey. The latter, Assistant-Quartermaster-General at Yenikali, was an officer of great experience, having served in Candahar and Afghanistan in 1841-2. He subsequently came into command of a brigade, and I succeeded him as Assistant-Quartermaster-General at Yenikali.

One day a man brought an Afghan medal into office; on it was inscribed "Ensign Carey, 40th Regiment." We could not make out to whom it could belong, never associating Ensign Carey with Brigadier Carey. The medal eventually reached him safely.

On November 25 all the troops were under arms. The Cossacks came in sight and burnt some villages; all passed off quietly.

I note that Majors Goldsmid, Vaughan, and Captain Hearn, all of head-quarter Staff, passed examinations in Turkish.

Landing stores seems to have been my chief employment. Amongst other things, 2000 sheep, which arrived in the *William Hutt*.

Poor Longley died at this time, and his effects were sold by auction. A pair of brass spurs fetched £2 16s. 6d.

A BRAVE ENEMY

A party of Cavalry went patrolling to the Spanish Farm, and my entry runs as follows:—"It appears that Major Macdonald in reconnoitring came across 400 Russian Hussars, and gave them battle with his eighty-five troopers. Very sharp skirmish. Sherwood wounded in the head, and left on the ground. Forty-five out of eighty-five troopers placed *hors de combat*. Macdonald escaped. It was a very gallant affair. Turks behaved very well."

Poor Sherwood, it seems, was carefully conveyed into Simpheropol. Major Goldsmid was sent subsequently under a flag of truce to make inquiries. He was escorted into the town blindfolded, and there found Sherwood lying dead, surrounded by every token of honour, affection, and regard, with Sisters of Charity watching the body. It was a most touching sight. The Russians could not have known that Goldsmid was coming and have prepared for his reception. It was the spontaneous work of Sisters of Mercy belonging to a brave enemy. The experience of Goldsmid was very trying; his escort came in suffering terribly from frost-bites.

The truth that one man's meat is another man's poison was here illustrated. By the next mail a box of warm clothing arrived for poor Sherwood. It was decided not to send it back, and, as the bill was inside, I agreed to hand over a cheque for the amount, and kept the clothing. I need scarcely say what a boon it was to me in the intense cold that ensued.

On December 15 frost seems regularly to have set in. I was down on the beach as usual, and saw the curious effect it had on the water. It seemed as if some unseen hand was sowing millions of the finest needles on the sea, which had become singularly smooth, a long waveless swell being the only indication of the recent storms. Presently these needles seemed to dart at each other just as if they had been attracted by a magnet. Then these different little masses collided with each other, and formed little saucers, the edges of which got crisp; finally these saucers adhered together and formed an undulating coating of semi-consistent ice. Next morning all was solid, but not too much so to prevent boats forging through.

Our activity was redoubled, and the shore became a living mass of fatigue parties. On December 20 the sea was frozen out two miles.

On the 21st we were under arms again, the Cossacks having appeared in numbers. Going round the alarm-posts was cold work.

I find that on December 22 I *walked* out to the *Weser* gunboat, and had a glass of sherry over the ship's side.

On Christmas day I dined with Brigadier Holmes, commanding Kertch, and Colonel Crewe, Deputy-Adjutant-General, who lived together. Young Glanville, such a nice boy, the Town Major, was also present. I think two others, but forget the names. We had indeed sumptuous food—the whole dinner, from soup to dessert, liqueurs, etc., from Fortnum and Mason. I was simply astounded to find walnuts, almonds, and raisins. Nothing seemed to have been forgotten, and my hosts were as good as their dinner.

About this time I lost my good kind Chief, Colonel Wetherall. He had been summoned to Sevastopol to take supreme control of the transport service. Never shall I forget his courtesy and forbearance. I was but a raw lad at my work, but I put my heart into it, and my Chief was satisfied. I never had one cross word with him. His successor, Colonel Morris, of the 17th Lancers, was an excellent substitute, but no one, to my mind, could have come up to Wetherall.

On the 26th I was engaged in blowing up the timbers of the wrecks I mentioned lying between Kertch and Fort Paul.

A curious incident occurred on the 27th. The *Jarrow*

was lying surrounded by ice, with heavy guns on board. Here is the entry connected with this day's work:—"Unloading heavy guns over the ice. Had a frame made like a sledge, on which a ship's boat was lowered, then the gun, weighing 56 cwt.; the whole was drawn over the ice until it was considered safe to unship the gun. We then placed it on its carriage, but at first the wheel cut into the ice, and the gun went over into the water; it was, however, recovered. All the others were landed safely." I have a lithograph done by Day and Sons after a sketch by Major Stack of this very incident.

My rations and forage caused me trouble at this time. The Commissariat were too overworked to undertake to deliver to individuals, or issue oftener than every third day. What was to be done? Three days' forage and provisions for Hearne and self was more than Percy could manage. I was at my wits' end; but on going home to lunch I found the admirable Percy, with his Yankee cuteness and experience, had solved the matter. He had taken half the barn-door off its hinges and fixed it on runners; then, harnessing a baggage-pony, had come home triumphant, looking for all the world like Robinson Crusoe on his raft.

Percy was indeed a treasure. One day, however, we had a difference; he got drunk, and in a quarrel was ill-used by some Greeks. I was called out of office to interfere, and in my wrath spoke unadvisedly and called him "a drunken thief." He sobered in a second, and said, " I never stole anything of yours in my life." I retracted my words, and got him quietly to go to sleep in the hay-barn. That was the only time we ever had words. I will finish off with Percy whilst I am on the subject. When the time came for us to part, and his passage had been secured, I paid him up, and gave him a £5-note as a present. He thanked me and said, "Look here; if ever you come to New York, you ask for Percy pilot, Sandy Hook, and I'll put you up at the Metropole at my own expense for a week." I've no doubt he would; he was a capital boy, and did not know the meaning of can't.

As debarcation had ceased, my work now lay amidst earthworks and entrenchments, and my recreation was a spin on the ice. It was very rough to walk on, except in places, where you would come across large patches of lovely ice.

"December 31.—Every living soul at the entrenchments. The General had intelligence of the approach of the enemy, but whether to attack us or only to occupy Arabat does not seem certain."

"January 1, 1856.—Alarm sounded at 5.30 a.m. Went round the picquets; very cold." Next day we were turned out again. I remember only too well the cold on turning out on these occasions.

So persistent were the enemy in these advances, that the utmost caution was necessary. General Vivian ordered one of the Quartermaster-General's Department to go out every morning with an escort to reconnoitre along the Simpheropol road, and report to him direct on his return.

This was simply fearful work. No words can describe the cold. Vaughan bore the brunt of this duty, which must have been very trying to a man after so many years of Indian service.

I had in my turn to go out reconnoitring. In addition to every stitch of cloth and fur I could command, I had my ankles bound round with wisps of hay. Poor Sherwood's fur-lined coat and seal-skin gloves and helmet came in very handy. Alas! to what base uses, etc. My seal-skin helmet was cut up eventually to make rabbits with big red eyes for the children.

This patrolling was ticklish work; one of our department exceeded the orders given to him, and got surrounded by the Cossacks, thereby causing a disorderly retreat, and the loss of five troopers killed or made prisoners.

On the 3rd the ships began cutting their way out to sea. It was splendid to see them crashing through the ice. We were now left with nothing but gunboats.

"Friday, January 4.—Went out with Tartars to patrol; awfully cold; saw nothing of the enemy."

To give an idea of the cold at this time, I may mention that one day, in passing, I saw a private of the 71st go to a pump and seize the handle; he dropped it in a second and wrung his hand. I went up to him, and found the skin taken off just as if he had seized a red-hot iron.

The entry for the 6th runs as follows: "As I was going to church I met Luther Vaughan, who told me the Russians were coming down on Fort Paul. Mounted at once and joined the General. Found the enemy had appeared in numbers. Saw some of them go and fire a village. Under arms for four hours."

My diary ends here; my 1885 book being finished, I inserted memoranda only occasionally. I am, however, in possession of the general orders issued from time to time to the force, which serve to recall events to my memory, and to fix certain dates. Amongst others I find I arrived at Yenikali on January 13, and took charge on the 14th as Assistant-Quartermaster-General.

A few words are necessary here. It seems that by the appointment of Carey to a brigade, a vacancy occurred in my department, and as I was the senior General Vivian promoted me. I thus became Assistant-Quartermaster-General of the Second Division, under my old brother officer, General Neill.

There was no end of bother about this appointment, for head-quarters at Sevastopol would not sanction it, as I was only a local captain and it was a field-officer's appointment. General Vivian, however, insisted that it was mine by seniority, and that I was entitled to it;

so eventually I was confirmed, and drew the pay and allowances.

I am almost afraid to say what I was drawing at this time, for in addition to my Crimean Staff pay my Indian pay also was running on.

Well, then, here I was snugly housed with Brigadier Carey, and as happy as a king. One always, I fancy, regrets leaving head-quarters.

Although in comparative comfort, I had no bed of roses. Work was incessant, but all with whom I came in contact were kind and considerate. No one more so than my General, who knew well what Staff duties were.

I remember a severe storm of wind and snow one night. Next morning an orderly came early with a note from Major Payn, commanding a regiment, asking me to come up at once. I went, and on knocking at the door was told to come in. I tried ineffectually to do so, but could not, and so begged them to open the door. Payn called out, "That's just what we can't do, so we sent for you." I found that the end window of the hut had been blown in, and the servant's room filled with drifted snow to the rafter. Payn and his second-in-command and servant had barricaded the other windows. A fatigue party soon released them, but theirs was only one sample of the huts of the whole division.

Percy brought in wild duck that he had caught, poor things, too weak to escape; they boiled down into good soup.

Brigadier Carey had two servants, a Frenchman and an Italian; the latter, named Placido, the idlest fellow I ever met. One day Carey called to Placido, whereupon his French servant with a grin said, "*Placido tranquille.*" Percy abominated Placido, and played him many a trick.

Though we were quartered in an excellent well-built house, and had rations of fuel according to our rank, the cold was intense. One day Carey broke his leg, and every comfort the hospital could supply was accorded to him. In the night he was very feverish and asked for an orange. I went to the cupboard for one, alas! it was frozen like a stone, and a bottle of soda-water was a mass of ice; this, too, in a room with a good fire in it.

The cold was intense. My moustache was always a mass of icicles when I went out in the early morning, but curiously enough the water for our baths in the morning was always warm. The well was so deep that the frost did not get down to it.

We had our alarms out at Yenikali, and I remember that one day when a tolerable force of Russians appeared in the plains, General Neill formed up in battle array on the glacis. The Russians thought better of it and retired. I do not think at any time they seriously thought of attacking our three fortified positions, but if they had caught us napping they would have most certainly warmed us up.

Our chief anxiety now at Yenikali was about our sea front, which was wholly unprotected. We knew from maps in my department that the distance from Yenikali to Taman on the opposite shore was two and a half miles, and had more than once been crossed by large bodies of troops, so that in this hard winter an attempt might easily be made to harass us on our sea front. To prevent this, batteries were erected commanding the passage.

Rations of rum and sugar were ordered to be issued to the Turkish troops at Yenikali at this time—which calls to recollection a most amusing scene.

It seems that very many men of our Division had been with Omar Pasha in Silistria, where they had a hard time; so that it was not wonderful that scurvy should set in. I think we had 1000 men at one time in hospital. Of course the proper treatment was rum and lime-juice, where no fresh vegetables could be procured; but the question was how to get the orthodox followers of the Prophet to touch any sort of alcohol. Neill knew the prejudices of Mussulmans as well as any one, and Gordon, our Assistant-Adjutant-General, was a sensible man; so they concocted a scheme between them. The Turkish officers in command of regiments were a most intelligent and amenable lot. The situation was fully explained to them, and then it was determined that the next day the principal medico and his staff should prepare the mixture, and that the General and his Staff, together with the senior Bimbashis (Colonels), should arrive at hospital, and formally taste the compound and loudly express their satisfaction at it, and then it was to be served out to the sick men.

The ruse succeeded admirably, and henceforth there was no difficulty in getting the men to take their medicine. It was an absurd sight, seeing the General and the grave old Turkish Colonels tasting this rum-punch, and wagging their heads over the punch-bowl.

We had our recreations, one of which was skating on a sort of inland lake, formed by the bank of sand thrown up by the waves during storms, which prevented the waters from the higher lands from gaining the sea. The lake was of considerable dimensions, and the favourite game hare and hounds.

Captain Moore of the 32nd, who subsequently did such prodigies of valour at Cawnpore, was always the hare, and no hounds ever could touch him. He was a marvellous skater, and used to lead the hounds a terrible game over obstacles, etc.

When the snow began to disappear we had excellent races at Kertch. I was then a very light weight, and got many mounts. In one race, when riding for Brigadier Holmes, my horse, when within a few yards of the winning-post, staggered, and I had only time to throw myself off when he fell; he had broken a blood-vessel, and the blood was streaming from his mouth and nose. Johnnie

Crymes, a Welshman, and Jack Day of the Royal Navy, were our best riders.

One horse, called the Greyhound, gained a splendid reputation. It was, I heard, originally bought by a storekeeper for a bag of small shot; then it changed hands for money, and eventually Pasley of the Artillery bought it, and cleared a good sum in stakes. I have by me another of Major Stack's lithographs showing the races going on, with the 10th Hussars keeping the ground.

The armistice had been signed, and we could now go roaming about for some distance from camp. I never shall forget the beauty of the flowers, as soon as the snow cleared off. As if by magic the whole earth became a carpet of bright blossoms: anemones, jonquils, hyacinths, tulips everywhere. As to Russian violets, I used to jump off my horse, and gather a handful, smell them, and then, alas! throw them away.

I went foraging about many Tartar villages, and, to my delight, found young onions and chives springing up, which were greatly appreciated in our soups and stews. I also found, in sandy places among the rocks on the seashore, sea-kale; this was, indeed, a treat. Young nettles and dandelions were acceptable after a long diet on salt rations. The former, boiled, did as a substitute for spinach.

Kertch was surrounded by interesting relics, and afforded a grand hunting-ground for archæologists. On the road from Kertch to Yenikali, which I traversed so many times, there stood a number of tumuli, and these afforded no end of amusement to the diggers, of whom McPherson, our P. M. O., and Major Westmacott were the chief. The British Museum, of which the nation may well be proud, gave us information as to the coins, etc., which we might find, and I think I am right in saying that we found some very precious ones. A book has, I believe, been published connected with these findings.

One day as I was passing a working party, the Engineer officer beckoned to me to come. On arriving I found that in excavating they had got into the heart of a most interesting tumulus. I put my head in the orifice, and there saw the almost perfect form of a female; so perfect indeed was it that the folds of the shroud were visible, as was the brooch that fastened it. The Engineer officer then directed the hole to be made larger, but at the first blow of the pick the whole thing vanished, leaving nothing but dust and the few accessories in metal and glass or pottery that were in use in those times.

Two curios found are still fresh in my memory. One was a gold (I think) brooch of a pattern recently revived, called the Marie Stuart, and the other was a key fitted into a finger-ring of exactly the same pattern as the present Brahmah. There is no new thing under the sun, says the Book of Books, and certainly we had a practical proof here.

After seeing that still figure lying in its grand solemnity, I ceased to pitch oyster shells, old farthings, etc. into these excavations, for diligent explorers to find and gloat over.

At this time, for want of better excitement, Major Payn organized a body of Irregular Horse. Every one who possessed a beast was supposed to join. Payn, on a splendid little pony, was our Commandant, and our dear General Neill was standard-bearer. His standard was one of his own huge bandanas tied on to his walking-stick. Our programme was as follows. After being told off we went through certain evolutions; then Payn would manage to form in line in some field with a low stone wall in front of us. He would then say, "Gentlemen, there's your enemy, charge!" and the whole line would go full tilt, and take the wall as well as we could in line. A breakneck performance, but worthy the old traditions of Englishmen, who if they cannot get shot by the enemy desire nothing better than to put an end to themselves by breaking their necks, or in some other mad way.

Payn was a good officer, and I was not astonished at his distinguishing himself during the Mutiny.

On April 5, 101 guns signalled the treaty of peace signed in Paris. Of course, now preparations were commenced for our evacuation of the Crimea.

Before leaving, our General gave a grand dinner to all the principal English and Turkish officers and heads of departments. All of the best that could be procured was bought up, and on the appointed day we assembled round the hospitable board.

I sat next to a Bimbashi (Colonel) of Artillery. I could not help laughing at the way in which wine was consumed. I remembered our qualms connected with the punch; however, I was told that the Prophet when he forbade wine alluded only to red wines, and all others were therefore not tabooed. Anyway these good Turks showed that their heads were hard. My companion, after dinner, in response to "fill your glasses," filled a tumbler half full of whiskey and topped it with pure gin, mistaking it no doubt for water. He mopped it all up, and never turned a hair. I wish the Turks and English would get on as well now as we did then.

General Cunynghame also gave a farewell dinner, which was in every way a great success.

A terrible storm came on at this time, and a large transport was wrecked. The effect of this storm was curious. The Straits of Yenikali run north and south; the wind was from the east; it blew the already disjointed floes of ice in great masses of many feet high on the western shore. I can after this easily believe in the power of an east wind, for no one who had not seen it would believe in the mountainous mass that was piled up along the shore by its force.

During the embarkation, which I had to superintend, it so happened that I had to load the *Minna*, a Danubian boat that had been purchased for our R.N. The Captain asked me to breakfast, apologizing for short commons, as he had been so long knocking about. All of a sudden an inspiration seized him. "Do you like cod-liver oil?" My answer was an emphatic "No." Then he said, "I love it, and I have just a small lot left which I keep as a treat, and I thought you might like it also." I appreciated his generosity, but take no credit to myself for any self-denial in declining it.

When my duties were ended at Yenikali, I rejoined head-quarters at Kertch. On my relinquishing command, General Neill was good enough to publish in Division orders his best thanks to me for "the ability, energy, and attention with which I had so assiduously conducted the duties of my department, and the great assistance I always afforded him by my most judicious and successful exertions."

This turned out of use to me afterwards.

We, of our department, had to hand over to the Cossacks each outpost as it was vacated. One day in giving over a post, I got into conversation with the Cossack Colonel; he was overjoyed at the conclusion of the war, for he said he had not seen his wife for two years. In further conversation I found he had a house in Kertch, and from his description I think it must have been the one Hearne and I occupied. I told him the house was in good order and in no way injured. I wondered if the woman shut up in the room next to Hearne's was his wife. We always handed over posts to each other with full military honours.

At last I embarked with others for Constantinople. We were delayed by an awful fog off the mouths of the Bosphorus, and could not hit off the entrance.

Our Captain fed us villainously, so I stopped his certificate at Constantinople, and he got compensation only for the days we ought to have taken in arriving.

We had cleared out so speedily that I had time after arrival at Constantinople to run up to Sevastopol. I made the passage on a steamer which was going to Balaclava. Just as we were starting, one of our department came to say good-bye. He wished me a pleasant journey, and added: "You have some nice passengers, amongst whom there is an American; mind you do not say anything to rub him up the wrong way." We were at that time having rather a nasty paper war with the Yankees.

A gentleman came up to me, and, seeing me in uniform, asked several questions about public buildings, etc. He seemed a nice sort of man, so I ventured to pass on the warning my friend had given me. The stranger laughed and said, "Curiously enough, I am that American." We became great friends. He was an artist, an uncommonly good one, and had been for some years making sketches in Egypt. His sketch-book was very interesting. Alas! he lost it at Balaclava, and, although I did all I could to try to recover it for him, my efforts were unsuccessful.

We had a Mr. and Mrs. Haliburton on board. An allusion was made to Sam Slick at dinner by the American, and the Captain, thinking perhaps something injudicious might be said, informed the American that Sam Slick's son was his next neighbour. Mr. Haliburton laughed and said, "No, I am no relation, but my wife is his daughter." It was curious. I formed a great friendship for these two most cultivated and interesting people, and we did Sevastopol together.

Arrived at Balaclava, I was utterly astounded that an army of such enormous numbers could have been landed and supplied from such (as it seemed to me) a narrow creek. In all I had read, I had never gathered any conception of the cramped space. The ships were lying beside each other like cabs and busses during a block in Fleet Street; literally, you could have walked from deck to deck. I now could understand the difficulties the transport and commissariat services had to contend with.

We made our way up the hill, and our first visit was to

Mother Seacole. She was a character well known to all the army. A dear fat bundle of clothes with a smiling dark countenance. She was in the throes of packing up, but would not be satisfied until we had had something to drink her health in. At that early hour Mrs. Haliburton did not care for stimulants; at last a bottle of lemonade was found, but no corkscrew. I knocked the top off with my sword, when the old lady laughingly said, "Bless the boy, he'd get liquor out of anything." She gave Mrs. Haliburton some tracts, but would not give me one, saying they were no good for me. I bought a gold five-ruble piece from her, which I now have on my watch-chain.

So highly was she esteemed by our people that a bazaar was got up in her aid by Lord Ranelagh; she had been so generous to our men that she had made no money at Sevastopol. The story goes that, whenever there was a big fight going on, she trudged out with all the liquor and provisions she could carry and gave them to the wounded.

We did all the sights of the place; the valley of the shadow of death, where any amount of burst shell could be collected—then Sevastopol itself. The walls of the dockyard and houses seemed to have had severe small-pox from the pitting of bullets. I was told that nowhere could any one be safe from them; they came through keyholes.

I stood on the brink of Inkerman, possibly on the very spot where my brother-in-law with his outlying picquet of the gallant Welsh regiment had stood when he was wounded. I could realize the deadly nature of the strife, and wished I had been present at that soldiers' battle.

Then we visited the cemeteries with their sad story, and then the trenches. On our way back we encountered a party of blue jackets getting big guns away. The process was simplicity itself. The gun was hauled to the edge of the incline leading to Balaclava. A sailor then mounted it cross-legged, with a fiddle, and the word was given, "Let the B. go," and it went, the tune only stopping when a catastrophe was imminent.

On reaching Balaclava I found a sentry performing gymnastics with his bayonet; he told me he was killing rats, and added, "Begorra, if I didn't kill them, they'd kill me." They were, I was told, awful; driven out of Sevastopol by starvation, they had found a land of Goshen at Balaclava.

I must not forget to mention having seen the so-called redoubts that the Turks were blamed for not holding. They resembled old Roman remains more than redoubts, and Colonel Wetherall, who was present at the battle of Balaclava, said that the Turks ought never to have been told to hold them. The Turks are not cowards, as has been proved a hundred times, and I think that the spontaneous evidence given in their favour by such a man as Wetherall should have some weight.

On my return to Constantinople I found things much changed. Yashmaks had been almost entirely superseded by the very thinnest veils, and it was reported that the Sultan said the sooner the English army was out of Constantinople the better.

Before leaving the land of the Crescent, I desire to say one word respecting my experiences of Turks. As far as I was concerned, I liked the Turks infinitely better than most of the Christians one met in those parts and at that time.

I own that the scum of the earth had been attracted there by the hope of a rich harvest. The Turks saw no harvest prospects, and were very much what they always were, apathetic and indolent. The Armenians were particularly grateful to us for assisting them in their desire to retain their holy places. Perhaps, of all, the Greeks were the worst—next to them the Jews.

As far as the Turkish soldier went he was simply admirable, and their officers with us were fairly good, but

I fancy, unchecked by supervision, they peculated sadly. As I said before, the bearing of the men towards me after my connection with them had ceased was most civil and soldierlike.

One question has puzzled me. Why were we not sent to Kars? When ready and splendidly equipped, why were we allowed to kick our heels about Beyukdere? and when keeping us in inactivity became a scandal, why were we sent to Kertch, where we were not wanted?

A certain red book with a lock and key, which was kept by the Chief of the Staff, and into which I was occasionally permitted to copy a letter, perhaps might tell us something; but my idea is that the secret of the fall of Kars has been well kept by those whose mouths were for good reasons shut.

CHAPTER X

HOMEWARD BOUND

I WAS quite a millionaire when my last pay and my passage-money had been handed over to me. I know I must have had £500 somewhere, for I consented to join an expedition under Speke, the great African traveller, who had joined our force, and £500 down was to be contributed by each one who joined.

We were to visit the Caucasus, and then make our way to Persia, visiting Dr. Wolff's missions on our way. The Royal Geographical Society promised a grant, I believe; but the Society for the Propagation of the Gospel in Foreign Parts seemed not to believe in us, and gave us no grant; so money was too scarce, and the project was given up.

It must be confessed that I was not as disappointed as I might have been, for I think I was more anxious to see whether the Circassians were as fair as they were reported to be, than to visit Dr. Wolff's missions.

As far as I can remember, passage-money was given to me, and I was left to choose my own route. I joined a party consisting of General Neill, his A.D.C. Major Warde, Beaumont and Ord of the Engineers.

I had no mufti with me, and it was not worth while to get any before reaching England. Moreover, we were told that if we travelled in uniform we got first-class tickets for second-class fare, so in uniform we travelled. We chose the Trieste route. On board I had a bad attack of pleurisy. Luckily, the then Governor of the Bank of England was on board, travelling with his own private medical man, who pulled me round in an amazingly short time.

We crossed to Venice at once, and put up at the Hotel Danielli, where we were nearly burnt alive by an idiot reading in bed.

The Austrians were in occupation in those days, and the hatred that existed between them and the Venetians was intense. My guide was anxious to get me to outwit the Governor in a very curious way.

I think I have seldom seen four finer or handsomer men than my four comrades alluded to, and as they stood together in the Piazza San Marco they were the cynosure of all beholders. I kept in the background, not wishing to spoil the effect. We did all the sights and operas.

When we were taking our tickets for Milan an unpleasantness arose. The man at the passport bureau demanded that we should take our caps off. We had not done so, as it is not usual; but we had saluted. We were very rudely ordered to do so. I forget how it ended; but it was an insult to our uniform.

At Milan we found no opera running, and the General was much exercised thereby; so he told the hotel-keeper we must have one. A manager was sent for, and a crier was sent round to say that *Lucia di Lammermoor* would be performed by special desire of his Excellency the General and the other English officers who had arrived. It cost us very little. The *prima donna* sang all her songs right into our stage-box.

I made a prolonged tour, visiting no end of interesting places. At Chamounix we met Dr. Chambers, and after that I think we scattered; indeed, Neill and his A.D.C. left me at Milan. I know I arrived at the 'Golden Cross,' Charing Cross, with only a ten-franc-piece in my pocket, and had to ask the landlady to pay my cab fare.

London is a very different place to me now from what

it was before I started for the Crimea, when funds were low and every penny was of importance.

I had been elected to the Junior United Service Club, so that my days and evenings were passed in comfort. The Club at that time was located as a temporary measure at Crockford's whilst the new house was being built. I did theatres more largely, and music-halls less.

I forget whether it was at this time or before that John Parry was at his best. To my mind, no one has come up to him since.

Later on I knew Corney Grain fairly well. He took me off at a private party one evening, giving a specimen of my agonizing efforts on the 'cello. On another occasion he told me the origin of many of his sketches.

At the time I am writing of, Albert Smith was in full force. My people had travelled with him, and whenever they went to see him, if they sent in our cards, he would introduce some scene in which they had all been present. I think he took off one of my sisters in a good-natured way.

But to continue my memories. Fechter was playing in those days, and his parlour-maid, who sat next to us on one occasion, told my brother that he often walked up and down the room for hours repeating only one sentence in English to get the pronunciation correct. I admired him immensely in *The Duke's Motto*, but he never got over his foreign accent when he said " I am here."

Jullien's concerts were, I think, on at that time, and I used to go constantly.

There were many rows between the military and civilians, got up by some idiot who thought the Guardsmen meant disrespect by not taking off their caps when *God save the Queen* was played. Of course they were right.

Jullien was the first man who educated the English audience to appreciate really good music. With a certain amount of charlatanism, he always introduced into his programme something good, and people soon began to like the good music best.

I can remember Vauxhall well, but that was earlier than 1856. Cremorne was in full swing. I never cared for it. Talking of Vauxhall, I remember a very thrilling scene there one night. A strong man was lashed by his feet and ankles to the top sail of a windmill, and was then to be carried right round. When he got to zero the thing would not work, and there he was head downwards. By great effort they got him to a horizontal position, which was worse. At last they got him all right, and then he was released. The spectators were horror-stricken. It was a gruesome sight.

Koenig was the great cornet-player in those days. I bought a cornet from him, and had lessons from him in a room in the Lowther Arcade.

Puzzi was the grand performer on the French horn. His wife, too, was a good musician, and taught my wife singing. The Duke of Wellington was very kind to Madame Puzzi, and used jokingly to tell her to drink lots of "porter-beer," as she called it.

Wright and Paul Bedford, with Madame Vestris, were inimitable at the Adelphi. Charles Mathews, Buckstone, and the Keeleys shone at the Haymarket. I remember seeing Mary Keeley as the blind girl in the *Christmas Carol*. She was so natural that she made me cry.

I think it was at this time that Miss Bateman was playing Leah. Never mind the time; the acting can never be forgotten. I have seen nothing to come up to it. *Punch* said that the boxes wept so copiously that the pit had to put up their umbrellas to keep themselves dry. I know I was too much overcome to be a pleasant neighbour, and the audience in departing looked as if they were suffering from severe influenza.

Reader, have you ever been in a crush caused by a

panic? I was once at the Alhambra. It was awful. My brother, who was next me on the stairs, said, "Fold your arms across your chest, and remain quite still." I did so, but I felt the breath being gradually squeezed out of my body. When relief came I heaved a big sigh, and then all was right.

As soon as my mother had returned to her old home, I started for Wales. On my journey I got into a carriage with card-sharpers. I, of course, declined to play, but was much interested in their proceedings with other passengers. They got out one by one, and I never could detect who were the pigeons, as each one on leaving declared the others to be the rogues.

My vanity was sorely tried, on reaching home, by our old doctor's wife. I had adopted the Napoleonic fashion of wearing my moustache waxed out into a fine point on each side. When the old lady saw me, she exclaimed, "Bless the boy! he looks for all the world like a goose with a quill through his nose"—a rather cruel custom practised around Wrexham, to keep geese from breaking through hedges into gardens. I dropped the goose system of dressing my moustache.

During this visit my brother-in-law, who married my sister as his second wife, came to stay with my mother; they were accompanied by a daughter of the first marriage, with whom I fell in love, this time desperately. As usual, the course of true love did not run smooth. The lady was an only child, and her father naturally did not care for her to go to distant lands. Of course I was properly in despair. So desperate was I that I actually offered my services to the *Times* as a war-correspondent in Persia, hoping to be put out of my misery with a pen in my hand and an ink-bottle at my button-hole.

Reader, are you surprised to hear that the *Times* did not accept my offer? I had no idea at the time that my own regiment formed one of the expedition.

Well, as death and glory were denied me, I did the very best thing I could, by applying to join the school of musketry at Hythe. What a jolly time I had between my moments of despair! What a nice set of fellows I met, all keen on their work, and enjoying their hours of relaxation all the more for being pretty well kept at it! We were lucky in having the great Whitworth and Westley Richards there experimenting. We had Conolly, V.C., Dormer, and Clive of the Guards, together with Palliser of shot and shell fame. Our instructors were painstaking and pleasant. My brother officer, Captain Daniell, was there, which of course was nice for me. We used generally to run up to town from mid-day Saturday until Monday morning's parade. On one occasion an officer missed his train, so had to come back. On reaching his quarters he found his soldier-servant in the bath, with master's clothes, clean shirt, etc., all ready to don. When he was clothed, he got the sack, and I hope returned to his right mind.

It was on one of these flying visits that I called to see my sisters, who were staying with a friend, when who should come in unexpectedly but the dear object of my affections! That sealed our fate. An uncle became our ambassador, and all was settled. I went back to Hythe to sigh no more—sigh no more!

We had a *liber veritatis* on the ante-room table, in which any story of a marked character told during the day was entered in exaggerated but not ill-natured form. The entries were endless and most amusing. I remember one or two as follows: " Lieutenant Palliser shot quail during the armistice with an Enfield rifle." It did not say that the rifle was loaded with small shot. Again, a certain ensign said he was off Gibraltar in an open boat in a storm when the waves were so high he could not see the Rock. I came in, of course. My story was that "my brother suffered excruciating agonies from headache;

physicians were in vain, until he tried parting his hair down the middle, when they entirely left him."

The book came unfortunately to grief as follows:—An officer of H.M. 60th described his sufferings from sea-sickness in going round the Cape to India. The entry ran somewhat like this: "Lieutenant X., H.M. 60th Royal Rifles, took one hundred days going to India, round the Cape. He ate nothing, and was sick every day. He landed in good condition." The narrator of this miracle happened to be late for dinner the day it was entered in the *Liber*, and as he passed through the ante-room read the entry. His wrath was great, and he gave vent to it by saying: "Some stupid fool has written a story about me. I beg to say I never told a lie in my life." That same evening there was another entry: "Lieutenant X. never told a lie in his life." The page was torn out, and then the book disappeared.

We had a good sweep on the result of our shooting. I was the favourite up to three hundred yards, but fell off at the long distances. I was, however, a marksman, and got a first-class certificate.

We used to go in state to church on Sundays, and sat in the Corporation stalls. Opposite was a large slab of marble, in which the goodness and virtues of Dame Catherine Deedes were recorded. It wound up with: "She was the mother of twenty-one children, of whom nineteen survived her." A friend of mine whispered, "Deeds, not words."

After leaving Hythe I went down to South Wales to do the billing and cooing. One day we were at the opening of a church, only too glad to be crowded out, and to enjoy ourselves wandering about and basking in sunshine, when a special messenger arrived with one of those ominous-looking envelopes marked O.H.M.S. This missive directed me to join my regiment at once. I was thunderstruck, and hurried off to London to see my old Chief, Sir

R. Vivian. I found from him that an outbreak of Sepoys had taken place at Meerut, and as a precautionary measure all officers on leave were ordered to rejoin. I told him that I was engaged to be married almost immediately, and asked if it would be safe to take a lady out; he answered: "Of course take your wife out; it will show your confidence in Government." And so it came to pass that our marriage was hurried forward—a circumstance I did not by any means regret; and as soon as practicable we set forth for the golden East.

Our ship, the *Colombo*, was full of officers returning from leave. We had, with other passengers, Generals Windham and Dupuis, and Colonel Adye, together with a considerable number of officers of the 9th Lancers. Everybody on board was anxious in reference to the scope and object of the revolt, but no one believed that anything really serious would occur. Those on board who belonged to native regiments in Bengal poohpoohed the thing, and assured us that all would be over before we arrived.

We disembarked at Alexandria, and went *viâ* Cairo to Suez. We had to wait a few days before the Indian mail-steamer *Bentinck*, which was to take us on, arrived. As was usual in those days, passengers overland only took with them such absolute necessaries as could be carried in small bags; our heavy baggage, portmanteaux, etc., were brought by some conveyance or other, so that much of it was never seen until arrival at the final destination. As soon as the steamer was signalled, we set to work to gather together our small belongings, and whilst so doing there was a knock at our bedroom door. The waiter handed me a card, and said the gentleman wished to see me. I went to the waiting-room, and found a stranger, who introduced himself as having just come from Calcutta. Hearing that an officer of the Madras Fusiliers was taking a young wife out, he considered it his duty to call and tell me that the regiment was far up-country, in the very thick of the disturbances, and that all India was in a blaze. It was most good and thoughtful of him, and the recollection of his kindness will never be effaced.

Here then was a predicament: I had only a few minutes in which to make up my mind. Two courses were open to me: either to take my wife on to Madras, and trust to being able to place her under the care of some friend, or else to send her back to her father at once by the same steamer that had brought us out. I need scarcely say that the latter was the one decided on. It was, of course, a cruel decision to announce, but she bravely accepted it, and did not add to my troubles by raising objections. No sooner had my determination got wind, than a gentleman, a captain in the Royal Navy, sought an interview. He told me he was going home from Ceylon on promotion, and if I would entrust my wife to his care, he would do all he could to ensure her comfort. I gladly accepted his offer, and he at once started off to get all the cabin baggage belonging to her that he could lay hands on. In this he was eminently successful, considering the short time available.

Thus, after only a few hours' notice, we parted, on the very day month on which we had been married. Well, one cannot expect unusually good luck to fall twice on the same anniversary.

My wife tells me that when she stepped on board our old friend, the *Colombo*, the purser started in amazement, thinking a ghost had appeared. Her time was well occupied in assisting to make up clothes for the poor fugitive ladies and children from Calcutta. Her greatest regret was that, owing to the paucity of her own personal baggage, she had little to give towards the general clothing fund; but her own sadness was somewhat alleviated by her sympathy with the greater sorrow of those on board, who had lost husbands, fathers, children, and friends—indeed everything.

CHAPTER XI

LUCKNOW

I NOW come to a period that demands the utmost attention. Luckily I am in possession of very many letters written at the time on the spot, but some are missing, having fallen into the enemy's hands; others went down off Galle in the P. and O. steamer that was carrying the mails. To the credit of the Post Office they were duly delivered, but in a state of pulp. How the addresses were deciphered is a marvel. The first is written from on board the *Bentinck*. By it I find I gave up my reserved cabin, and had Colonel Becher and Major West as cabin companions.

Powys of the 9th Lancers, like myself, had left a young wife, and we became friends. I was glad of this sympathy—yes, more than glad, for I found the ladies on board, if they did not actually cut me, were, to say the least, very cool. I discovered that the cause of their resentment was my *brutal conduct* in sending the "poor creature" away; that it was "all nonsense, there was no danger," etc. In this they were backed by those officers on board who belonged to native regiments. I could not help admiring the loyalty of these men to their old comrades; mistaken they were, but they would not cast away their belief in the fidelity of their men.

The real cause of offence was, that my having acted as I did seemed a reproach to others for not having done the same. The wisdom of my act was proved, not only by subsequent events, but by Lady Canning's diary, in which she so loudly laments the influx into Calcutta of husbandless ladies.

The heat in the Red Sea was quite abnormal; all slept on deck, the ladies being partitioned off by sails across the quarter-deck. One morning Dr. White overheard a Lascar say to another, "Never mind, the Governor-General's body-guard are ready to rise, and then every white man in Calcutta will be murdered." Dr. White jumped up and asked the fellow what he meant. The Lascar denied having spoken. He got two dozen on his bare back all the same.

On arrival at Madras I was ordered to embark immediately on board the H.E.I.C. steamship *Coromandel*, which was taking a Madras native regiment to Bengal. I had only three days to spare, which I spent in visiting the wives of brother officers on service. I found all Madras ringing the praises of our regiment. Neill was a sort of demi-god; money was pouring in on all sides in aid of the families of the killed; already 28,000 rupees had been collected. The newspapers called Neill "the saviour of India," for had it not been for his promptness Allahabad would have been lost.

I left everything not absolutely necessary at Madras, and embarked for Calcutta. I found that, in consequence of the lateness of the arrival of the order for my passage, no accommodation had been provided for me. I was miserable—no cabin and no bed; the decks were crowded with the Madras Rifles, and the only place assigned to me was a bath-room wherein to put my baggage. Here was a come-down from Quartermaster-General of a Division to a cabinless outsider! Of course I could have claimed accommodation according to my rank, but I preferred to nurse my sorrow in silence.

Captain Campbell, who commanded the *Coromandel*, was a singularly nice man, and to him I owe any small favour that it was in his power to grant. I got no sort of civility from any one else.

We had to put in to Coconada to land some Rifles, if necessary, as an outbreak was reported to have occurred there. Here I heard of poor Neill's tragic death whilst entering Lucknow. It caused me real grief, and I felt that my own prospects were greatly blighted.

On September 16 I landed at Calcutta, after having had a sharp attack of influenza; for two days I was really very bad. In going up the Hooghly we passed the *Golden Fleece* bringing nine hundred men, not before they were wanted. We gave them a cheer. I reported my arrival, and asked to be sent up at once by *dâk*, that is by relays of horsed carriages.

Calcutta was swarming with officers awaiting orders for transport. Several of my *Bentinck* friends were at my hotel. Cator and a lot of the 9th Lancers officers had already started fully armed, and with one hundred rounds each of revolver ammunition. There was a chance of the road being blocked by rebels, and they would have to fight their way through.

Every officer travelling *dâk* was allowed one hundred pounds of luggage, to include food, cooking utensils, etc.; not much room for neckties and collars. The roads were so congested with officers hurrying up to join their respective regiments, that I was told my turn could not come for several days.

I was greatly exercised as to uniform, not knowing what my regiment was wearing. In Burmah, owing to our clothing never having been sent from Madras, our men were literally in rags; they had to borrow from each other to appear on parade for guards. As the Royal Navy had a good supply of serge, our Colonel got permission to buy some, and our regimental tailors made it up, so we wore a most suitable and comfortable uniform of blue serge. I determined to get a tunic similar to my Burmese one. This was greatly admired by Colonel Little of the 9th Lancers, who was very kind to me, and wanted to know how I came to be wearing such a garment. All new arrivals in Calcutta were wearing brown holland blouses with their distinctive facings.

I found Calcutta quite as enthusiastic as Madras about my regiment. Neill's memory was cherished, and all the stories about him retold—how he had locked the station-master in his own office, and put sentries over the engine-driver, etc. One was told me that I had not heard before. It seems that General Neill wanted a pair of binoculars, and went to the shop of a leading jeweller to buy them. He tendered Government notes in payment. The shopman hesitated at taking them, and asked if Neill could pay in silver. "Oh, I see," said Neill, "you have lost confidence in Government. I will soon restore it by asking the Governor-General to allow me to place a couple of my men as sentries over your shop." The man was horrified at the idea of two of our men being quartered on him, and took the notes without more ado. I believe Neill reported this to the Governor-General.

Neill's arrival at this hour of the deepest gloom and despondency was like a ray of sunshine. I can well imagine what a power he was amongst the feeble advisers of the Governor-General. His Crimean experience had given him a justifiable self-confidence, and he knew he was backed by a thousand men on whom he could rely. Neill felt equal to the emergency, and I have always thought the moral support brought by his presence was in no way less valuable than the material advantages gained by his subsequent victories. Calcutta seemed to me still terror-stricken, and the general opinion was that the advisers of the Governor-General were very inefficient. Sir Patrick Grant was the one brilliant exception.

On the 19th I got my orders to go by rail to Raneegunj, and then proceed by *dâk*. At Raneegunj I met my old Crimean friend, Major Austen of the Artillery, and Colonel

Russell of the 84th. These two were to be my travelling companions. We had two *dâk* carriages, one for Colonel Russell, the other for Austen and self. By lying head-and-tail-ways we managed pretty well, the more so as we were never long in the carriage together, for we had to keep "sentry go" in turn, three hours on and six hours off. Colonel Russell took the first watch. When on duty we sat beside the driver with our pistols ready.

The grand trunk road to Cawnpore was desolation personified; wires cut, villages still smouldering, and the hand of havoc apparent everywhere. We had several alarms. Once the horses of the leading carriage refused to move. We thought it was an ambuscade; it turned out that a tiger had recently crossed the road, and the horses scented the danger. We coaxed them over, and then all was right. On another occasion the horses in Colonel Russell's *dâk* took fright and tried to leap over a parapet. One succeeded in getting half over. We had to cut him loose; then, after mending the harness, we proceeded. If any one wants to know what *dâk* horses were like, let him get *Curry and Rice*, by Major Atkinson, R.E., to which I have already alluded.

We halted from time to time at the various rest-houses to get food and change horses. Every rest-house had its visitors' book, in which any complaint or remark could be entered. Alas! how many quite recent entries were made by hands already cold for ever!

I was amused by an entry as follows: "Major Renaud and party, Madras Fusiliers, passed through; road quiet." The next was: "Lieut. Gosling and party, 1st M. F." Then some wag had written: "There goes the goose after the fox."

At Allahabad, Colonel Russell got news that 15,000 Gwalior rebels were crossing the road, so extra precaution was necessary. They wanted us to halt, but we determined to push on. Allahabad had many interests for me.

It was the scene of Neill's first great achievement; then, so many of our men lay buried in the ditch: they had succumbed to cholera, hard work, and exposure. I visited the hospital, and found seventy-four of our men there, either sick or wounded. They were so glad to see me, and made much of my having been in the Crimea.

During our onward journey we passed the scene of the action at Futtypore, where Renaud of Ours so distinguished himself. General Havelock in his despatch said: "First on the list I must put Major Renaud of the Madras Fusiliers, whose exertion at the head of the advanced column I cannot sufficiently praise. His coolness and conduct in the action are equally entitled to my highest commendation." Nothing now remained to mark the battle-field but two disabled guns.

At last we reached Cawnpore. It is not easy to describe one's feelings on nearing the place, the very name of which even now makes one shudder. Then all was so recent that the tragedy almost seemed to be re-enacted before our eyes.

The history of the massacre is too well known to require any comments or remarks. I was painfully interested in hearing of the stupendous deeds of heroism done by my friend Moore of the 32nd, the man who skated so splendidly. It was said that when the enemy grew bold and brought their guns too near, he called for volunteers, and with a sponge-staff in his hand sallied forth, and literally mowed them down. I can easily imagine the dismay he caused, for not only was he a man of magnificent physique, but he was also maddened with grief at the loss of a young wife. He was the leading spirit of that marvellous defence.

From my letter, written at Cawnpore, I gather that I got several mementoes from the entrenchments and the massacre house. I will not enumerate them, and I am glad they were lost with other things of mine, when the

Gwalior rebels subsequently attacked Windham there, for they could only be valued as relics of a sad, sad time.

I will, however, give a portion of the said letter, as it may be interesting. I wrote as follows: "I send you a verbatim copy, spelling and all, of some writing on the wall in the room where the poor ladies were murdered. It is scratched with a pin on the plaster, and is written by some soldier's wife. The 15th of July alluded to was the day when the first massacre took place:—

"'Country men and women remember the 15th July 57. Your wives and famelies are here in missery and at the disposal of savages, who has ravished both young and old and then killed us. Oh! Oh! my child my child. Countrymen revenge it.'"

Under was written: "We will! a soldier."

The excitement here was intense: every blade of grass seemed to call up some sad memory. Of course Neill's conduct in meting out such exemplary punishment to the rebels was much discussed. It was said that besides making the murderers clean up the house in so degrading a manner, he hung hundreds on a gibbet erected in the garden of the fatal bungalow. Of course this was mere hearsay. The number hung must have been very great. I remember one of our men sending in a large money-claim for rope used in hanging rebels.

I have an interesting photograph of the Bungalow, taken immediately after the frightful occurrence. It merely shows the house with a large tree which was felled to cover the well into which the bodies were cast, and over which the beautiful monument now stands.

Conversation here naturally turned on the deeds of Outram and Havelock. It was said that sixty-five officers had been killed or wounded in the advance. It was also reported that the garrison was hemmed in by 80,000 rebels with many guns; if so, our work was cut out for us.

I now, to my great joy, met Taylor of Ours, and with

him was attached to H.M. 75th Regiment, to do duty until we reached our own men in the Alumbagh. The 75th were sadly off for officers, having lost so many at Delhi. The regiment too was over done. One of the greatest hardships of this campaign was the necessity for using again and again men who had already done their full share of work. It could not be helped.

As we were now on the verge of active service, I cautioned my wife not to believe in any reports of my being killed, as telegrams were very hazy at this period, and, as I said, "there were many Parrys and Barrys hanging about."

We were now busy getting guns and baggage across the Ganges. I watched the main column crossing the bridge of boats, and noticed how distinct the regiments in scarlet were by comparison with those wearing karkee (dust-colour).

The Nana Sahib caught seven of our spies one day, and, after cutting off their hands and ears and splitting their noses, sent them back to camp.

Taylor crossed the Ganges with me at twelve noon. What a sight our camp was! Our fighting force numbered barely 3500, but was accompanied by 20,000 camp followers, independent of scores of elephants, camels, mules, bullocks and carts, etc. The scene was indescribable, reminding me of the transport corps at Balaclava, with a mixture of Greenwich Fair.

I now continue my narrative more closely on the lines of my diary.

"October 31.—Brigadier Grant joined yesterday. We marched this morning about sixteen miles. On arriving at our camping-ground, I was ordered on outlying picquet, so had to march off without breakfast. A cheroot and a biscuit did very well till some arrived. We had no tent, but a clump of trees afforded a good shelter from the sun. A party was sent out to a village near, which was said to be hostile. The women and children had been removed, which showed they anticipated a fight. About eighty men were killed; some, I am afraid, innocent. We lost one Sikh killed, and a 93rd Highlander wounded.

"November 1.—Marched to Bunoo.

"November 2.—Marched very early; was detailed with Captains Brook, 75th, and Lightfoot, 84th, for advanced guard. We had scarcely got two miles when we were halted and told to wait for orders. As our camp colourmen were marking out the ground, they were fired on by the enemy, who were posted in a village in front. The cavalry and horse artillery of the advanced guard galloped up, and like lightning a heavy fire was poured into the village. We were then ordered to advance skirmishing, and had only just deployed, when two of our men were wounded from shots fired from loop-holes in the mud walls. We were ordered to lie down under cover until more guns were brought up; then after a few rounds we advanced with a rush, and the village was in our hands."

Just then, Colonel Russell, seeing me, and probably knowing no one else by name, told me to go back and tell the gunners to cease firing on the village, as it was in our hands. I ran back, and, just as I reached the guns, I tripped up and came head over heels, much to the amusement of the gunners. I gave my message, and was about to rejoin, when I found I had lost my revolver. I had to go back to the scene of my disaster, and there found it. As I was going through the village, two sepoys came right on me; they were both armed with muskets. It was a case for immediate action, so I shot one with my revolver, and the other bolted, thinking, I suppose, that I had soldiers near to back me. Just then I heard firing behind me, and found it was only Sikhs who had come in and were blazing into the roofs of the houses, in hopes of dislodging Pandies, who were very fond of hiding in the thatch and remaining quietly there, until they could get a shot at an officer or some person of consequence. They were said also to hide in the huge grain jars, just as Ali Baba's men did.

At this time, my own party under Brooks having gone goodness knows where, I joined a party of the 84th under Captain Rolleston. The shots of the Sikhs in the village came dropping around us: so Rolleston cleared out, and we became a gun-guard.

Our duties now were very light; we marched when the guns advanced, and lay down when they halted. During a halt a small body of cavalry was seen hovering on our right. As I was a Hythe marksman, an Enfield was handed to me to have a shot, whilst the artillery officer watched the result with his field-glass. My first shot at 900 yards made a party of five of them move off, and the bullet of my second at 1000 yards at a single horseman was said to have gone under the horse; the rider put spurs into him and went off. We saw no more cavalry afterwards. As we continued our advance we came across dead Pandies and wounded horses; I noticed we never came across a wounded Pandy!

At one place we came to a sugar-cane brake, and some Sikhs went in to cut some cane. Three were severely wounded by sepoys lying concealed there. I saw one Sikh holding his arm up; it had almost been severed from the shoulder; it was a horrid sight. We had no time to go in and clear the brake. Next we saw three Pandies lying in a group, killed by a round shot. In crossing a nullah I got a splendid ducking. The chief mischief done was to my ammunition and revolver.

By this time we had come up to another village. We gave it a few rounds, and then passed through it. It was nearly empty. We found two women, whom the Sikhs at first wanted to kill, but were easily persuaded not to do so; we also took three men prisoners. Another hour's advance brought us up to the main body. Here Rolleston had to give in from the effects of the sun, and Taylor was sent to replace him. The artillery had some grub in a tumbril, and they gave me a lump of bread and tongue which I shared with Taylor; some brandy-and-water was also tendered, and gladly accepted.

Whilst we halted in this village a most amusing scene occurred. Some of these jolly Highlanders woke up an old sow with a young sucker. The hunt after them was most exciting; the old sow dodged between the Highlanders' legs, upsetting them right and left. At last the sucker was caught, and borne in triumph under a brawny fellow's arm, the pig emitting a series of squeals that did not unworthily represent the pipes of the gallant corps. We captured in this village a brass nine-pounder and two tumbrils.

The troops were by this time completely fagged out, so we returned to our original village. On our march back Colonel Russell came to me; he told me his horse had had its leg broken by a round shot, and asked me to put it out of its misery. I saw the poor beast, but could not shoot it, so got a drummer to do it. What strange creatures we are!—I could shoot a man at sight, but not a wounded horse. Our fight lasted altogether about seven hours, so we were glad to get back to breakfast. Our loss was two officers wounded, half-a-dozen men killed and twenty wounded. So ended the battle of Maragungh.

We halted on the 3rd, and on the 4th I was on picquet, and heard heavy firing in the direction of Lucknow. A few shots were exchanged with the enemy on the 5th. Whilst on outlying picquet next day, some prisoners were brought in, but as they seemed harmless villagers, I interceded for them, and they were released outside our videttes.

On November 7, news was brought into camp of the battle of Futtypore, and that Sir Colin had nearly been taken prisoner at Shergotty.

The Sikhs and Punjabees were astonished at the Naval

Brigade; they looked on them as a species of Irregular Horse, and could not understand their white shirts being outside their trousers. The enemy said we were hard up for troops, and had taken all the firemen from the steamers.

I was on outlying picquet next night, with strict orders not to allow any firing unless absolutely necessary. I posted my sentries, and gave orders accordingly. In the early dawn bang went one of my sentries. Off I hurried to the spot. There was no indication of any enemy, so I told the man not to fire again. Presently off went another bang. This time a field officer arrived, and slated me because my men were disturbing the camp. I could not help it. I doubled sentries to restore confidence, and remained with them. I found out next morning, when relieved, that the men had some cause for their uneasiness, for a man named Kavanagh had come in from Lucknow disguised as a native, to give Sir Colin a map of the route he was to take in entering. A most gallant act, which was eventually rewarded by a V.C.

Kavanagh told us that Outram's force was suffering from cold, the men having only the clothes in which they stood. Tea-leaves were smoked instead of tobacco, and the men were on half rations. A round shot had killed three ladies the day before. We were all anxiety to get on and relieve the sufferings of these poor creatures. We had not long to wait before getting orders to move.

Whilst advancing on to the Alumbagh we were fired on; we made a detour to the right, so as to get on the enemy's flank, but they moved so as to avoid our guns and infantry. Our cavalry got amongst them, and killed forty, taking two guns. Our loss was trifling. The Alumbagh was a large building, situated on a plain some little distance from the suburbs of Lucknow; it was surrounded by gardens, enclosed by a high wall. In this building Havelock had left all his sick, wounded, and baggage, under escort of a rear-guard, composed of detachments of all the regiments under his command, whilst he, with his main body, forced his way into the Residency, and reinforced Sir John Inglis. Time itself will scarcely efface the memory of this gallant but awful achievement, which, whilst emblazoning the scroll of England's fame, caused unutterable sorrow in so many homes.

The Alumbagh in turn became surrounded and besieged. It is not too much to say that the defence of the Alumbagh under Colonel McIntyre was scarcely second to the defence of the Residency. I know competent judges who considered it much the more exposed position. Had the enemy concentrated their whole energies against it instead of against the Residency, the condition of the small force that held this outpost would have been very critical.

On our arrival we became a part of this heroic band, and met many of our brother officers and about one hundred of our men. I was on picquet that night with Taylor and Dobbs; a most awful place, a ruined village in a clump of trees, with high elephant grass growing close up. I remembered the Sikhs and the sugar-cane, so warned our sentries to keep a sharp look-out. The Pandies came very near us, and fired all night, but did not hit any of us. In the morning, after having had our dram and some biscuit, we started off to join the column.

The details of the 84th, 90th, and 1st Madras Fusiliers, which had been left in the Alumbagh, were now formed into one regiment, called the First Battalion of Details, and with the 93rd Highlanders and Sikhs (Loodiana) we formed a brigade under Colonel the Hon. Adrian Hope of the 93rd. The battalion was commanded by Major Barnston of the 90th L. I., a regiment well known to fame from the part it took in the Peninsula.

Our advance was necessarily slow, and our halts frequent. We bore entirely to our right, so as to get round the enemy; we heard from time to time heavy firing in front, and the monotony of the march was occasionally broken by the dashing past of bodies of the 9th Lancers or field guns.

We were not brought into action until quite noon, when we had arrived at a place called the Dilkoosha, a large palace standing on a considerable eminence, and surrounded as usual by a high solid wall. Here we halted until a breach had been made, and then in we poured. The enemy retired firing; their shot fell amongst us. I remember a round shot falling amongst the 93rd Highlanders, who were on our right. It did considerable damage; in its course it struck the musket-barrel of one of these splendid fellows, and drove it clean through his head. Three were killed and many wounded. After the first second there was not a move in the ranks; the officer called out, " Tell off again from the right," and it was done as quietly as on parade.

Colonel Græme, in speaking of this incident, said it made on his mind the impression of a large stone being thrown into still water; a disturbance where it fell, and then in a few seconds all still and placid again.

We were then ordered to advance on the Martinière, a splendid building, erected by a General La Martin, as a college for orphans. It was said that the King of Oudh, in whose service the General was employed, coveted this building intensely. The old General knew this, and in order to frustrate the accomplishment of any evil designs after his death, ordered his body to be interred beneath the central dome. This was done, and thus the building was rendered sacred from the purposes the King might have had in his mind's eye.

I remember the excellence of the artillery practice as we advanced, and that in consequence the place fell easily into our hands.

Our regiment of Details, which by the bye numbered some 700 men, was ordered to occupy this building; but just as we had got comfortably settled, an order came for a further advance. The object in view was the capture of a strong position, known as Bank's Bungalow. The 93rd and ourselves got into column, and advanced under cover of a heavy fire from Peel's guns. The storming party lay down behind the guns, until a parting salvo had been fired; they then rushed on, but found that, in consequence of the canal having been dammed lower down, the water was so deep that it was impossible to cross, and as it was getting dark we retired.

A curious incident occurred during the rush to the front. A gun went off by accident, blowing away the gunner, and causing some men of the 90th, who were right and left of the gun, to spin round like teetotums, and eventually fall down.

We now bivouacked in a large clump of trees near the Martinière, and awaited further orders. We remained there that night, and were much harassed by the continuous fire from Bank's Bungalow. Luckily the shots were high and did us but little damage; the small branches of the mango-trees suffered most, and they came tumbling down upon us. Had we remained there long enough, we should have been buried in leaves like the Babes in the Wood.

Towards morning the firing ceased, and we ascertained that the house had been taken by the Sikhs, under Captain Keane, in a most masterly manner. Seventy of them crept out silently, passed the enemy's outposts unobserved, and rushed the place without firing a shot. It was said Sir Colin gave them £50 as a reward for their trouble.

All next day, Sunday, we lay in this wood more or less under fire. We were not uncomfortable, and being old campaigners had excellent food. Not so some of the other detachments, and I remember being amused at the way in which our society was sought when the savoury smell of our stew reached the nostrils of our hungry comrades.

On Monday the 16th we were up at daybreak, and after

a hasty breakfast had our dram served out. I always carried mine in a soda-water bottle covered with leather by a strap round my neck, and could therefore take a pull at it when I thought fit. We advanced in due time, making a wide detour to our right, so as to avoid the canal, which had been dammed higher up.

And now let me once for all say that I do not pretend to give even an outline of the general operations. I know nothing of what others were doing; I had enough to do to attend to our own business, so that none need be offended if I omit to record any gallant and plucky deeds done by them. Everything seemed more or less confused, and the positions we occupied were so confined and surrounded by houses or walls that it was impossible to get a general view of our surroundings. Sometimes we were in a veritable labyrinth, at others in a more open space. Occasionally we got a bit of information concerning others from some Staff officer or orderly passing by, and such I shall record if I have reason to believe that it was correct and of interest to the reader. Otherwise I confine myself to my letters and to my memory in cases where important events have been overlooked.

In due course we entered a sort of labyrinth of narrow lanes, lined on either side by low mud huts. We halted from time to time. As the firing in front grew more rapid, dhoolies began to pass carrying their occupants to the rear. When the face was visible, we knew it was only a case of wounds, but when the face was covered up we knew that the spirit had flown, and that only the empty carcase which held it was being carried to its burial. This halting and merely looking on was miserable work. Occasionally we were diverted by a Staff officer hurrying by, who shouted out some scrap of intelligence.

At last our turn came to move on, and we presently found ourselves in front of a huge square building, surrounded by a high wall well loop-holed, from which came a murderous fire; indeed so much so that we were ordered to place ourselves under cover, until some guns came up to breach the wall.

Soon they came up, and I can remember very distinctly the artillery officer in command hurrying to and fro with his arm in a sling. He had evidently been wounded, but was still to the fore, and now seemed to bear a charmed life.

We were at this time on the extreme left of our Brigade, with the 93rd on the right. At last a practicable breach was made in the south-east corner, and the 93rd and Sikhs rushed into it with a yell. Our regiment of Details wheeled round to the left, and got opposite the south main entrance, the door of which was guarded by a strong earthwork. Lieutenant Lawrence Græme of Ours was the first man over. The men swarmed after him, and tried to force the door, which was locked, so a rifle was put to the keyhole and fired, thereby bursting it open. One man got in, but was overpowered, and the door closed, shutting him in. Another private got it partly open again, and in so doing lost his fingers from a sword-cut; at last it was forced, and we got in, to find our comrade still alive but covered with bayonet wounds.

Just as Græme got into the gateway, an officer of the 93rd, leading his party, came running along the inside from the direction of the breach. Some of the enemy turned on him, and while he was engaged with one, another raised his tulwar. Græme tried to warn him by calling out, but in vain; he got a slash over the face, which seemed to slice the skin, causing a great piece to fall down over his face, blinding him with blood. I fancy this must have been the officer who got the V.C. for being in at the breach first.

All this time the 93rd and Sikhs were busily at work. The building was crammed full of regular sepoys, and the

93rd and Sikhs fired volley after volley into the dense mass, until nothing was left but a moving mass like mites in a cheese. In the centre of this building was a sort of substantial summer-house, in which the rebels had stored ammunition and gunpowder. Our fire caused this to explode, thereby hurling destruction on all sides, unhappily injuring some of our own men. It was said that several officers and men were wounded by bullets from above, and, on looking to see where the shot came from, found that a woman (probably one of the Queen of Oudh's Amazons) was quietly firing down on them from a tree; she was speedily dislodged. The scene of havoc was simply indescribable; there was no escape. The 53rd were on the north side, Sikhs and 93rd on the east, and we were on the south. There was, I believe, no exit on the west.

Whilst this carnage was proceeding, I was standing with some of my men at the south-west corner. We saw that some rebels had managed to scale the wall, and were flying across the open plain in the direction of the Kuddum Russool and Shah Nujjif. Our men opened fire on them, when suddenly a sergeant cried out, "Don't fire, they are women," and the men ceased firing. I mention this as it was a remarkable act of self-denial on the part of men infuriated at the recollection of Cawnpore. All this time a fire was concentrated on us from the numerous buildings surrounding us, occupied in force by the enemy. Later on a shell burst over us, and killed poor Major Barnston, who commanded us. As I have said, I was wearing a blue serge tunic with an outside pocket, into which I had placed my watch, which was suspended by a chain fastened outside. I felt the watch drop to the bottom of the pocket, and, on looking, found the chain cut in two. It was a narrow shave. When the work of destruction inside had been completed, and 2000 of the sepoys had been killed, the men of the 93rd and Sikhs were recalled, and we had an hour's rest; during which time, no doubt, Sir Colin was making arrangements for a further advance.

I had now time to look around me, and take note of our position. In front there was a plain, not unlike Woolwich Common, on the opposite side of which stood a solid-looking building in the shape of a mosque, with a row of low mud huts, thatched with grass, running along the side. To our left, some strongly-fortified houses, and to the right, a curious-looking mound, called the Kuddum Russool. The main road ran right across this plain, in front of the main entrance to the Secundrabagh, past the main entrance to the Shah Nujjif, till it eventually reached the Residency, the object of all our desires. During this interregnum much was being done by others. Captain Peel, R.N., had brought up his Naval Brigade with their heavy guns; an attack had been made on the Kuddum Russool by the Sikhs and others, and it was captured.

A curious story was current at the time in connection with this building. It seems that Sir Colin wanted reinforcements, so an order was given to send up another regiment to the Kuddum Russool. The orderly of the 9th Lancers, who was to convey the message, knew that Colonel Russell commanded a Brigade, but had never heard of the Kuddum Russool. Fortunately he repeated his orders thus—"All right, sir, a regiment to Colonel Russell," and so luckily the error was corrected. Upon how little the fate of a force may sometimes rest!

But to return to our doings. The Shah Nujjif promised a considerable amount of trouble. It seemed a solid, bulldog-looking place, that would require much hammering; for not only was the mosque itself built of massive masonry, but it was surrounded on all sides by cloisters opening inwards, the outer walls of which were ornamented by a sort of openwork design executed by the omission of bricks in a certain set form. Every one of

THE NAVAL BRIGADE 191

these openings formed a splendid loop-hole to those concealed inside.

The Naval Brigade was brought on to the plain with their heavy guns, and it is no exaggeration to say they advanced in skirmishing order without the slightest support. Such a sight had never been seen before, and probably will never be seen again. It was splendid, and gave one a good idea of what our sailors were made of.

Sir Colin arrived on the spot at this time, and was horrified to see the guns so exposed, so our detachment was ordered to lie by in reserve, in case any rush was made on the guns. We took up our position under cover of a small mud-built building, which abutted on the main road; it probably had been a police-station. In front of us lay the plain, with the Naval Brigade serving their guns in the coolest manner. Whilst lying here, young Lord Pelham Clinton was brought to us wounded; I very nearly finished him by putting my bottle of grog to his mouth, and thereby choking him; he had been struck by a jingal ball, and received a severe contusion. At this time, too, a round shot struck a tumbril, and it exploded, injuring several blue-jackets. Captain Peel took the thing very quietly.

The firing of the big guns had been admirable, but very ineffectual, for the walls already alluded to were sheltered by the row of mud huts, which also in turn served as a cover to the enemy's skirmishers, who occupied them. Every round shot fired simply went clean through the mud wall, doing little or no damage, but leaving an extra loop-hole for a musket to fire from.

This state of things could not be allowed to continue, therefore Sir Colin called for a party to go and burn down these huts. I was near at the time, and called for volunteers; nine of my men came out. Sir Colin himself told me what to do, and to get a piece of port-fire from Captain

Peel. This I did, and off we set. The distance we had to traverse was insignificant. As soon as ever I got into the first hut I put the port-fire to the roof and fired the grass, then on to the next; but, alas! no sooner was a blaze well established than my men seized lighted brands right and left, and set fire to every hut around. We were instantly in a circle of fire. The dry materials blazed like tinder; one of my men's pouches blew up, and what with fire and smoke it was impossible to go further, so I ordered a retreat.

Just as I got on the main road, who should I meet but Sir Colin himself with some of his Staff. He called me, and said, "You have not half burned the huts, sir." I answered that I could not burn more on account of the fire. Sir Colin turned on me like a wild tiger, shouting, "D—— your eyes, sir, I will not allow you or any other man to tell me the fire is too hot!" I was simply speechless; I felt as if I could cry. I looked at General Mansfield, who happily caught my meaning, for he said, "I think the officer means the fire of the burning huts." "Yes," I cried, "I was not afraid of the other fire, but one of my men's pouches blew up, and we were so surrounded by flames that I thought it better to retire." Sir Colin said, "All right, sir, it was my mistake," and so I returned terribly crestfallen. I lost three men out of the nine who accompanied me in this work.

A most curious thing happened in connection with this burning. I found three or four men of the 53rd Regiment lying dead in these huts. How on earth they came there is a mystery I have never been able to solve. The regiment was, as far as I could ascertain, far away on our right; the huts I burnt were on our left front, and consequently at a great distance from the place where the 53rd was. There was no mistaking the identity, for the number and facings were clear enough.

I made my way back to the place where our men were

sheltering. I had hoped to get some credit for the work I had done, but I got nothing but growls. Just then Sir Colin came, and, dismounting, sat down near us under shelter. He recognized me, and called to me and said: "You must not mind what I said just now; I quite mistook your meaning; sit down." Then, pointing to McBean, the Adjutant of the 93rd, who was sitting near, said: "Let me introduce you to my friend McBean, a good Highlander, and a grand soldier." Accordingly we nodded to each other. I shall never forget the broad Scotch accent in which he spoke those words. Thinking I was no longer wanted, I saluted and retired. I think Sir Colin grew impatient at the losses we had sustained in our attempts on this place. Allison had been severely wounded, beside many others; so an advance was ordered.

Up to this time we had acted simply as a gun-guard: we had now to join the remainder of the regiment of Details, and take part in the forward movement. I have the whole scene in my mind's eye as clearly as if it had occurred but yesterday. It was the only thing I ever saw that fulfilled my idea of a real battle.

The whole force was on the outskirts of this plain, when the 93rd, covered by our battalion as skirmishers, and protected by the incessant firing of the heavy guns, were ordered to form line. My company, under Captain Taylor and Lieutenant Dobbs, was in support. Then with a cheer the Highlanders, led by Sir Colin himself, advanced with a rush. It was a glorious sight, but alas! what a reception they got! The whole loop-holed wall I have mentioned became one sheet of flame: *the fire was hellish.* In a second every field officer was dismounted, either wounded or with his horse shot under him.

We had just reached those beastly huts; to have advanced further would have been madness, so we were ordered to lie down under such cover as we could find. Luckily these same huts came in useful now as a shelter.

o

In this advance poor Dobbs was mortally wounded: a bullet went clean through his thigh, shattering the bone and piercing the other leg. We carried him under cover, and left him in charge of a sergeant. Just then a sergeant of the 93rd crept up to us. I found he had a very curious wound: indeed, I may say four wounds. He was evidently in the very act of firing himself, when a bullet struck him in the left fore-arm, went through it, and then passed clean through the fleshy part of the upper arm near the muscle, thus making four holes. I bound him up as well as I could, and left him with Dobbs, with whom I shook hands and said, "Good-bye for ever!" He was quite calm, and gave me a loving message to his family.

Our position now was very critical. What was to be done? How could we carry away our dead and wounded, and so hide all trace of our losses? Peel's guns were ordered to come up to the front. Lieutenant Duncan with a party of our men helped to drag one. Lieutenant Daniel of the Naval Brigade was killed in this advance. The guns opened fire, but after half-a-dozen rounds Captain Peel pronounced that a breach could not be effected.

During an interval Lieutenant Salmon, R.N., with a coloured seaman called Snowball (*lucus a non lucendo*), managed to climb some palm-trees that grew amongst the huts, and discovered the enemy bolting through a gateway on the far side. The welcome news was given, and instantly the winter of our discontent became glorious summer. The 93rd rushed round to the main entrance, blew in the door, and became masters' of the place. The two gallant sailors eventually gained a well-merited V.C.

On entering the Shah Nujjif I saw what a strong place it was, and how ineffectual our chances of breaching were. A party of the 93rd were told off to hold the place; the remainder of the force retired to bivouac near the Secundrabagh. The loss in this one operation was 150 out of 800.

We were scarcely settled down when Sir Colin came up. He asked for Captain Taylor, and complimented him on the work done by the detachment, making special mention of the burning of the huts by the party under Jones-Parry, and as a compliment said he wished the company to form his guard that night.[1]

Personally, I feel that Sir Colin really made more of the service than it required, in order to make amends for having sworn at me when labouring under a misapprehension of my meaning. He could swear when he liked!

We had now time to think of food, and a most excellent dinner we had, consisting of a splendid beefsteak, which Solomon, my servant, had cut off a gun-bullock that had been knocked over by a round shot, and which he had carried all day in his pocket-handkerchief. Solomon, so named by me on account of his wisdom, was a splendid servant, and had ever an eye to our comfort. I shall have a good deal more to say about him hereafter.

Of course the events of the day were discussed, our losses first of all; and no one was more regretted than poor

[1] As this incident is of a personal nature, I have considered it necessary to verify it, and therefore append extracts from letters unsolicited which bear on the subject.

General Taylor writing to me on the 28th May, 1878, says:
"I have not forgotten your plucky performance in burning down those lines in front of the Shah Nujjif where the rebels found shelter. Men have got the Victoria Cross for less eminent services than that many a time."

Lieutenant-Colonel Reginald Coleridge Parry, who was also present at the time, writes:
"I remember Lord Clyde coming up and asking for the Company. Taylor came forward. Lord Clyde complimented him on the work done by Jones-Parry, and as a mark of recognition told Taylor to furnish his guard that night."

Dobbs, such a quiet good fellow. I think every one felt that he was of all of us the one best prepared to go. Then Major Barnston, our commanding officer: the little we had seen of him had won our esteem. I felt a special interest in him, for his family and mine were known to each other. We learnt Colonel Russell had been severely wounded. He was a tall man with a very long neck, round which he wore a black silk handkerchief with his coat-collar down. A round shot caught him on the back of his neck, and took off the flesh without cutting the handkerchief. He was paralyzed for a time, but eventually recovered.

Two thousand sepoys had been killed in the Secundrabagh. Their bodies were hauled out in batches by elephants and thrown into a ditch, and then covered with earth by the Sappers. It was said that an artillery officer recognized one of his native officers amongst the rebels, and reproached him with being a traitor to his salt. The fellow spat in the officer's face, and was immediately run through the body.

One thing struck us very forcibly, and that was the cessation of tom-tom beating, bugling, etc., around—very different from the night before. No doubt the enemy had something better to think of than noisy demonstration. The stillness was almost painful after the incessant roar of cannon during the day. Taylor and I slept under the same blanket; mine was laid on the ground, and his covered us. We had a most excellent night. So ended the memorable 16th November, mentioned by Sir Colin in his dispatch as follows:

"From the morning of the 16th, until last night, the whole force has been one outlying picquet, *never out of fire*, covering an immense extent of ground. The storming of the Secundrabagh and Shah Nujjif has never been surpassed in daring, and the success of it was most brilliant and complete."

Our work, however, was only half done, and much more ground had to be won before we reached our destination.

Next morning (17th Nov.) we were up at daybreak, and stood under arms until ordered to advance. In our new position we were too much exposed to round shot, so we were removed under cover. From the absence of firing on our part it seemed to us that the remainder of the force was also unemployed. No doubt a good deal of reconnoitring was going on.

At 2 p.m. a message came from Sir Colin that he wanted volunteers for a particular service. Taylor called his company out, and with it Reginald Parry, Woods, and myself. We were drawn up in the main road before alluded to, when Sir Colin rode up. He said he was pleased to find we were for this duty; he told us that before leaving England he had dined with her Majesty, who had spoken to him particularly of the gallant deeds of the Madras Fusiliers. He then said that the work we had to do was to carry ladders and planks to bridge over the moat round the 32nd mess-house, a building of considerable strength, and held stoutly by sepoys. The work only required steadiness, for our advance would be masked by a hail of shot and shell. He added: " If you do the work well, I will give the V.C. to the officers, and recommend the men for a handsome gratuity."

As soon as the ladders and planks had been brought up by the Engineers, the 90th and Sikhs advanced skirmishing. We shouldered the ladders and planks, and off we went. There was a roar like thunder around us: we were indeed under cover of a heavy fire; and had not gone many yards when all of a sudden there was a cry of " They're bolting ! " The skirmishers made a rush, down went our ladders, and off we too went tearing until we reached our goal; and found the place in the hands of our friends.

It was a nasty place to look at, and I for one felt glad it had fallen so easily. It seems that the enemy, after the lesson of the Secundrabagh, had thought it dangerous to leave themselves no means of retreat, and had left a drawbridge down. The skirmishers, seeing this, made for it with a rush, whilst the enemy cleared out by another exit.

This important post was given over to the 84th, and was, I think, twice attacked afterwards. An officer of the 84th gave me an amusing account of the last attempt to regain possession. The enemy had collected in large numbers under cover of some buildings; so near that their conversation could be heard. A dispute was going on as to who should lead the assault. At last it seems that a leader was chosen, and then came the cry from the others, "Chullo Bahadoor! Chullo Bahadoor!" "Go on, sir; lead on, sir!" At last Bahadoor did lead; he was a very fat Subadar. He had scarcely advanced a few yards when one of the 84th hit him right in the stomach, and he went pop like a ripe gooseberry; then all the rest bolted under cover like rabbits.

After the loss of the 32nd mess-house, the game of the Pandies was all up. We took position after position till about 4.30 p.m., when a deafening cheer rent the air, which announced that Sir Colin and Sir James Outram had met and shaken hands. This cheer was taken up in succession all along the line, and, as it went further and further off, it sounded like a faint echo of the first grand cheer. Thus, after three days' continuous fighting, our object had been accomplished.

That night we occupied the Moti Mahal (the House of Pearls), in which the Zenana had stood. I am sorry to say that the bedding there contained an abundance of those vile things which troubled the Egyptians of old. I remember next morning Adrian Hope, our Brigadier, coming up to us in very nude condition, whilst at our morning toilet, and saying: "I'd advise you fellows to look to your flannel shirts, mine was full of lice." So it proved with ours, but an hour or so in the sun made them fairly wearable. Strange to say, that genus does not get into the heads of the people, but beards had to be shaved off afterwards. The smell of dead bodies around us was awful.

We were hard worked there—all kinds of fatigues. We were comparatively out of danger. Two men were killed the first day. Shot and shell came whizzing round, and occasionally logs of wood chained together were fired from a mortar. These were called "whistling dicks"; they amused us, and did no harm. I find by my diary that we were much occupied in sending in necessaries and comforts to the women and children in the Residency.

Curiously enough, the first man of the garrison I met was my old school-fellow and chum, Mecham. He was an excellent specimen of the condition of the defenders, for he looked more like a greyhound than a man; he was as thin as a lath, and his eyes looked sunken into his head. No wonder, for in the first few months he had gone through untold dangers and miraculous escapes. He had only escaped being murdered by his own regiment by a narrow squeak; then he had weathered that awful battle of Chinhut, and finally, had been blown clean out of his own lines into neutral ground by the explosion of the only mine that the enemy had succeeded in firing. All the others had been countermined and destroyed by the indefatigable exertions of Fulton, McLeod Innes, and others. Poor Mecham, his troubles were not yet over. We were glad to meet, and subsequently he got posted to do duty with us until his services were required elsewhere.

It seems during these days a council of war had been held, and an evacuation of the Residency decided on. This was kept a profound secret.

I now come to the 19th. During the day numbers of women and children of the garrison were streaming out under escort through our quarters. I was much struck with the amount of finery the soldiers' wives of the 32nd Regiment had heaped on their bodies, and the trash they were carrying in their hands, and this under a somewhat heavy fire, for I saw more than one woman wounded in the retreat. The enemy still held the Kaiser Bagh (King's Palace), and many important commanding positions, from which they continued to fire on us. When I speak of retreat, I only allude at this time to the women and children, who were being sent to the Alumbagh for safety.

A very sad and pathetic incident now occurred. I was sitting on guard near a gateway, when I saw Spurgin of Ours, who had been Brigade-Major to Neill, escorting poor Mrs. Banks and her children. She was clad in such mourning as circumstances would permit, for she had lost a good and brave husband early in the siege. She looked the picture of sadness, holding her infant in her arms. Her little boy was clinging to her dress, and was unable to keep up, so Spurgin took him up in his arms and carried him. If ever a painter wanted a subject worthy of genius, here it was to hand. That one little scene can never be forgotten; it brought the horrors of war, alas! so clearly before my eyes.

This passing out continued, and on the 22nd I was on gun-guard with the Naval Brigade in the advanced battery. I do not remember ever having such a jolly time. I was nearly killed several times during the day, but only from laughter. I knew most of them from having been on gun-guard during the day of the storming of the Shah Nujjif, and they were most friendly. A sailor is a splendid fellow—twice as good as a soldier. Their jokes and their extraordinary childishness in many things were killing. Whenever they got a bit of loot, such as a hurdy-gurdy or banjo, they always offered it to their officers first. They had a French piano, which was kept going all day by any one not actually on duty.

I remember a brass shell striking the muzzle of one of our huge guns; it burst with moderate force, and a piece struck one of the blue-jackets in the side. The explosion looked nasty, and I thought the poor fellow was cut in half. They carried him under shelter of the rampart, and a doctor attended to him. It was only a contusion, but there he remained lying until a quartermaster came by and looked narrowly at him. He then gave him a kick, and said: "Bill, you b——, you ain't dead yet; get up and do your work." The man got up with a grin, and went off highly pleased with himself at having got a slant off duty.

Our orders were to breach the wall of the Kaiser Bagh, in order, as we supposed, to make it practicable for an assault next day. We had, I think, six guns in position. I never saw such firing. The guns went off all together in a salvo, and then down came a portion of the wall just like a slice of cheese. I do not know how far the Kaiser Bagh was from our guns; I should say, from recollection, about 500 yards. The building was of florid architecture, and over a principal gate stood a huge effigy of the god Mars, or some other allegorical figure. This was too tempting a mark for Jack, so a gun was trained on it. Lieutenant Young, the gunnery instructor, laid it, and the shot took off the right arm of the figure. The second shot took off the left leg; the third shot hit the iron bar on which the figure had been set, and bent it so that the figure was in miserable-looking plight. This larking, however, seemed to have been too much for Captain Peel, who had been quietly watching the proceedings unknown to us. Down he came in wrath, telling them to stop that nonsense, and go on with the breaching. I have never seen such splendid artillery practice, and feel it almost impossible to make any one believe that such accuracy could be obtained from such large smooth-bore guns.

As the day wore on, an ominous and weird uneasiness seemed abroad. Nothing was said, but somehow, I cannot explain why, I felt that something important was going on, and that it was for some reason kept secret from us.

I saw, too, quite easily, that the same idea had caught hold of the men. Towards evening the rocket-tubes were withdrawn. This was a terrible blow to us, for we simply adored the rockets, and could perfectly realize what the enemy felt when one came whizzing amongst them and then burst.

The big guns still went on breaching; then a Staff officer came and spoke to the senior naval officer, and the guns were limbered up one by one and taken off. My men wanted to accompany them, urging that we were their gun-guard; but my orders were to hold fast, and not allow any firing unless absolutely necessary. As it grew darker my men occasionally fired, evidently to keep up their spirits. Staff officers came time after time to tell me not to fire—that it only brought down a counter-fire from the enemy. Of course, every time a man fired, he swore that there was a sepoy right on him.

All this time there was a dull rumbling noise, as the tramp of men marching in our rear. The men got panic-stricken, and declared they had been forgotten—they were sure all the others had gone away, and begged me to march off.

Reader, I have gone through some unpleasant half-hours in my time, but this beat all. These men had never hesitated to go forward against any odds, but a retreat was a different thing. It was a terrible strain, but I told them what were my orders, and that I would obey them. Just then, luckily, the same Staff officer came up, and told me, in the hearing of the men, that our turn would come next, and I was then to form up without any noise and follow him.

And so a few minutes later we moved silently from our post, and were, I think, the last body to leave the position that Outram and Havelock and Inglis had held so long. We marched silently in fours through deserted buildings until we reached the main road. There we found a column halted, which we joined. Gracious! how glad I was! We soon moved on, until we got into the sandy bed of the canal, or river, and there we lost our bearings, and wandered about half the night. At last we were ordered to halt and pile arms. Some one rode off to reconnoitre, and just then we heard a bugle sound, which gave us the direction of our comrades; we made for the sound, and were soon in the very wood we had occupied during our first advance. At daybreak we got clear of the suburbs, and eventually reached the plain of the Alumbagh.

Only one man was missing out of the whole force; he seems to have slept through everything, and on waking in the morning found himself alone. He succeeded in rejoining unmolested.

It seems that the enemy were too busy mending up their breaches during the night to take much notice of us, and, in the morning, finding no firing from the Residency, suspected treachery, and only realized the truth about mid-day, when we were all safe and sound at the Dilkoosha, and Sir Colin, the ladies, children, sick and wounded, well on their way to Cawnpore.

So ended the relief of Lucknow—a feat that, to use the words of Sir Colin, was achieved " by fighting as hard as ever fell to the lot of the Commander-in-Chief to witness, it being necessary to bring up the same men over and over again to fresh attacks; and it is with the greatest satisfaction that his Excellency declares he never saw men behave better. The movement of retreat last night, by which the final rescue of the garrison was effected, was a model of discipline and exactness. The consequence was that the enemy were completely deceived, and the force retired by a narrow tortuous lane, the only line of retreat open, in the face of 50,000 enemies, without molestation."

CHAPTER XII

ALUMBAGH

IT was not with unalloyed pleasure that we found ourselves encamped on the plains of Alumbagh. Many were the growls and regrets at relinquishing the Residency; these came chiefly from the members of Outram's and Havelock's force, hardened warriors who would have fought on till they had less left to them than the traditional Kilkenny cats. They argued that a great blow had been struck to our prestige; that the women, children, sick and wounded could have been passed to the rear as already described, and have been sent on to Cawnpore with the Commander-in-Chief in the same manner; whilst the Division left now to hold the Alumbagh would have been a sufficient force to hold the Residency against all odds, and so obviate the necessity for the recapture of the city. This is a question for experts to determine; at the time sanitary reasons were given as the cause of relinquishing our hold of the position. However, here we were, and there was nothing to be done but to make ourselves as safe as possible.

I have never thought sufficient attention or credit was given to the holding of this last remnant of our footing in Oudh. No doubt the interest of the public was drawn off from us to the movements of the Commander-in-Chief, and so a very important, and, indeed, from a military point of view, noteworthy, performance was lost in oblivion. Very many years after, a paper was read at the Royal United Service Institute, entitled 'A Tactical Study,' by

Captain Sir James Seton, Bart., of the 102nd Royal Madras Fusiliers, in which attention was directed to the extraordinary achievements of this Division of observation under Sir James Outram, G.C.B.

I have it now before me, and so valuable do I think it to military students that I would gladly print it as an appendix, were it not marked "for private circulation only," and as the writer, alas! is dead I cannot get permission. I have, however, no scruple in using it, as it confirms in a singular manner the accuracy of many of the entries in my diary.

Not only had Sir James Seton access to the letters and despatches of Sir James Outram, but his statements are confirmed by evidence of Generals Sir John Spurgin and Sir D. Dodgson, who are, I am glad to say, still living.

Well, our position lay from east to west in a direct line across the main road to Cawnpore, facing Lucknow; our right resting on the somewhat dilapidated mud fort of Jelalabad; and our left on a village the name of which I forget. The Alumbagh now became our front centre outpost, and was just about one mile from our head-quarter camp, and exactly the same distance from a strong position held by the enemy, called the Yellow House, which Havelock's force have good reason to remember.

The right Brigade, to which I belonged, consisted of H.M. 5th, 84th, and Ourselves. On our right again there lay a mud village, which was occupied by the Sikhs, under Colonel Brazier. The left Brigade comprised H.M. 75th, 78th Highlanders, and 90th L.I. In the centre were the artillery and head-quarter Staff.

In addition to these infantry regiments we had four squadrons, chiefly composed of mounted men of a military training fresh from England, who had been hurriedly put through some sort of drill. Add to this three field batteries, only one of which was horsed, the other batteries, together with a garrison battery, being drawn by bullocks;

we also had a company of Madras Sappers. So thinned had the regiments become from constant fighting, that the whole force numbered scarcely 4500, and with this we had not only to hold our own, but also an important position called Bunnee Bridge, twelve miles in our rear, leaving only 4000 all told to defend ourselves against the incessant attacks of the enemy, who numbered at one time no less than 80,000 organized infantry, 7000 cavalry, 13,000 irregulars, and 100 guns of various calibres, making a total of 100,000 men, no small odds to meet on an open plain.

Luckily we had certain impassable swamps, which protected our flanks in a measure; we had well seasoned men with stout hearts; and, above all, a General in whom we had confidence, and who never let any one feel that there was the slightest cause for anxiety.

I can see Outram now, riding along the lines when an attack was going on, smoking as usual a huge cheroot, stopping now and again to speak a cheery word to some officer or sergeant, or offer a cheroot to some private who looked as if a smoke would be a treat to him. Others may say what they like: Outram was my man, and knitting-needles will not make me alter my opinion.

Of course the first thing to be done was to make ourselves as safe as we could. After the positions of picquets had been selected by the General and his able Chief of the Staff, Colonel Napier (afterwards Lord Napier of Magdala), we were told to use the pick and shovel as much as the rifle and bayonet; so with earthworks, trenches, abattis, etc., we entrenched ourselves much after the fashion of Zulus, and soon got to understand our duties.

One thing I specially remember, and that was that no one was to relinquish his picquet or outpost under any consideration whatever; if seriously attacked, reinforcements, Sir James said, would arrive, and we knew that what he said would be done.

We had, I think, about a dozen picquets or posts to hold and to man; these required about 800 men by day, and over 1000 at night. The pressure put on the men of a force consisting of only 4000 may be imagined, but the actual state of affairs was in reality much more serious, for we were eternally harassed by attacks which necessitated the calling out of reserve men to strengthen picquets, whilst the remainder of the whole force stood to arms. When a portion of the force was employed on convoy duty to the outpost already mentioned, twelve miles in the rear, we had only 1500 reserve men available to withstand the combined attacks of the enemy, made, as they usually were, simultaneously at several points. I mention these facts particularly, for I feel sure we none of us knew them at the time; and although the Commander-in-Chief was fully informed of our difficulties, as is shown by Sir James Outram's despatches, he seems to have taken little notice of them, and certainly gave as little credit as was possible to our commanding officer, for having successfully held the position with so inadequate a force.

Sir James, in the despatch alluded to, represented to the Commander-in-Chief, "that without metaphor or exaggeration he was obliged to do that with companies for which in former times a whole battalion was deemed insufficient." This expression was called forth by the news that a most desperate attack was to be made at a time when many of our force would be away on convoy duty. It must also be mentioned that we were absolutely devoid of means of transport; we were consequently immobile, and, had any disaster occurred, we had nothing to do but relinquish our camp, and retire on Cawnpore fighting inch by inch.

Convoy duty seems to have been the main bone of contention between Sir Colin and Sir James, and surely it was not unreasonable to point out that convoy duty was scarcely to be expected from a force consisting of but

1500 men off duty, often worked night and day. As a matter of fact, guards, outposts, and picquets could only be relieved every seven days, and often the men only went off outlying to go on inlying picquet.

My own impression is that Sir Colin was at this time amply strong for any work he undertook in our rear, and could well have spared us one regiment to make the convoy and other duties less severe.

But no murmur or shadow of anxiety was ever permitted to pass outside the sacred bounds of the head-quarter Staff. Sir James was not only always cheery himself, but did all he could to relieve the monotony of camp life by organizing sports and amusements for the men.

I must now go back to incidents more immediately connected with myself, and carry on my narrative by means of my letters and diaries. Our first thoughts on getting into something like shape was for our own comrades. Poor Colonel Stephenson of Ours had succumbed to a slight wound he had received at the commencement of the siege; he really died from want of nourishment, and passed away the day after we reached the Residency. Grant and young Bailey, both twice wounded during this campaign, were in a most critical state. Grant had done wonders in keeping down the enemy's fire from the Clock Tower. Barclay and Fraser were doing well, and Colonel Galway was just off the sick list. General Havelock died immediately after the relief had taken place, and was buried under a large mango-tree in the garden of the Alumbagh. I have a photo of his grave, done immediately after his burial.

I see by my letters that we had expected to be recalled after the relief; we had lost seventy-five killed and one hundred and fifty wounded in the last two months. I think our regiment and those glorious 78th Highlanders suffered most. The garrison we had relieved looked pale and careworn—indeed, utterly done up.

It took some time to learn the position of our picquets and posts, and the various duties in connection with them. This was no easy matter, for the positions were so strategically chosen, that every picquet flanked and was flanked by some other picquet, and it was necessary to fully understand from what quarter aid might be expected and where aid was to be given in case of an attack. I have often wondered since what owls the enemy were to leave us unmolested at this critical juncture; they were no doubt occupied in looting what remained in the Residency, or in quarrelling amongst themselves, and were totally ignorant of the smallness of the force left by Sir Colin. Perhaps they did not even know that he had himself gone.

We at this time heard of Sir Colin's victory over the Gwalior rebels at Cawnpore, and of the fact of his only just having been in time to save the bridge of boats across the Ganges. I also learnt that my baggage, that had been sent up after me and left behind at Cawnpore, had been looted or burnt. We also learnt that the rebels in Lucknow were quarrelling amongst themselves, and were in want of all kinds of ammunition. This latter information proved quite untrue.

Up to this time, although Instructor of Musketry, I had taken my regular tour of picquet and other duty, and as the captains were scarce had always had a Captain's command. So great was our paucity of officers owing to deaths, that mere lads just from school on joining had to be put on duty before they had learnt their drill, and often these splendid specimens of English public school boys commanded parties, which in ordinary circumstances would only have been entrusted to officers of great experience.

Sir James Seton mentions that many important portions of his pamphlet were supplied to him by a mere youth. and I remember hearing that one fledgling, on being told he was too young to go on the most dangerous of all our outposts, cried and said he was quite old enough to be killed the same as any other officer. His argument carried the day, and I have no doubt he was the boy who so fully entered into his work as to be able to give such valuable information to Sir James.

But to return to my subject. As I have said, up to this time I took my regular tour of duty. I was now called on to assume my duties as Musketry Instructor. It may seem strange that in such times, and with such a paucity of officers, any one could be spared off general roster. It happened in this way.

My regiment had been sent to Persia to take part in that campaign, but, arriving only just as peace had been concluded, were ordered back to Madras, where in about a week they were ordered to re-embark for Calcutta to assist in quelling the Sepoy revolt. Instead of their taking their old muskets, the new Enfield was sent on board ready packed, and thus on landing at Calcutta they found themselves armed with a new weapon, with the nature and merits of which they were wholly unacquainted. No instruction could be given on board ship, for the arms, though on board, were not yet served out, and as, immediately on landing, the regiment hurried up in detachments to Benares, any kind of drill was impossible. Notwithstanding all this, that the new weapon fell into good hands is amply proved by the following anecdote.

My regiment, following the precedent of the Burmah campaign, had their forage-caps covered with blue muslin as a protection against the sun, and were known as the Blue-caps. We were at this juncture the only regiment fully armed with the Enfield. Companies of other regiments were armed with the new rifle, but so far as I know we were the only regiment completely armed. It so happened that after one of our splendid victories over the Nana Sahib, under the glorious Havelock, a despatch was picked up, in which the arch-traitor warned the

Begum in Lucknow to "beware of a regiment wearing blue caps, for they fought like devils, and had muskets which killed before the report was heard."

But all this, good as it was, proved in a very small measure what the weapon really was capable of under proper instruction. Men in the hurry of action and from want of habit constantly forgot to reverse the cartridge, causing considerable mischief. The cartridges served out at this period were most defective. They had in those early days an iron instead of a wooden plug, and this constantly went clean through the bullet, leaving a leaden ring behind it. I always wore a pouch-belt, and carried such implements as were necessary for extracting these rings; frequently a man brought his rifle to me saying it would not go off, and I extracted as many as four rings left behind from four consecutive bullets. Then again, from the action of the iron plug or some other cause, the bullet bulged out and split the barrels constantly about six inches from the muzzle. Many of the rifles so injured had the barrels shortened, and did good work afterwards; but whilst we were in the Residency so great was the dislike of our men to the rifle, that they begged to have the old musket served out again, which was granted. Personally, I found the sights to be the greatest stumbling-block. The men took the higher numbers on the back sight to indicate velocity or penetration, and I frequently whilst on picquet during an attack heard one man saying to another, "I say, Bill, give the d——s the 900," thereby of course giving an elevation that would make the fire very ineffectual. At last an event occurred which needed immediate attention. A picquet of ours fired (I think) 27,000 rounds in one night. I went to see the spot next morning which the enemy were supposed to have occupied. It was in a clump of trees. I could find no trace of any loss having been inflicted. I found one pair of slippers, and the ground literally strewn with small branches. I then got permission to interview Sir James Outram, explained the whole situation to him, and said that, if he would only sanction a small amount of ammunition being spent in instruction, I would guarantee that there would be a saving in the end.

Sir James not only sanctioned my having the ammunition, but at once offered a prize of fifty rupees to be competed for monthly by all the regiments in camp. My Colonel gave me small squads every day to instruct. I set up targets, taking care that every shot went in the direction of the enemy, and had the satisfaction of seeing my men win Sir James's prize twice during our stay at the Alumbagh. This is how I became relieved from picquet duties, and had to superintend musketry drill.

It was after this interview that Sir James asked me to dine with him. He was regularly in the habit of asking two or three officers of his Divisions to share whatever little luxuries he might happen to have. I do not think he had ever more to offer than ordinary rations, with the addition of good coffee and tobacco.

On the occasion referred to, whilst we were smoking after dinner, there was a slight commotion outside the tent. Presently Colonel Napier went out, and returned with what seemed to me the end of a quill in his hand. This he gave to Sir James, who laughingly said: "Oh, here's the *Court Journal;* now we shall know what these rascals intend doing!" He pulled out a scroll of paper, and read out to us that an attack was to be made in force on a certain day—that the feint would be on the left, but the real attack on our right. And so it happened. At the same dinner Sir James said that, if Sir Colin had remained twenty-four hours longer in Lucknow, the Begum would have given in—she had been advised to do so.

At this time I got a most complimentary letter from my old Chief, Sir Robert Vivian, to which I shall refer later on; in it he commented on the deeds of our regiment, of which he was then Colonel-in-chief.

It must not be supposed that we were ever free from annoyance at the hands of the enemy: they kept up a fire more or less day and night. We were absolutely indifferent to it. One gun, christened by the soldiers Nancy Dawson, sometimes threw a shot amongst us which did damage.

On Christmas Eve we had blankets served out to the men, and, as some were on guard and could not take them, there were three spare ones, of which Raikes, Taylor, and I got one each. This on the top of a good dinner induced me to take my trousers off when I went to bed. Now the firing of heavy guns by the enemy or ourselves never troubled us; but the firing of rifles meant mischief, for Sir James had issued stringent orders that no sentries were ever to fire unless in face of absolute danger. No sooner was I in bed and asleep than crash went a volley of rifles. Then came, "Guard, turn out!" and bugles sounded the alarm. In forty seconds the whole brigade was under arms, and then such a clashing of cavalry and dashing of guns! Oh, it's worth being a soldier sometimes to see the way our cavalry and artillery can come into action! To see Olpherts handle his guns was perfect bliss.

Well, after a bit of firing things quieted. Next morning we found that the enemy heard our working-parties making rifle-pits, and sent out feelers; this alarmed the covering parties and caused the turn-out. The most amusing part was, we heard the enemy fancied that we were going to attack them, and immediately limbered up and bolted. So afraid were they of losing a gun, that they always kept their horses and bullocks ready harnessed close at hand, to take them away if threatened.

On December 29 they were very quiet, and of course we were suspicious. It turned out that they were moving guns, in consequence of one of their chiefs having been cut in half by one of our shells. They, however, came back again to the tune of 6000, with eight guns; we let them be, as they did no harm. The villagers by this time had gained confidence, and were bringing in fruit and vegetables.

I do not intend to carry my readers (if I have any) through all our endless attacks; it would take acres of paper. I shall merely content myself with referring to those which were of unusual importance. As I have said, the firing continued day and night. It is on record that an artillery officer, during a ten days' tour of duty at the Alumbagh, noted 2107 cannon-shots fired, 360 of which either struck the building itself, or fell into the enclosure; and a field officer also kept a record of a seven days' tour, which showed a daily average of 126 shots, thirty-three of which entered the enclosure. The "whistling-dicks," as the men called them, were a source of amusement rather than danger, and were not counted. But to return to attacks: the grand attack promised on January 1, 1858, turned out a fiasco—nothing more than solos on tom-toms, and many hundred shots into the Alumbagh.

I see that about this time I was asked to write for the Madras *Athenæum*. I do not remember doing so. Nothing seems to have been recorded but gossip until January 12, 1858. On that day the enemy came out, bringing with them two light field-guns. A shell from one of our batteries killed the officer in command and sixteen men: they retired. The enemy then attacked our left. The only casualty on our side was poor Gordon of the Bengal Artillery, whose head was carried off by a round shot at the Alumbagh. An artilleryman saw it coming and warned him, but I suppose Gordon thought it would drop short.

We now come to the attack of which Sir James had received intimation. We breakfasted at daybreak, and then quietly awaited events to shape themselves. The enemy evidently had good information as to our movements, for they generally selected days for an attack when our force was weakened by escorts for convoy duty. On such occasions we used generally to send over 500 men; consequently, our absolute fighting force, irrespective of picquets, was only 1500 men; with this we resisted an attack, along the whole of our front, by 30,000 men.

Of course, as Sir James had been informed, the attack commenced on the left. It was brilliantly overcome by the left Brigade. At the same time a very strong force advanced to the half-way picquet between the right Brigade and Jelalabad. Our two weak regiments went to the relief with two guns, and obliged them to retire; they caught it splendidly from the Alumbagh in so doing.

To give an idea of the work we had to do, the area we had to defend, and the swarms the enemy had at their disposal wherewith to threaten us, I must mention, that no sooner was this action over, than a new attack was made on the left, chiefly by cavalry, and was only discontinued at 4 p.m. Then news arrived that our bridge post, twelve miles in rear, was threatened, and one hundred poor worn-out fellows had to march out to reinforce the troops there. So serious was the attack this day, and so completely did it show the power of the enemy to annoy us, and the force at their disposal to bring against us, that Sir James asked for one or even half a battalion more to reinforce us, and save our being left so weak when convoy duty was imposed on us. At this time, I believe, the Commander-in-Chief had 20,000 British and 18,000 Nepaulese troops.

My entries at this period are not over cheerful. These constant alarms seem to have worried me, and I was longing for one big fight, and so get the thing over. I also note that I was going to send in a pattern of a new pouch to Government. I really quite forget all about it; even the entry recalls nothing to my mind.

Colonel Russell, to my great joy, was about to return in command of our Brigade. I had an intense admiration for him as a really excellent man and good soldier.

The enemy on the 13th were most obliging, and left us alone. We heard their loss on the last occasion was 400. They were desponding, for though they attacked us at four points, they found us ready at all, and guns opened on them before they could form line. Colonel Berkeley told me that, so admirably were our picquets posted, they completely flanked each other, and these fellows could not come near without being under a cross fire.

We heard at this time that the Vakeel of the Nawab of Futtyghur had been taken prisoner by the Commander-in-Chief, and after suffering considerable indignities was hung. It was said he blew ladies from guns at Cawnpore. By a letter dated January 25, I find that we were still continually harassed, and that a grand attack had been made on us with unusual boldness and persistency. General Outram, as usual, had full information concerning the disposition of the enemy's troops. They came on, led by a fanatic, whose naked body and face were painted to represent the monkey-god Hanuman;[1] he had also a tail.

The principal movement was against what we called our half-way picquet, between our right and Jelalabad. They came on in grand style, deploying, etc. We were so used to these attacks, that no notice was taken of them until they got to about 400 yards from us; then they got a volley which completely staggered them. The monkey-god got a wound that cut him across both eyes, and down he went; the remainder bolted, leaving their leader and others on the ground. The poor fanatic, taken prisoner

---

[1] The name of the monkey-god gave rise to a curious typographical error in the *Times*. Dr. Russell had written, "led by a fanatic bedecked as Humayon." The *Times* printed it "Bedekodos Humayon." We could not understand who the gentleman with the Greek-sounding name could be—it caused much amusement.

by the Sikhs, was carefully tended, and I heard afterwards that they made quite a pet of him; but I notice Sir James Seton in his pamphlet says the monkey-god was mortally wounded. I think my version is the right one.

The attack on the left, which continued longer, was also brilliantly repulsed, whilst a cavalry threat on our left rear was checked by horse artillery and cavalry. These successes were all very well, and our losses were trifling, but then they could afford to lose any number, as they were being reinforced day by day. At this time it was said they numbered 100,000 fighting men in the city. Their losses in the recent engagement was said to be heavy. A break appears here in my letters; they must have been lost or have fallen into the enemy's hands. I must therefore continue my narrative from my diary or from memory.

Camp, Alumbagh, January 25, 1858.

Since my last entry we have had much trouble and anxiety. These horrid Pandies threatened to attack us on all sides, and as our rear is but ill defended, we should only have repulsed them at a great loss to ourselves. However, the last attack they made on our position cost them so dear, that they have contented themselves with threats. That attack must have cost them 1000, for it continued all day, and we let them come up close to our guns, and then we poured in grape and canister. Our loss was six or seven wounded. The enemy fired 730 round shot at us during the day, and they fired 2110 during the week; they never do any harm, and they are now all bolting.

They began by fighting among themselves as to who should have the honour of attacking us; neither would own that they did not like the post of danger. Then they fought about pay, and finally the Begum has quarrelled with her brother, who is disgusted with her proceedings. She is not living a very virtuous life. When her brother reproached her with it, she told him not to interfere; that she had a right to follow her own inclinations in all things. The consequence is that there is a split in the camp, and all are bolting; they say that three zemindars and 9000 men left last week.

Yesterday there was a report of their moving their guns and magazines, which I believe to be perfectly true. The benefit to us is that we get no more attacks, and are permitted to sleep, eat, etc. in peace. It is a great comfort to feel so secure; not that one ever had any fear for the whole, but yet any one might suffer, and the suspense and anxiety were very trying. We still have our heavy firing, but then we are so used to that, that it means nothing. John Pandy practises at us, and we at him. The escape of these 9000 rascals may perhaps cause no end of trouble, but I don't think it will, for I know that the townspeople hate and fear them, and when once they are out of Lucknow they will make terms for their city. Lucknow being ours, the country will soon settle down, the zemindars will only be permitted to hold their lands on condition of giving up all Pandies.

I fancy Sir Colin has too much sense to work his Europeans during the hot weather, but will content himself with resting on his oars until the next cold season, and then if there are any budmashes about, setting out a fresh campaign against them. Our day will, I think, be over with the fall of Lucknow, for all seem to be of opinion that we have done our work, and ought to go back to quarters; and then there will be such a meeting of wives and husbands!

I have been very busy at target practice; it is uphill work unteaching men. The recruits that joined at Madras were, owing to the emergency of the service, sent into the ranks before they were drilled, and the consequence is that what they have learnt they have learnt badly, and it is difficult to set them right again.

Colonel Russell now commands our Brigade, and Lightfoot has fallen into command of his regiment, the 84th. This morning we had rifle practice for a prize of fifty rupees, given monthly by Sir James Outram. One of our men got the prize last time, but he failed this time: he shot very well, but he lost one shot through carelessness.

A report came in yesterday that the Nana Sahib had been taken, and that he was going to be hung immediately. I hope it is true. They seem to be hanging their share of Pandies at Delhi. No one knows the Chief's movements, but it is certain that the country is settling down wonderfully. Henley is made an extra A.D.C. to General Windham. The General is sadly cut up at his failure at Cawnpore. It was a mistake, but more has been made of it than there was any occasion for.

Report says that the H.E.I.C. is defunct, and that we are now under the Crown. I hope it will not interfere with our pay; if it does not I do not much mind. There is a "shave" in camp that we are to go to England for three years to recruit; if they give us Indian allowances I shall be very glad.

News of the Commander-in-Chief comes in very slowly. The Pandies are quiet, and the Calcutta people say that negotiations are going on with the Oude people. The Moolvie, or head priest, is in durance vile, and a proclamation has been issued by the Begum threatening death to any person who assists him. The 79th Highlanders are expected daily, and the Commander-in-Chief in ten days. Something must be done very soon, and I really believe that there will be an awful slaughter; anything is better than being obliged to hunt them down and kill them in cold blood; if we can get them to stand, all will soon be over.

Sir Colin brings 100 siege guns with him, and if that does not settle matters I don't know what will. I am so glad that young Havelock has the pension of £1000 a year; he is a fine fellow.

I wonder when I am to get the Medjidee, and if they think of giving a medal for this business.

February 7, 1858.

Our enemy is out of spirits, and though he talks of attacks, he never carries them out. Convoys are coming in constantly now with "material," and we are busy making fascines and gabions. Everything is tending towards a siege; we are to have 120 guns in position, and Sir Colin hopes to batter the city to pieces. A conference is going on at Allahabad between the Commander-in-Chief and the Governor-General, so things are coming to a crisis.

February 12.—To-day 800 Sappers arrived in camp; we expect the 79th, 38th, 1st Bengal Fusiliers, and some heavy guns to-morrow. Operations must commence ere long, but I anticipate little or no resistance; if they make any, the operations will be those of a regular siege, and will extend over a lengthened period.

I see by Outram's despatch that he had only 1400 men when we were last attacked; it seems miraculous that we escaped. I expect to see Stephenson of the 79th in a few days. Bill Ward is with the 42nd.

A servant of Spurgin's has just escaped from Lucknow; he says that on the occasion of their last attack, they blew away from guns four officers who were prisoners. One was Captain Orr, the rest not known by name. They always reported after their attacks that they had driven us away and annihilated us. Spurgin's servant says that they have a most wholesome dread of our fellows, the "Blue Caps"; they call us devils, and say that we kill before we shoot; they mean that our bullets hit before the report of the musket is heard; they once said that they had even made us run.

They have no large guns in the city, only jingals.

They have loop-holed every place, and the city is very strong, the garrison enormous: upwards of 100,000 men; and all have swords or guns. All this seems terrible enough, but when one considers that they will have 150 big guns against them, and be shelled night and day from distances out of range of their muskets, it seems as if all the power was on our side.

Everybody has confidence in Sir Colin's not being foolhardy, but taking position after position quietly. I am neither sanguine nor an alarmist, and I sincerely believe that the taking of Lucknow will, by God's mercy, cost us little loss of life. Hamilton and Woodcock are both promoted, and the former has gone home sick.

Sunday, February 14, 1858.—No valentines to-day.

Two companies of the Royal Sapper Corps arrived this morning; they will be very useful in getting things ready for the siege. All the rest of the force is ready, and only awaits Sir Colin's order to move on this place. Three Infantry Divisions have been told off, and they consist of twenty-one regiments, numbering, say, 15,000 Europeans; then there are the artillery, engineers, and cavalry. Independent of this large force there will be Frank's Brigade or Division, Jung Bahadoor and his Ghoorkhas, and most likely Chamberlain's Division.

We shall have plenty of men for fighting, but not enough to invest the place properly, that is, so as to let no one escape. I quite look forward to the excitement of a siege if there is to be no more street fighting; that was fearful work. Yesterday 400 men arrived in Lucknow, and seeing the state of affairs there they bolted.

The Begum has issued a proclamation to the effect that all our reinforcements are shams, and that we only pitch tents to make a pretence of having more men, added to which our guns are *wooden;* she will find out her mistake.

Our Division is the 1st, and is commanded by Sir James Outram, G.C.B. It consists of three brigades, viz.:

1st Brigade, under Colonel Russell, composed of H.M. 5th Fusiliers, 84th, and 1st Madras Fusiliers.

2nd Brigade, under Colonel Franklyn, consisting of H.M. 78th Highlanders, 90th Light Infantry, and the Ferozepore Regiment of Sikhs.

3rd Brigade, under Colonel Hamilton, with the 38th, 53rd, and another Queen's Regiment.

February 19.—Our news here is much as usual. The reinforcements that were collecting in Bunnee have been withdrawn for some secret purpose; they are, I suppose, going to attack some force. In the meanwhile stores and munitions of war are arriving daily; commissariat stores are literally pouring in, and the Engineers are hard at work making up pontoons, etc. The enemy have annoyed us a good deal lately, and promise to do so for some time; but that is just the reason why I do not believe in a single attack.

On the 16th, in the morning, they sent out cavalry to try to cut off a convoy, and in the evening about six o'clock they commenced a regular attack. It commenced on the left, and the firing was very heavy. Being beaten back there, they tried the Alumbagh, and we were obliged to reinforce it; finally, they retired amid a shower of shell. The firing ceased, that is, as much as it ever ceases, at about 9.30 p.m., and then we are able to get a little dinner. I was nearly sick for want of something to eat, having had nothing but a bit of toast since nine o'clock at breakfast; however, a cigar and a nip of arrack soon put me straight, and a peaceful slumber made me forget my woes.

At 10 a.m. on the 17th they commenced an attack on our right at Jelalabad, but were driven back; we remained under arms until one o'clock. It was a cool day, so it did not much matter.

In the evening they tried to turn us out again, but we fired lazily at them with big guns, and that disheartened them. Our losses as usual were very slight; in fact the main body was never under fire, only the picquets, and they are under cover and so escape. The Pandies have no shelter, or else they would do us more harm; they sometimes fire a shell or two, but they are evidently scarce, and when fired are invariably fired high.

I am sorry to say that we had two serious accidents on the last occasion of our being turned out. There were several trees where our regiment was posted, and the men got on the branches to look on and see the fun. Amongst others Mecham, who is now doing duty with us, and a Sikh, were on a tree, and the branch gave way. Mecham fell with the branch on him, and was literally doubled up; another second, and he would have been suffocated; however, he was extricated, and is now tolerably well, but in great pain from bruises. The Sikh fell amongst some brushwood, and a stick went right through his cheek. Mecham has had some wonderful escapes; he was blown up in a mine at Lucknow, and escaped with only two others out of seventeen.

We have had a good reinforcement of officers to our regiment. Young Seton, who was A.D.C. to Havelock, and who was wounded at Cawnpore, has returned. He was shot through the jaw, and has lost ten teeth, part of his tongue, and a great part of his lower jaw. The bullet came out under his left ear near the collar-bone. He has a pension of £70 a year for his wound. He can speak very plainly, and manages to eat; if he were not a plucky fellow he would not have come back so soon, as he was strongly advised to go to England.[1]

February 21.—We have been plagued by these brutes a

[1] Sir James Lumsden Seton subsequently joined the Germans during the Franco-German war, and obtained the Iron Cross for conspicuous bravery at Gravelotte. He was compelled by the Duke of Cambridge to send in his papers, he having disobeyed the orders respecting our neutrality.

good deal lately. Yesterday one of their tumbrils blew up, causing great consternation. The day before one of our shells set a village on fire, and so frightened the fat Jemadar in command, that they had to take him off in a palanquin.

Yesterday news came out from Lucknow that two regiments had sworn to penetrate into our camp, and that all the police corps were to attack Alumbagh with one hundred and thirty scaling-ladders, and that the regular army were to be ready in rear to shoot any man who turned back. The Begum gave out that if her troops did not sleep in Alumbagh, she proposed poisoning herself.

In consequence of these terrible threats, we expected a vigorous attack. They began firing at two o'clock this morning, but we never returned their fire; whilst at church parade, they moved to our left and commenced firing. A battery and some of the military train went out after them, then the "alarm" sounded, and all the men had to run away from the parade.

It was strange to hear a clergyman preaching the gospel of peace on earth, whilst guns were roaring and cavalry and artillery moving to the front. It reminds one of Marlborough's service before action.

I do not know what is going on; our Brigade is not turned out, but there is a terrible row going on. One ceases to mind these things after a time. We had bad news the other day; the Commander-in-Chief was expecting an attack again on Cawnpore, so had recalled his troops from Bunnee, but it appears now all is serene again. A feint on Cawnpore would delay us here terribly. Franks is supposed to fight an action to-day near Fyzabad. I hope he will gain a brilliant victory; he is evidently near, as five regiments left Lucknow yesterday to oppose him. It is a strange life to lead, ever being in sound of musketry and guns night and day. The attack is at last over, and we are supposed to have caused great slaughter amongst our enemies. It is sad to have to feel such pleasure in hearing of the death of hundreds of them. They are a bitter, cruel, wretched enemy, and I feel it difficult to think humanly, much less Christianlike, towards them.

I have drawn a plan of Lucknow for you; it is a rough sketch, and only took an hour or so to do, but it may serve to make you understand our position. You will perceive what a large extent of ground we occupy, but then it would not do to allow these fellows the chance of holding Jelalabad, Alumbagh, or Alumnuggur. Our attack to-day was chiefly on the left, where I have put a village; we got round the village, and cut off their retreat to their own lines. They came also from the yellow house round to Jelalabad, and got a pounding there. You will understand the position of the Madras Fusiliers, as I have marked it very plainly. I fancy our next advance will be entirely on the left.

February 22.—Our enemies got a terrible thrashing yesterday; they must have lost about four hundred killed and wounded. I think we lost two or three wounded only. We expect the Bengal Fusiliers in here to-day.

February 24.—The Bengal Fusiliers came in all right, and are a great addition to our force.

Sir James Outram told us yesterday that he expected Hodgson's Sikh Horse, two squadrons of H.M. 7th Hussars, and a troop of Horse Artillery in to-day, and doubtless they will come all right, and then if these rascals dare to leave their entrenchments they will surely catch it. Sir James got authentic intelligence that there were upwards of five hundred killed in their last attack; upwards of one hundred died of wounds after they were taken into Lucknow.

Only fancy how safe we must feel with all these troops and such good defences, when at first we had only a few hundred and a bare plain before us! We have got our carriage issued, so that our move must take place soon. Colonel Franks has gained a victory at Tanda, and captured six guns. Maund Singh, one of the most powerful nobles of Oude, and one who gave us much trouble and anxiety, has joined us.

Brigadier-General Grant gained a victory yesterday, and took two guns, and Sir James has gone out to-day with all his cavalry and a horse-battery to try to intercept the fugitives from escaping into Lucknow after being beaten by General Grant. Nothing could be more cheering than the news from all sides.

February 26.—So far had I written when I was turned out by these vagabonds, and I have only been able to recommence to-day. We have had a tremendous fight and attack, and have taken two guns. We were fighting on and off from 6 p.m. to 4 a.m. this morning. Our loss is slight, three officers and about fifty men.

We fought this battle out during a most awful duststorm. It was simply blinding; both sides ceased firing, for neither could see a yard. We piled arms and stood easy. I was much amused during this interregnum. A very funny fellow of my company, named Jimmy Hurd, professionally a dog-dealer in Whitechapel, went up to a very zealous, newly-promoted corporal, and said, "Come, corporal, own you're a d——d coward, and would like to run away out of this." There was something inexpressibly comic in Hurd's face, and I am sure that most of us felt that he had pretty nearly hit off our sentiments. The corporal did not see the joke, and said, "Back to the ranks, sir!"

The troops are daily arriving, and we are in perfect safety, and can thrash these fellows out of their skins if they dare to come out. To-morrow we move ground to the Dilkoosha.

THE KAISER BAGH OURS

Dilkoosha, March 15, 1858.

We arrived here quite safely some two hours ago. I was rather tired, having got up at 3.30 a.m., but the change has done me good already.

Yesterday evening we received the glad tidings that the British ensign was floating over the Kaiser Bagh. The news at first seemed too good to be true; however, it was officially confirmed, and we now hold the Imperial Palace of the Kings of Oude. The moral effect that this blow must have on the people will be surprising, more especially as many were waverers before, and now will decide immediately in our favour. There has not been a shot fired to-day, and the city up to the Kaiser Bagh is given up to plunder.

Some say that the game is entirely up, that all are deserting. I know that all the Alumbagh cavalry and horse artillery moved off in some direction at 2 a.m. this morning, being ordered by a telegram in pursuit of fugitives. Others say that hostilities have ceased, in order that Sir James Outram, in his capacity of Chief Commissioner, may offer the townspeople the option of ransoming their city. Another report says that we are only moving our guns, so as to shell the city better.

However, two things are certain, namely, that the Kaiser Bagh is ours, and with it forty guns, and an immense quantity of ammunition; and secondly, that numbers of the enemy left the city last night. The taking of the Kaiser Bagh seems to have been one of the pieces of good fortune that attends our arms, or rather one of those marks of favour that have been so abundantly poured on us.

The Sikhs had been to take a place called the Imaum Barah, in rear of the Kaiser Bagh, and the Pandies, seeing this, feared a second Secundrabagh, and so made safe their retreat at once by bolting. The place is terribly undermined, and our great fear now is from them.

Some of the 10th were blown up yesterday, but only a few, and most of them are doing well. Captain Cator was wounded yesterday slightly; he is unfortunate.

The place seems alive with troops. Our loss is really very slight; I don't think altogether that we have lost one hundred men and officers. We have now only the town to take, and Sir Colin knows what street fighting is too well to let his men be used up in that way.

Our Ghoorkha friends must be potting away at imaginary Pandies, for I hear firing, and I am quite sure that there can be no one in between us and them. They do not seem fit for much, but Jung Bahadoor makes the most of them, and when they say a position is impregnable, he sends them back, and says they are not to return until they have taken it.

Lucknow, March 21, 1858.

I may relieve your anxiety by telling you that the city of Lucknow is fairly in our possession, and that we are now quartered in a huge mosque in the very heart of it, undisturbed by any firing or annoyance beyond an occasional shot from some budmash or robber.

I think in my last I had just time to mention that we had been ordered to the front. We marched on Monday morning, and took up our ground just in front of the Dilkoosha, very near the Martinière, and on the left of the grove of trees under which we had remained to be fired at on our last entry into the city.

On Tuesday morning I went to Banks' house to see what sort of a place it was, and also to look over the city. I met Laurie of the 34th, an old Hythe friend, there. Shortly after breakfast we got an order to proceed to the 32nd mess-house, which is near the Kaiser Bagh, and which, though very strongly fortified, had fallen into our hands without any trouble. We had scarcely got up to the place, when we found the 23rd Fusiliers following us, so our Major, imagining something was in the wind, halted on the main road, instead of going up to the mess-house.

It appeared that the Residency was to be attacked that day, and we hoped to have formed part of the attacking column, but we were ordered to remain as a reserve. The attacking column consisted of the 23rd, 2nd Bengal Fusiliers, and the 79th Highlanders, Sikhs, Sappers, Horse Artillery, and Middleton's Horse Battery. They formed up in column on the main road between the Kaiser Bagh and the Moti Mahal, whilst we were formed up on their left. Whilst the preliminaries were being arranged, we got some breakfast *al fresco*, for our first breakfast had been a very spare meal.

I met Henry Stevenson for the first time in my life there: he was acting Brigade-Major to Brigadier Douglas. We had only time to explain who we severally were, and make an engagement to meet again; then we had to go on our different roads.

From the mess-house tower we saw the advance admirably, and a very pretty sight it was. The 23rd were in their China frocks, then came the Bengal Fusiliers all in blue, and finally the Highlanders in their feather bonnets and kilts, all looking so nice. The column wound round through the different buildings until they came to the Residency, and then the guns opened fire.

We could soon see the effect of the shot, for the Pandy cavalry and infantry began to swarm on the iron bridge in full retreat; they seem to have been headed by Walpole's Brigade on the other side of the river, for they began scampering back again, and then our fellows gave chase, and they dispersed far and wide.

The column continued to push on, until it had taken the Residency, Machi Bawan, and stone bridge, thus holding a good half of the city without losing a man. We had remained at the mess-house and observatory all the time, but in the evening we were ordered to hold an old palace on the river's bank. Whilst at the observatory, some prisoners were caught with slow matches, evidently lurking about to spring mines; our fellows rammed greased cartridges into their mouths, and then shot them. You cannot imagine how infuriated our fellows are, and being in sight of the old Residency, where they suffered so much, nothing can restrain them.

General Franks was at the observatory during the business, and told us that he had heard us spoken of as a most gallant regiment, praise which he seldom gives to any regiment but his own.

We had a jolly bathe in the river, in spite of dead Pandies being in it; it was a luxury after being on that sandy plain at Alumbagh so long. I went to see some of our old battle-grounds: the 32nd mess-house was enormously fortified. I do not think we could have taken it under twenty-four hours' shelling. The Shah Nujjif and Moti Mahal were also well fortified; and the Kaiser Bagh, of course being their central position, was quite a fort.

I met Vaughan and Lords Clinton and Kerr of the Naval Brigade, and a host of old friends, and had a long chat with them. Clinton was the middy to whom I gave brandy when he was wounded in the last entrance. I went over the Residency; they had pulled down much of it, and had quite destroyed the church.

After another bathe, I went up on the top of the Palace to see the shelling, but was soon ordered down as we were to advance; we were to take the palace of the ex-Minister of Oude. It was exciting, as we were now advancing on a part of the city hitherto unknown to us. We marched merrily along, amidst camels, horses, carts, guns and tumbrils, until we got to the Machi Bawan, a strong fort, held originally by Sir Henry Lawrence, but blown up and destroyed when he found he could only hold the Residency. Up to this the road lay through ruins, for all this part of the town had been held during the siege by the mutineers, and pounded from the Residency, and subsequently had been under a cross fire from our guns at the Kaiser Bagh, and iron bridge.

We next got into the main bazaar, and such a sight I never beheld. Every house was gutted, and turned inside out; the street was strewn with furniture, palanquins, cooking-utensils, cloth, silks, velvets, and satins, some of the most costly description, painted and embroidered. Sailors passed and repassed, with embroidered muslins wrapped round their heads; camels walked slowly by with gorgeous silks hanging down, trailing on the ground. It was a perfect pandemonium, a chaos of loot.

Every here and there we perceived a fair sprinkling of dead Pandies, evidently showing that either shells or Europeans had been at work. I have never seen such a queer sight as that which·surrounded us: pictures, tinsel, wearing apparel, chiefly female, and all gaudy, lying in heaps; casks of sugar, bales of wool, heaps of tobacco, tubs of ghee, all in masses.

We advanced to the large mosque in the centre of the bazaar, and then halted for the column to form up. It was here, whilst standing with the others in a group talking, that I noticed a very fine goat. He seemed uneasy; presently he backed for several yards, and then came at me with a rush. Luckily my sword was drawn, and I received him on the point, or assuredly he would have smashed my legs. We found out he was a fighting goat, kept to amuse the neighbourhood. His end was, I think, curry for our men.

We were this time placed between the 79th and the 23rd, and at last started off. We went winding round though several streets. Suddenly we halted; the order was passed down for water-carriers to go to the front, and just as they were going, a dull heavy noise was heard, and we were enveloped in smoke. A mine had been discovered, and before the Engineers could damp the powder, some lurking blackguard had sprung it. The cry was then raised for dhoolies and stretchers. I am sure that no one ever saw such an awful sight. Those who were least burnt ran wildly screaming down the street perfectly naked, with their skin hanging about them in loose shreds. One poor fellow went rushing about quite blind, his eyes had been blown out; others, dead, were carried off in dhoolies; natives who had been as black as ink went by quite raw, and Europeans quite black.

The doctors said that there was only one who could live. One officer, an Engineer, was found, lying in a corner, just alive and quite blind; another was never seen, only his sword was found; a third was buried that evening. I never saw such a frightful sight, it was worse than the Secundrabagh, because there they were dead, and here many were still lingering, and we could not shoot them to put them out of their agony like Pandies. This unfortunate event caused some delay; but we finally got on, passing through horrid lanes, where one might be shot any moment from a loop-hole.

Our destination was the palace of the ex-Grand Vizier, Ally Nukee Khan, an arch rebel and crafty scoundrel. On arrival I was left with half a company to hold a gateway at the end of one of these lanes, whilst the others went on and got into the palace without any opposition; the fellows were cowed and would not fight. On my post I began a minute examination for mines. I found the earth loose in a house, and a smouldering fire burning on the floor.

I was in a precious fright. I moved the men, and then set to work to put out the fire, which we accomplished in a short time. I then got hold of an Engineer officer, who pronounced he did not think there was any mine, so I was comforted.

In all probability Sikhs had been there looting. They had a most ingenious way of finding hidden treasure; if the mud floor seemed in any way disturbed, they poured water on the spot, and if the water sank into the ground they then pushed their researches further, if the water did not sink there was no need to dig.

I found a quantity of powder in an adjoining house, which was instantly destroyed. After placing my sentries I looked round for some place in which to pass the night. It so happened that a very substantial two-storied house was close at hand, so I put the men in the lower rooms, and occupied the upper ones myself. My men now commenced prowling about in search of loot; they brought in a most miscellaneous assortment: pickles, jams, etc. They offered me many things; the only one I accepted was a roll of Horrocks' longcloth, which, cut into strips, served as towels, for I was hard up for such things.

The main body of the regiment had occupied the Minister's palace, and were having a good time looting. I am afraid to say what treasures they got hold of. It seems that the old scoundrel of an ex-Minister had only just time to escape. He had been taken completely by surprise. The bed on which he had been lying was still warm, and by the bedside on a teapoy stood a silver ewer of sherbet. I have the ewer now. I bought it from a soldier, and a book of a curious but most filthy character, which he had evidently been reading. The framework of the bed on which the old fellow had been lying was covered with a thin coating of silver, which was quickly stripped off and rolled up into portable packets.

But to return to my own picquet. Towards sunset a field-officer came round, and inspected my arrangements, then gave me the parole, and the inevitable injunction to allow no firing.

Ours was not a very disagreeable post, but it was a nervous one, for I knew that the place was infested by budmashes, and we were in a labyrinth of narrow lanes and alleys, unlike anything ever seen in a European town or village. Early in the day I found an old fellow prowling about, so took him prisoner.

In addition to placing sentries at every important place, I patrolled every hour; the sentries were of course loaded, but had strict injunctions not to fire. Whilst visiting sentries I heard shots in rear, and on hurrying to the spot, I found that three sepoys had come down the road, never dreaming that sentries were near. They advanced too far, and one of them had been shot, the other two escaped. It was now growing dark and I heard another shot; this time there was a prisoner. It seems that the sentry had seen two persons trying to escape. He fired; the man got away, but the woman fell down unable to move for terror. I took her to the main-guard, and placed her in a corner of my own room, speaking kindly to her, and telling Solomon to do all he could to reassure her, for I felt convinced that she could scarcely be other than a villager. I had fruit and water placed before her, but she took no notice of anything; she merely swayed her body to and fro, groaning as if in pain.

Firing at intervals continued in the same quarter, and of course the inevitable field-officer came down to know the cause. On this occasion I had a reasonable answer; we had taken two prisoners and shot two men.

It was now near midnight. My sentries had been doubled, and there was a comparative lull, when all of a sudden I heard the crack of a rifle, followed by another in the old quarter. I hurried off. The sentries assured me that they had seen men running past, and had fired; they added that they knew they were surrounded by rebels, and had heard them talking. I asked where, and they indicated a certain spot. I went with my corporal, and found a well, and on getting a light saw something moving. I called to the object to come out or I would fire down, and then by degrees we captured a party of six: two old women, two young ones, two children—one old woman

carried a baby. I told them not to fear, that we did not
hurt women and children, and took them from the main-
guard to my own room. No sooner had they entered,
than my former prisoner flew towards the old woman carrying the child. I thought she was mad, and would have
interposed, but she tore open her jacket, and pointed to
her breasts which were full of milk as proof that she was
the mother of the child. She seemed to devour it in her
joy at its recovery. I assured them of their safety, and
gave them all they wanted; they were very grateful, and
made the children come and bless me, and said they
would always pray for me. The rest of the night was
quiet, and would have been peaceful if the mosquitoes had
not taken up the running.

Next day I sent all my prisoners over under escort to
Sir James Outram, who had by this time established some
kind of civil government. The old man promised to stay
in my service: he did so for two days, and then bolted.

Here I must pause to comment on a serious subject,
namely, the awful responsibility that was placed on us in
cases where prisoners were taken on outposts. Of course
any kind of trial was impossible, and to guard even one
under such circumstances was not feasible. I know that
it was customary merely to say, "Take them to the rear,"
and that meant all and everything; but to those who had
to give that one order, it was a terrible ordeal, for even in
our moments of greatest excitement or danger, with me
there still lurked the dread feeling of shedding innocent
blood. To my mind, although I dare say in hasty moments
I may have said or written otherwise, my admiration of
Outram's clemency was intense. I think, on the whole,
being shot at oneself (especially if not hit) was better
than saying "Take him to the rear."

With daylight my men recommenced looking for loot: a
marvellous collection they got. I heard the head-quarter

people got six thousand rupees in hard cash, besides any amount of silver ornaments and shawls. Sladen, who was a past master in looting, got endless plunder, amongst other things a first-rate English barouche made in Longacre for the ex-Vizier. One company was said to have come across thirty thousand rupees, together with no end of swords, daggers, etc. I unfortunately got little or nothing. I did not go in for looting; it was to my mind too dangerous a game. You never knew whom you might meet in an obscure place, and when the other looter thought you intended an attack on his possessions, there was a very speedy and safe way of settling the question of ownership. It was currently reported at the time that Hodson, of Hodson's Horse, was shot by a comrade whilst looting.[1]

A very curious story got abroad that Hope Johnston, on Lord Clyde's Staff, whilst engaged in carrying an order, was appealed to for protection by the women of the Zenana in the Kaiser Bagh, that they handed him a casket of jewels as a recompense for his kindly services. He left the casket with the women, whilst he sought a safe escort; when he returned, women and casket were gone. I wonder if it was true.

Much of the loot which officers got was purchased. The shortest and surest mode of purchasing was the promise of a bottle of brandy. Some absurd prices were given. I have entries of an officer of the 84th getting an elephant of solid silver, worth £100, for £3, and a diamond worth £5000 for £140. Then again, per contra, sometimes a bit of glass from a chandelier was sold for a diamond at the price of a genuine one. Sladen of Ours got six medallion portraits of the Kings of Oude on ivory, set in pure gold, with massive chains, for a mere song. He also got three diamond brooches, of which

[1] This seems to have been false, but it was the current report of the hour.

more hereafter; his loot was said to be worth a thousand pounds. He was extremely superstitious in some matters. I remember his buying a sapphire ring from a soldier; he wore it for a day, and something unfortunate occurred during the time of his wearing it, so he gave it away as unlucky. I must now leave loot, and go back to our work.

The city was by this time free of sepoys and fairly free of budmashes. General Grant was vigorously pursuing the fugitives, and had captured sixteen guns, whilst Brigadier Campbell seems to have allowed no end of the blackguards to slip through his fingers. About fifty of the Begum's women came in, and it was said that the pretty ones showed their faces to our picquet. Can it be possible? I wondered where they would be housed, for there were nothing but men about in the city, and these fine Court ladies were very helpless.

I remember going to see Cator, an old Crimean friend, in hospital; poor fellow, he was wounded badly in the left arm. He had been wounded in the right in the Crimea, and had a stiff joint, so that he could not get his hand near his face; he was smoking a cheroot placed in a cleft piece of bamboo, which he could then get to his lips. He was wonderfully cheerful. What a good fellow he was, and what a sad end! I also saw one of the Engineer officers who had suffered in that terrible explosion; he was a sad sight, and I do not think he lived.

We had no firing at this time, and were admirably fed, thanks to the Commissariat, which, without any exaggeration, was splendidly worked.

One morning a fat, greasy native, mounted on a horse, and followed by several retainers, tried to pass my picquet. I happened to see a rifle in the hands of one of the followers, so I stopped them; they had a pass from some one in authority, but I took the rifle all the same, much to their disgust. It was an Enfield, and had been cut down, evidently one of those alluded to as having been split in the Residency. Fancy allowing natives to go about armed with our own rifles after the twelve months' experience we had had. There were many white idiots let loose on us in those days; but anything was better than throwing the responsibility of disposing of prisoners on us.

I must now go back to loot; it is an interesting subject, especially to those who are successful. I remember a gallant comrade with a strong Hibernian accent coming to me, and offering me a gigantic drop from one of Ostler's chandeliers, brass fastening and all, as a "foine diamond, your honour," for ten rupees and a bottle of brandy. He came down eventually to the brandy alone. A grand piano was offered also dirt cheap; perhaps this was the very one alluded to during the exodus from the Residency in October, by an officer who implored me to let him have a working party of my men to help carry it out, as "it was such a favourite of his wife's." As at that very time ladies and women were streaming out actually under fire, I need scarcely say circumstances over which I had no control, etc., etc. My own loot consisted of that one piece of Horrocks' longcloth I have already mentioned. I do not think I got another thing with my own hand. I got an ornament off the belt of a scoundrel that I think Bogle of the Artillery had shot, and a button off the coat of a sepoy of the 22nd Regiment, who had paid me the compliment of trying to shoot me, but luckily I went one better! By purchasing I got a few things, notably a lovely Nepaul pony, such a perfect beauty, it was like one of Flaxman's war-horses in miniature, pure white, the mane and tail stained with henna. I gave £5 for him to one of our men, who said he "*found it standing outside a house, and asked who it belonged to, and as the man could not tell, he took it.*" No doubt the man could not tell, possibly he had not breath left in him wherewith to answer questions. This perfect specimen I intended as a present for our Empress Queen, but after a day or two Solomon came and told me that it would not eat ordinary hay and corn, such as the Commissariat supplied, but loved boiled rice and sugar; this I could not get, so it was a white elephant, and I sold it to some one, who I fancied liked white elephants, for £25. I also bought a horse for £5. As Instructor of Musketry I was entitled to forage and horse allowance, I think at the rate of £3 per month, so a horse at £5 was not an expensive luxury. It was sold to me at Commissariat price, for stray horses were a drug in the market. It evidently had been the property of some rebel sowar of an irregular cavalry regiment. I named it Ossian! No, reader, not after the poet, but after the Latin word "Os," for it was skin and bone, a veritable Ossy 'un! He proved a nugget, as follows:

It may be remembered that the city was given up for forty-eight hours to loot; this is said to have been arrived at in the following manner; mind, I do not vouch for it. It was said Sir Colin intended his dear Highlanders should have the honour of taking the Kaiser Bagh, and also the first pickings of loot therein, but, alas! another brigade saw their opportunity, and went in; so the poor Kilts were done! To make up for this, forty-eight hours' loot was allowed; that was the *on dit* of the day. Be that as it may, it so happened that Sladen had looted a very superior barouche in the Vizier's palace, but could not get it out within the prescribed forty-eight hours. No sooner was time up, than strong picquets were placed at all the principal gates, as a sort of octroi, to prevent any loot being brought in or taken out of the city. These picquets became an object of interest, and would have made the fortune of a certain class of artist. There was piled up in front of the guard house every imaginable species of apparel, furniture, *bric-à-brac*, etc., awaiting the arrival of the prize agent, who would take them away, to be eventually sold for the benefit of the whole force. Curiously enough, the force itself was the only thing sold, for the money obtained by sales never was accounted for. Well, what was to be done? The barouche was there, only awaiting transmission to our new head-quarters. Sladen, being a man of resources, came to Seton, the Adjutant, and then to me, and said if we would assist by the loan of our horses, we should share in the sale of the carriage. We gladly consented, and at the appointed time Ossian the base born met the well-groomed charger of the Adjutant. Of course, on being introduced, they squealed and tried to bite, neither had ever been in harness; that did not matter, we were going to show them how clever they were unknown to themselves! We found harness, and had placed it on, when, alas! there were no reins. What was to be done? The glorious Seton was equal to the occasion; he had his saddle and would ride postillion. Never mind boots, that was a secondary consideration, and thus one difficulty was overcome. The next, a still more serious one, was not so easily surmounted. No doubt, his Excellency the Grand Vizier took his airings by a different route from ours: we had to thread the alleys alluded to, and the passage was in parts so narrow that the boxes of the axles touched the sides; luckily they were mud, and a little persuasion got the barouche past. At last, having overcome many more difficulties, we arrived at the junction of an alley with the grand trunk road, where, some hundred yards further on, the great gateway stood with its picquet. Here a council of war was held. We knew that to pass the guard in cold blood was impossible; no amount of asseveration that the barouche had been looted within the prescribed time would avail; it would be answered by "Sorry, old man, but you can't pass." At last it was determined to rush the post. Seton was the prime mover, he cried, "Get in, and I'll make a dash for it."

Now it so happened that in those days, men and officers dressed as Providence permitted; uniform in the sense of uniformity of dress was nowhere. Seton was in a shell jacket, I was in blue, and Sladen in kharkee. Seton mounted, and Sladen and I sat in the barouche with arms folded, doing "toffs." When within a hundred yards of the guard, Seton licked the horses over the head and ears, and set them off in a fine gallop. Then we heard "Guard, turn out!" shouted by the sentry, and like lightning we were received with a "present arms," and we were past; they had mistaken us for the Commander-in-Chief. When at a safe distance, we looked over the back of the barouche, and, as Ingoldsby described it, we "put our thumbs unto our nose, and stretched our fingers out." It was a brilliant success; not only had we secured our loot, but we were the only regiment possessing a carriage and pair of our own, for Ossian and the charger were made in future to do constant work.

Well, I had better end the story of the barouche. Some time afterwards, whilst at mess, the mess-sergeant came and said a gentleman wished to see me. I went into the ante-room, and saw a Staff officer, an A.D.C., I think. He began by saying: "I was referred to you, I think you have a barouche." "Oh Lord," I thought, "here's a go, the whole thing has come to the General's ears, and we are in for a court-martial for breaking past a guard." "Barouche," I said, feigning complete ignorance, "you mean a sort of carriage?" I told him I would make inquiries. "Do, please, for Sir James Outram wants to buy one to convey two ladies to Cawnpore."[1] "Oh," I said with alacrity, "I understand

---

[1] The ladies were, I think, Mrs. Ord and Miss Jackson, who had been hidden in the city by a friendly native. Their rescue was accomplished by Lieutenants McNeill and Bogle of the Bengal Artillery in the most gallant manner. I do not remember that they got the credit they deserved.

now; I'll see to it at once." I consulted Sladen and Seton; the price, a stiff one, was fixed, and the money paid; and so ended our barouche. But we were not going to be without some sort of regimental carriage, so we looted the cantonment hearse from the Residency, and so with Ossian and the charger, and with Seton as postillion, we had many a moonlight drive. The best part of these drives was coming across obstacles, such as poles with lanterns hung to them, indicating that roads were being mended, or mines filled in; then the word was passed to passengers, who sat *outside* with their legs dangling down like veritable undertakers' mourners, and, indeed, just as jolly, to hold fast, and a charge was made, and horses, hearse, and passengers were taken over at full gallop. I think we were dispossessed of the hearse eventually, because some one required Christian burial. Ossian went to some one else, at an improved price, " warranted quiet in harness." My! but they were jolly days in spite of everything.

Sladen and I as usual chummed together; we occupied a good-sized room over the gateway of a palace, I think called the Furreed Bux, and we were very comfortable. We were still dependent on the Commissariat for our daily bread and for liquor, that is for our ration of rum. Solomon used to take two soda-water bottles, and our allowance just filled each bottle. A soda-water bottle of rum all to oneself seems a lot, doesn't it? But just try it campaigning, and it does not go far. I remember so well we used always to take half at mid-day, and half just reached the W of the soda-water on the bottle, so we came to make it a joke that we were only to go as far as W. The second dram we took in the evening.

We were much annoyed by the horrid stenches that reached our nostrils. We could not make out where they came from. Sladen, who was at the time acting quartermaster and interpreter, was responsible for the cleanliness of the quarters, but he declared he could find out no cause. One morning we spied a hand sticking out of the earth in the ditch below, and found that about twenty sepoys had been hurriedly buried there, and were beginning to make themselves as disagreeable in death as they had been in life. Lime and more earth made them less objectionable.

It was at this time that an amusing scene took place in reference to the diamond brooches that Sladen had looted. He told me that a native had made him an offer for them. I examined them, and more veritable Palais Royal trumpery I never saw. Sladen declared they were genuine diamonds and worth a lot. Two natives came by appointment, and the brooches were produced. I must say that they never for a moment disputed the genuineness of the stones. They came day by day after the manner of natives, and talked and haggled; they wanted to test the gold and the stones, but Sladen would allow neither. He would only sell two out of the three, and the price arranged was £25 each. Before concluding the bargain they asked permission to bring a celebrated lapidary, who had recently arrived from Cawnpore, to see the brooches; this was granted, and the lapidary came. Next day the money was brought—a certain number of Company's rupees, a lot of Oude rupees, and then bits of bar silver were weighed against rupees to make up the total sum due. The brooches were then handed over. Two days after we heard a sound of lamentation, and found our two friends wringing their hands and praying for mercy. The brooches were all a sham. They got no mercy from Sladen; we talked the matter over, and he declared that the brooches were genuine, that these two jewellers had come day after day merely to examine carefully so as to make imitations. As I have said, I always thought them false, but I cannot account for a lapidary being deceived.

I must enter another incident that occurred whilst we

were living here. One day Solomon came and said a soldier wanted to see me. A soldier always meant a white man. I told him to show the man up, and presently in came a sergeant of the 38th, always a particularly smart regiment. We were ragged enough as a rule in those days, this man was a pattern of neatness, it was quite a pleasure to see him. I asked what I could do for him; he smiled and said, "Don't you remember me, sir, I'm Private A., late of your company." I had good reason to remember him, for at Tonghoo he got me into a nice scrape with the Colonel. We then had a talk. He said that I had always been kind to him, so finding himself near his old corps, he thought he would come and see me. I complimented him on his improved fortunes, and asked the cause of his failure in our regiment. It was the same old story. An indifferent company officer and a dishonest pay-sergeant. Private A. was sufficiently educated to understand his account, and detected a fraud; from that time his life was a burden, he got callous, was twice flogged, and eventually discharged as an incorrigibly bad character. He landed in England just as the Crimean War commenced, and re-enlisted in the 38th, and went out to Malta. He was made a lance-corporal almost immediately; he had a good company officer and rose rapidly. I learnt afterwards from the Adjutant of the 38th that he was the prospective sergeant-major, so excellent was his character. Moral: "Never too late to mend." I came across another very similar case at Templemore, where the subject of gross injustice determined to live it down, and became not only sergeant-major of a crack regiment, but had a commission offered to him, which he had refused, taking instead a very good Staff appointment. I think most bad characters are amenable to kindness, and in many cases their downward career commences in brooding over an injustice which a little inquiry would have remedied. In my time young officers were as much in the hands of sergeants as magistrates often are in these days in the hands of policemen.

It was somewhere about this time that I saw the division go out under General Walpole on its unfortunate mission. It was a sight never to be forgotten. Three regiments of kilted Highlanders formed one brigade under our late Brigadier, the Hon. Adrian Hope, who, poor fellow, was killed; the other brigade consisted of four regiments of Rifles. Of course a division of seven regiments was unusual, but the component parts still more unusual; they looked simply splendid, fit for anything.

Lucknow, May 10, 1858.

The night before last we had a most fearful dust storm; Sladen and I were sitting smoking our cheroots, and the whole sky was a blaze of lightning. Suddenly a gust of wind came, we rushed into the room, and it was as much as we could do to hold the doors until we got rope to tie them, and then the wind snapped some wire like twine. The dust covered everything and literally filled the room, so that we could not see each other. Hair, eyes, nose, mouth, all were crammed with dust. I congratulated myself that you were not there, for your hair would have cost you no end of trouble. The wind was blowing from the west, so we opened our east windows to let the dust out, but we were sold, for the wind changed and we got a fresh dose; however, it was only for a very short time, for the rain came down, and then it was so delightfully cool. Little damage was done, and I was soon asleep, forgetful of all wind and dust. Next morning I went out for a tremendous walk, a thing unprecedented, as generally when drill is over it is too hot to walk. Sladen and I went to the Kaiser Bagh and saw all the lions.

Yesterday I went to church at Banks' Bungalow; a West End preacher named Baldwin preached; he gave us a very good sermon, but he was very theatrical, and introduced so much of the Classics that it might have been an essay.

We are sadly off for news. I do not know what the Chief is about, or even where he is; however, we have columns enough in all conscience, and these people are being hunted down.

I went to see the tomb that has been put up to poor Dobbs, and the men we lost coming in with Sir Colin; it is erected over the pit where they were all buried. We are going to have one put up in the Residency over poor Neill and the officers and men; it will merely mark the spot, for I am afraid all the graves were opened there.

We hear that General Penny is dead; it is strange what a number of senior officers we have lost; this war has cost us more generals than any other, it shows that they are well to the front.

Lucknow, May 15, 1858.

We have had a few alarms lately, for the Begum and Moolvie are moving about: some poor fools actually imagined that Lucknow would be invested again, but such is a simple absurdity. Of course it is in these fellows' power to give us no end of annoyance, in fact the campaign has resolved itself into a guerilla warfare, and so it will continue until overwhelming troops are sent out. But our enemy has now no power to inflict serious injury on us; his resources are getting daily more crippled, and he has not time nor material to repair them withal; his sulphur must be waxing low, and caps and lead at least must have run short. News is every day received of our successes, and in the rains the enemy will be obliged to seek shelter somewhere, and then we shall be able to catch them. Rain does not injure our percussion caps or cartridges, but it does their matchlocks.

A telegram yesterday informed us that Bareilly had been taken with great loss to the enemy. Brigadier Jones and Sir Colin moved on it from different points, and as Jones approached on the north he heard Sir Colin's guns pounding into the cantonments. General Grant took three guns and some ammunition, and killed from 100 to 300 of the fellows down south. Sir Hugh Rose and General Whitlock have also been successful in their tours, so that we have every reason to be thankful and satisfied.

The weather here is tremendously hot, the perspiration streams off one, and the prickly heat is very annoying, but thank heaven it is very healthy weather. I have no pains or aches of any kind, and our men are very healthy now, though we have had small-pox rather badly.

Did you perceive that my letters smelt of smoke terribly a few mails ago? I used to fumigate them for fear you should get it. We lost many men, and one day when I was writing to you the sergeant came and told me that Private Daniell wanted to make his will, so I had to leave your letter and go to make it for him. Poor fellow, he was an awful sight; his face was black with dried-up pustules. I had to sit by his bedside and make out his will, and then he signed it. I took the precaution to light a cigar before I started; I could not smoke in the sick man's room, but I lit it again when I came out, and took care to fumigate your letter well. The man died two days after; I did not like to tell you at the time, but now it is all over, and there is no fear.

May 16.—Yesterday's General Orders contained an extract from our dear good Queen, in which she thanks the army for their unprecedented exertions, and deplores the heavy losses that they have sustained. She certainly takes great interest in her soldiers, and it is quite a pleasure to serve her.

Sir James Outram has sent up £300 worth of books, rackets, cricket bats and balls, etc., to the regiment, and has ordered all the leading papers to be sent regularly to the sick. He says in his letter to the commanding officer, that he is only too glad to be able to record his admiration and his appreciation of the services rendered by the regiment.

I don't know whether I told you that I had made some experiments in my professional line whilst at Alumbagh. Well, I sent in a rather elaborate report, and made it pretty with sections and diagrams.[1] It was sent in to the Adjutant-General, and now I have received a copy of my own report. The Government have printed it and sent it to the Court of Directors, and to the Inspector-General of Ordnance. Lord Harris, as Governor in Council, says, "In his Excellency's opinion the suggestions of the Instructor of Musketry of the 1st Fusiliers are deserving of serious consideration." I am really very much pleased, as it is a great compliment to have your report published and copies sent to all commanding officers. I hope that it will get me an appointment.

May 29.—Poor Hargood died a few days ago of a severe fever, he was only ill two days. He was a lion of a soldier, and had been in everything from the first to the last; he had been Havelock's A.D.C., and was then made Outram's; Havelock loved him, and gave him as a dying charge to Sir James. Poor boy, bullets were charmed, but the unerring finger of sickness was pointed too surely at him. Another good soldier gone.

I am afraid that our chance of getting back this year is getting smaller and smaller. The secretary to Lord Canning wrote to one of our officers, that it was the intention of Government to relieve us after the rains, but the Madras Government has since been ordered to send out recruits, which certainly looks like another cold season here; besides, the country is so very disturbed that it is impossible to send troops away. I am in quite as much doubt as you are, one cannot tell what a day may bring

[1] I have not the faintest recollection of this wonderful production. How curious it is that such things escape one's notice.

forth; one blow might settle all, or our remaining quiet might perhaps induce the people to give in; they are too much harassed now, and this hunting down system induces petty warfare.

Lucknow, June 11, 1858.

Here we are without any orders for a move, but I have still hopes of our being moved to Cawnpore. General Grant goes out with a very strong column to the north to a place called Nawabgunj, where they say that there are some 10,000 of the enemy with sixteen guns. The misfortune is that in all probability they are off long before this.

June 13.—General Grant's column made a forced march yesterday night to surprise the enemy this morning, but I hear that Pandy was bolting all yesterday. It is a farce trying to catch these fellows unless they are surrounded.

June 22.—Just as I was preparing a budget of good news, all my hopes are withered. I expected the regiment would be ordered in to-morrow, but alas, I find we have to remain in camp out at Nawabgunj all the monsoon. It will be a wretched time, and we shall be cut off from all communication with the world. I shall, however, be able to send my letters regularly into Lucknow for posting, as a set of runners have been put on between Nawabgunj and Lucknow. We are only sixteen miles from Lucknow, so I dare say things will turn out better than we expect. It is rather a hard case, that a regiment which has had no cover to its head for fifteen months should have another monsoon in the open, while other regiments have been in clover all the time.

Camp, Nawabgunj, June 28, 1858.

There is a report that the 2nd Madras Regiment is coming over here to relieve us, and the newspapers have it so. Sir Hope Grant said that we should never see Lucknow again, so I suppose it is intended that we march from this place, *viâ* Fyzabad, to Calcutta. I like this place now, for I feel so well and strong. The country is quiet, and everything looks very well.

July 3.—Reports of the capture of ringleaders are rife, and we hear every day that the country is quieting and people are beginning to cultivate their land. Nothing could be more like peace than everything around us, and I do trust they will use conciliatory measures and not incite the people to rise. Lord Canning's proclamation is, in my opinion (in spite of all the great authorities opposed to me), quite just but very impolitic; whether it would have been in the end wiser to have bowed and become conciliatory is a matter time will prove. It is certain that the Chief Commissioner has the power and will to show mercy to all except those whose hands are stained with English blood, shed in cold murder.

Lord Ellenborough is no loss; he has so many political enemies, and is detested by the Civil Service out here, so he would have the whole body and Press of India against him; and his own policy was so inconsistent and doubtful, that he would have not only to be cautious regarding present acts, but have continually to defend past deeds and opinions. Lord Stanley is, I fancy, a good man.

I am building a house, and I hope it will not cost me more than £7; it is worth £7 to be dry and comfortable instead of crowded up in a small tent, with a burning sun by day and rain at night, so I do not look upon it as extravagance. I have now no pretty flowers to make my tent look nice, but perhaps after the rains I may get some. The Rifles have made gardens outside their tents and huts.

July 12.—On the evening of the 10th I got another touch of fever, which laid me up till this morning. A one day's fever is not very serious, but it utterly prevents writing, and indeed, I was so light-headed from quinine, that if I had dictated a letter it would probably have been most unconnected, considering that I fancied I was a door-frame, and that I could not get my various pieces to unite properly.

Everything is going on tolerably here. On the evening of the 9th a very severe storm broke over us, and continued for some hours. It regularly flooded our camp, and it was in going about nearly naked to look after the men's tents that I got my fever. Our mess-tent happened to be pitched on the side of a tank or lake, considerably above the ordinary high water-mark. However, so excessive was the rain, that the tent was soon surrounded by water, and had it not been embanked well with earth, we should have had a very cool floor. Two of the officers' tents were literally flooded, and they had to sleep through the night surrounded by a foot of water. Three out of four of the tents of my company had a foot of water in them; in fact, you never saw such a deplorable state of things. It certainly was strange to dine and breakfast surrounded by water, with all the trees standing at least two feet in water; the poor squirrels and monkeys thought it no fun; they had gone up the trees to eat mangoes, and were made prisoners. I saw several little grey squirrels come down the trunks of the trees, and put their noses to the water, then run round to the other side and try that. At last, finding no escape, they ran up again, squeaking and making a great noise. A large cobra was caught in one officer's tent in a basket; the servant went to open the basket, and he heard it hiss, so he ran away, got a light, and looked; there the beast was, so he shut down the lid, locked it, and waited till next morning, when the animal was despatched.

The huts that we were building stood pretty well. I had only just begun the walls of mine, so that little damage could be done. The chebutra, however, suffered, being much cut up by the rain, but even that evil was mitigated by my having taken the earth to make it from drains which I cut, thus my drains supplied my material for the foundation, and afterwards saved it. Some others dug holes to get their earth, and forgot their drains, so that the water flooded the chebutra and washed away great portions.

July 14.—The house progresses rapidly; all our timber is up, side-posts, wall-plates and all, and our roofing is on. The walls are about three feet high now, and we shall soon run them up; we shall then only have to cut the walls straight, and plaster them over with a native mortar, viz. cows' dung, chopped straw, and fine mud; it is very wholesome, and gives the place a *dairy* smell. The floor will be covered with rough knobbly gravel beaten in, then plastered, and then matted. The walls inside and out will be white-washed, so that everything at least will be clean. We shall have bath-rooms also, which will relieve us from the necessity of sitting down in public, and having water poured over us, the only way one can have a bath out in the jungles. It is really quite wonderful what a thousand little comforts or luxuries this wonderful house will bring us, things that we have long done without, but which one again wants, immediately they are within reach, far more keenly than we should if we had never been without them.

I shall be very glad to get out of this place, for though it is high and precludes the possibility of our being flooded, yet being on the banks of this tank, the water sends forth a malaria, and the wind carries it into our tent, and so gives us fever.

Fancy, Mr. Baldwin rode out on Saturday from Lucknow, good eighteen miles, having to cross swollen streams with no bridges, and extremely treacherous, to give us service on Sunday morning. He visited, the same day, fourteen hospital tents, giving an address and reading some prayers in each. He gave an open-air service on Sunday morning to the troops, and then rode back to Lucknow to serve his own church in the afternoon. He is a civil chaplain, so is under no necessity to do any military duty, but he is a queer, zealous man, and is, I am sure, a very good one. He works like a slave, but he is so funny. He preached standing on a six-dozen chest that had contained beer, and in the middle of his sermon he shouted out, "I say, can you men out there hear me? for I see you looking about as if you could not."

They talk of an amnesty here. I think it compromises our dignity, and will do no good, for the people will not believe us. The Begum wrote in answer to the Chief Commissioner's letter the other day, "I consider I am quite justified in trying to place my son on the throne. The annexation was an unjust one, the treaty with England was broken by you, and I never will believe an Englishman again."

They hear from England, first, that their land is to be confiscated; then, that the people of England say it is not to be confiscated; next, that the annexation is a just one; and then, that it ought to be annulled; and so on, until no Englishman out here understands our policy, and how on earth can a native?

Fyzabad is said to have a force of 16,000 men collected there, but I never heed any rumours of collecting forces; the better they collect, the more chance there is of our catching them, always supposing we have not too many of "Old Khubardar's"[1] combinations, with Brigadier Campbells to carry them out.

Beni Madoo, a powerful chief, is within ten miles of Bunnee, and had the impertinence to come and settle a dispute regarding the right of possession of a village which is only four miles from the said Bunnee; he killed one man, and put the other in possession. Rather impudent, certainly.

[1] A nickname given to Sir Colin, meaning "over cautious."

There are great chances of the country quieting down during the rains.

Nawabgunj, July 21.—This force is under orders for Fyzabad; just as our house was finished the order came; however, there seems to be a doubt about it, but whichever way things turn out I do not go, as I have been very unwell with fever and dysentery.

Dr. McLelland, whom you may remember on board the *Colombo,* called on me yesterday; he is doing duty with Hodson's Horse. He told me that General Windham had dined with them just before starting for Cawnpore, and was very bumptious, saying that he had written to the Duke to tell him how things were being carried on in this country. He seemed particularly jealous of Outram, and wanted to know who he was, and why he held so many appointments. What he meant to ask was why he was acting in a civil, political, and military capacity at one and the same time. The answer is clear: because he was the right man in the right place.

July 25.—The weather is nice and cool now, heavy rain having fallen yesterday; the house leaked in two places, but not materially; when the thatch swells it will be all right.

Dr. Thornton of the Bengal Fusiliers is living with me; he had a miserable little tent, and was not well, so I offered him house-room; he is very quiet and will not bother me. I knew his brother in the Crimea; he was Assistant-Quartermaster-General of the Artillery, and was a very nice fellow.

July 27.—I managed to walk out yesterday as far as the 90th lines. Everything is much changed, and I miss the order and tidiness that existed when the Rifles and ourselves were here. We built, and therefore took a pride in our lines, and were studiously particular not to mar the effect by any dirt or rubbish being left about. The new-comers found their huts built, and seem to care but little about them.

You are quite wrong in supposing that Sladen and I quarrel. We understand each other perfectly. We have our times for study, and our times for sociability, and they are kept with singular precision. As soon as the after breakfast weed has been discussed, each retires into the recesses of his own room for the transaction of public business, or the study of any subject that may be the occupation of the period. The one o'clock bugle is the signal for lunch, and a glorious chat over a second cheroot; this hour is especially an hour of idleness, and very frequently ends in lying down and sleeping, or in giving up oneself entirely to some light reading. If any particular study or business is being carried on, of course the afternoon must be devoted in like manner as the morning; but now that Hindustani does not claim our attention, and neither of us have heavy office duties, the afternoon is spent very much as fancy dictates.

Dr. Brougham sent me two quail for my dinner a few days ago, but as they were alive I had not the heart to kill them: so I cut their wings, and have given them a box to live in; their names are Jack and Jill, but whether they are two Jacks or two Jills I cannot state.

You ask me whether there is any marked difference between the Queen's and the Company's officers. I do not think that there is any difference in the class from which our officers and those of the Queen's army are selected; every man in the Company's service has brothers, father, or relations in the Queen's, but I think the constant active service, and the numerous independent commands which fall to the lot of the Company's subaltern officers out here, make them the better soldiers of the two. They are not so agreeable or polished, owing to the long absence from home and its associations. I do not believe that more jealousy exists between us and Queen's men than exists between us and our comrades attached to native regiments. Of course we consider ourselves superior to sepoy officers, though only the merest accident places us to European regiments; still a greater amount of discipline is necessary with Europeans, and English instincts are more closely preserved. We have better chances of seeing service, and the greater advantage of being always in good stations with other troops under the eye of a general officer, which of course prevents our growing lax. The Queen's men enjoy the still greater advantage of home service; nothing causes such deterioration as long service away from home.

The Royals in India, except crack corps, certainly give themselves great airs. The Indian *Punch* has had no end of good hits at them. One I remember well; the wife of an officer of a native regiment required an English nurse, and all but concluded an engagement with the wife of a soldier of a Queen's regiment. When asked why she declined, she answers, "No, ma'am, it is not the wages, which is perfectly *satisfactuary*, but it is my husband who has objections to my taking service with the lady of a sepoy officer." Good isn't it?

I think in the matter of rewards our service has been unfairly treated. No honours were ever conferred during the Punjaub and Sikh campaigns, except when their omission would have created a positive scandal. In this campaign our services have been fairly acknowledged.

One great grievance still exists, and that cannot well be remedied. Our promotion is so slow that constantly subaltern officers of from ten to fifteen years' service are serving under Queen's men of four and five.[1] A curious case occurred to me. An officer of the military train, who had not even got his commission when under my orders at Yenikali, superseded me at the Alumbagh. He was most unwilling to do so, and was as nice as could be,

---

[1] These remarks were written before the Amalgamation. I retain them because they represent, I think, the feelings of the Indian army in those days.

but of course when I found out that he was my senior I could do nothing but hand over the command of the picquet to him.

Durreabad, August 16.—At a moment's notice we left Nawabgunj, to replace H.M. 53rd Regiment here. The notice of the move was only received at 9 p.m. on the 13th inst., and we marched at 3 a.m. on the 14th, making three marches to this place. We literally had to wade out here; the rains have flooded the whole country, and it is one vast lagoon. I enjoyed the march very much. "Cardigan," my new horse, carried me superbly; he jumps beautifully, and I have had three offers for him.

Durreabad, August 20.—Here I am still, doing duty with the 1st Bengal Fusiliers, and anxiously expecting my tent from Fyzabad. News has reached us of a fight at Sultanpore. We lost three men wounded and two horses killed; the enemy, one hundred killed and twenty drowned in trying to cross the river. Our force is not strong enough to push on to Sultanpore itself, but has long ere this been reinforced by the Rifles and Brasyer's Sikhs.

There has been a slight skirmish here. About 2000 of the enemy tried to cross the road between this and Nawabgunj; the Kupperthulla Rajah and his contingent, who are stationed here, went out after them; the enemy exchanged shots and bolted, the Kupperthulla contingent following, but unable to come up with them. A few dead matchlock men were found.

I don't know whether I told you about the chief man of the police-station near Nawabgunj bringing in the head of one of the rebels. He was rather alarmed at going back again, as he said a large force was in the vicinity of his post, and that he was sure to be attacked out of revenge. He was told to go back and not be afraid, as support could always be sent to his assistance in case of an attack; he went back reluctantly, and now the poor fellow has been barbarously murdered. It appears that they did come down, and managed to creep into the Thana police house, cutting up five of the policemen and disabling ten others. The chief man has not been heard of, but it is supposed that he was taken off to the rebel camp to meet a more cruel fate. I consider our conduct in this matter infamous and cruel. If we detach parties, we ought either to give them orders to retire on an attack being made, or else be prepared to support them. I wonder how we expect any natives to adhere to a side that cannot even protect them.

I went out coursing foxes to-day, a most unsportsmanlike proceeding in England, but quite legitimate out here where there are no fox-hounds. We put up a hare, but she got into cover before the dogs were well laid on. I saw two jackals, but they are seldom good running, and they bite the dogs so fearfully. A brace of partridges got up, and reminded me so of home.

Tell all your friends that General Peel and Lord Hardinge were quite wrong in their statements to their respective houses. The ammunition sent out is very inferior.[1]

Durreabad, August 26, 1858.

I start for Fyzabad to-morrow morning with a strong escort. A party of recovered men of different regiments are going on together, with a treasure party of the Rajah's force, the whole under command of two officers of this regiment. I have thus a nice escort and pleasant society. I am not at all disinclined to go to Fyzabad, as I hear it is a pretty place and well worth seeing. Colonel Payne, who commands H.M. 53rd at that station, is an old Crimean friend of mine, so I am sure of being kindly received.

The proceedings of the last few weeks have been anything but satisfactory. Troops have been hurried hither and thither without any definite plan, the men are

---

[1] The report was that the condemned ammunition from the Crimea was sent out here.

THE RAJAH OF KUPPERTHULLA

tired, sick, and disgusted, and there is no excitement to keep them up. In every case we are just too late, and our movements resemble the efforts of a wayworn traveller endeavouring to catch a will-o'-the-wisp. At the same time it keeps Pandy on the trot, and prevents their reuniting, drilling, and collecting revenue.

The landowners, or rather holders, are cultivating extensively, and so all chance of a famine is I trust averted, a consummation devoutly to be wished for, as a famine would inevitably be attributed by the ignorant to our misrule. Quarrels among our enemies seem to be fashionable. The Begum has cast adrift her paramour, Mr. Mamoo Khan, and, although expecting an addition to her family immediately, has taken some one else for better or worse. This of course has caused a great rupture, as Mamoo Khan possessed some influence. The Begum is, I fear, a very low, common woman; in fact her origin was the streets of Lucknow, and Mr. Mamoo Khan was an amorous butcher.

Wazeer Ali and Musahib Ali have quarrelled about some trifle, and split up into two parties. Another leader has been killed for not paying his men, a difficult matter when the shiners are not forthcoming from the landholders.

In fact, altogether things look like a final arrangement before the cold weather even commences. No recruits have been sent up to us, so I suppose we must go down to them; an argument which is supported by Edmondstone's promise, and the reports current here.

I went the other day to call on the Rajah of Kupperthulla; I had sent to ask for an audience, and he granted it, so at 6 p.m. Dr. Brougham and I were transported from the top of an elephant to the Durbar tent. The Rajah was very polite, came outside to receive us, barefooted, all according to Cocker. I got the seat of honour, and talked enough for everybody. His Highness could speak English, but preferred Hindustani, an arrangement that suited me;

he spoke his language to me, and I answered in mine. He had ascertained my previous history, after the manner of natives, and asked much of Turkey and the Crimea. On the whole I was pleased with him; he seemed an honest, straightforward man.

You may never have heard of Kupperthulla, I think it is a small district to the north, up in the Punjaub. The Rajah pays 2,035,000 rupees to Government every year. On the outbreak of the mutiny, he saved two important stations for us by marching down and occupying them. For his services the 35,000 rupees were given up to him in perpetuity, and for the use of his troops now he gets annually two lakhs. The Government also presented him with two years' revenue, so he has feathered his nest by his loyalty.

I went with Maxwell to reconnoitre a fort the other day; we found it surrounded on all sides by a fringe of dense jungle, bamboos, and prickly thorns; so thick was the jungle that no one but foot passengers or a single horseman could make their way through it. Near the fort we found an open glade, so very pretty, and there were some wild peacocks feeding there, which on our approach gave a scream, and flew into the trees very lazily. The fort appeared formidable, but it was uninhabited, so we returned home.

Next day we went to shoot the peacocks, but we flushed them too soon, and they would not rise after, but ran under the bushes like pheasants. Two days we tried, but unsuccessfully. I found lots of beautiful ferns and flowers, amongst others the *Gloriosa superba* and a very fine *Euphorbia*. You will be glad to hear this, as it proves Oude to be a very beautiful and rich country, and gives one an opportunity of looking up hiding Pandies. But joking apart, I do not go into any danger in these excursions, so you must not fancy that I do.

Fyzabad, August 31, 1858.

After a most charming march we arrived here yesterday. The Brigadier was very kind, and offered me an escort to enable me to proceed on at once, but as the party only halt a day here, I preferred going on with them, and we start to-morrow.

The force has left Sultanpore, and most likely I should have been detained there to wait for this party after all, and as there is no immediate fighting going on, I considered that a recovered man might take a day's rest. I am delighted with the idea of going with Wheeler and Warner; they are such nice fellows, and our party is a very happy one. We always take a set of quoits with us, and when we arrive at our halting place, we have a game until the tents are ready. Our marches have been dry, but rather long, or I should say slow, for the men we have with us are all recovered men, and cannot march fast. We generally marched from 1 a.m. to 6 or 7. I do not like turning out at 12 o'clock; however I get a cup of tea and a cheroot, and I am happy enough.

Fyzabad is a very pretty place; the river is a magnificent one, a mile broad, with lots of alligators and turtle. The ancient city is named Ajudea, and is the oldest and most sacred of all the Hindoo cities. It is quite in ruins now, and is only resorted to on account of the sacredness of the shrines, which are still partly kept up.

We went there this morning and saw a lot of fanatics and ugly old men; they smear themselves over with lime, and then sit perfectly motionless receiving alms. I longed to try the effect of a bamboo on some of them, but, poor wretches, they are not worth a thrashing; our treatment of these people and their religion is most singularly inconsistent. We went to Maun Singh's temple, and happened to see him there; he is a shrewd-looking little man, but of no very striking appearance. We also went to Hanuman's temple; he is the monkey-god, and it was a fanatic from this place, and dressed as Hanuman, that led a most severe attack on us at Alumbagh. You may remember the fact of his being wounded and taken prisoner. The god is an image of a most hideous half man and half monkey, painted vermilion, and decked out with silver and gold and jewels. The people are utterly under the priests, and believe in all kinds of absurdities. The most sacred shrine is patronized almost entirely by the ladies who desire children; it is considered a sure specific, better than Tunbridge Wells even.

The people of Ajudea venerate the monkeys, and thousands are seen skipping about; some are enormous. It is very funny to see the little ones riding on their mothers' backs, and jumping from bough to bough.

The turtle also is very sacred; they believe the world is supported on a turtle's back. The turtles come up to the steps of the temples which lead to the sacred water in hundreds to be fed, and are easily caught. Our soldiers behaved disgracefully, for they caught the turtles and turned them on their backs, and then called the priests to come and look at their gods " a-kicking like anythink."

Solomon is going to bathe there; he is a Hindoo, but a very lax one; he does not believe in idols, but only considers that the God of the Universe is named Ram. I do not think that he understands anything about his religion. Please to send out his watch as soon as possible; I think Bennett's £6 one would do, and mind have an inscription put in it, saying that it is given as a reward for his faithful services during the Mutiny.

I am very well now, and the marching agrees with me wonderfully. Do not get the views of Lucknow by Mecham,[1] as I have ordered two copies to be sent to Herries.

[1] Poor Mecham succumbed eventually to his wounds and the shock his system had sustained, not, however, before he had published a most excellent series of views of Lucknow, dedicated, by permission, to Her Majesty.

Sultanpore, Sept. 9, 1858.

I arrived here safely yesterday after a very pleasant march. We started from Fyzabad very early one morning, and had scarcely got two miles out of cantonment when a deluge of rain fell. You would have pitied me had you seen me crouched under a tree, more like a mass of dripping clothes than an animate body. My boots were literally filled up to the tops with water. Animals could not stand such a beating rain, but turned their poor tails to it. Of course we had to return and try to get a dry suit, but I never got my *dry*, really dry, clothes or bedding until four or five days later. The rain continued, and the atmosphere was so damp, that it was impossible to be comfortable; fancy sleeping in a damp bed smelling like a potato hut. The rain detained us several days at Fyzabad, and we got very tired of remaining in such a damp hole. At last we effected a regular start, and our march was a very pleasant one.

I had a good deal of work to do at a place called Budassah: the road through the village reminded one of Fetter Lane, under repair, after a thaw; it was knee deep, and very narrow. Our convoy met a return convoy in the village, as ill luck would have it, and the whole lot came to a deadlock; to go on or turn back was impossible. I had only the alternative of making a new road, so, like Alexander of old, I cut the knot, and much to the annoyance of the proprietors, I got the head man of the town and some workmen, and we cut right through the village, destroying three mud walls and a couple of hedges, not to mention trampling down standing grain.

I paid compensation, and the people stood looking on in mute astonishment at a man who could by his nod make ducks and drakes of their houses and lands, and then pay for the damage done. I got my convoy through, and then gave permission to have the road closed, in order to prevent further damage being done.

Whilst halting at Syree, at about 9 p.m., two sowars rode in, and informed us that the enemy had come down on the road, and killed some people, burning and plundering in all directions. It became necessary to look to the safety of our position, so picquets were put out, and every precaution taken against surprise. The sowars were detained to accompany us, and give us information. In every direction we found the villagers very much frightened, and in a state of considerable excitement, and much damage had been done. It seems that a party of sepoys crossed the road near a place that was being repaired by some of our coolie workmen; they killed one, then looted the village, wounding two of the chief men in it. We came up to the place of disturbance, and found the body of the coolie laid on the ground bathed in blood; his brother was kneeling beside it, swaying himself to and fro; on our arrival he began a terrific howling, for which he got a good slanging and a promise of a thrashing, which stopped his roaring. It seems very cruel to treat these people so, but they are regular humbugs, and always begin a dry cry whenever any one is near to hear them, and they invariably end with a begging petition for money. I dare say those very scoundrels had not lent an ear to the entreaties for mercy of some of the poor fugitives from Fyzabad or Sultanpore. However, it is now our policy to protect them, so we gave them all the assistance we could.

A little hump-backed man came from a neighbouring farm with some milk as a present, and he gave us very good information; he was a shrewd little fellow. Wheeler determined on following the rebels, and he and I and fifty men were about to start, but news was brought to us that they were encamped near a fort with two guns and 2500 men; it was not safe to risk a skirmish with them, though without their guns we could have thrashed them well. News came in that evening that we were going to be attacked; the result would have been anything but advantageous to Jack Pandy, and I suppose he thought so, for he never came near us.

Next morning we marched to Bhurtipore, and met a force under Colonel Payn of the 53rd, which had been sent out to clear the road: finally we reached this place yesterday morning.

Sultanpore is or was a beautiful place; the Pandies have burnt down the cantonments. The affair here was utterly mismanaged. There were myriads of Pandies, and they offered battle three days running; on the fourth day it was accepted, but too late in the day, and they bolted, and darkness prevented our following them up.

Camp, Sultanpore, Sept. 22, 1858.

This country does not agree with me. I feel that I never can be well, or even in passable health, whilst this constant exposure is carried on, but set me on the hills for a year, and then at some quiet station, and I do not see why I should not enjoy as good health as ever. I do not like to go away while there is any chance of service, but still on the sick list I am of no use.

I went out riding this morning, and from the deserted gardens of the ruined houses here I gathered a very pretty bouquet. I got pink and white oleander, a yellow flower like stephanotis, a kind of variegated foxglove, roses, balsams, and peacock pride, an Indian flower that I never saw elsewhere.

September 26.—General Michel has gained a great victory over Tantia Topee, and has taken 26 guns.

October 2.—I can only write a few lines, as I am too weak to sit up long. After many consultations it has been ascertained that I have a low fever, and I have to be treated accordingly. I am too weak to stand, but am in a fair way to recovery.

Sultanpore, Oude, October 5, 1858.

It is said that Lord Clyde intends sweeping out Oude with nine light columns, which are to break up any large bodies of the enemy, and then he says that the police must hunt them down. There are five cavalry, and twelve infantry regiments of Oude police, so they ought to be able to settle the business.

October 7.—I am still progressing favourably, and hope to get out in a palanquin to-morrow. I cannot stand long without tottering, but I hope strength will soon return.

October 8.—The enemy got a mauling at Selimghur the other day, 700 were killed, also three swells, one a brother of Musahib Ali. The game is utterly up, but it may take time to checkmate the brutes. What twaddle the English people talk about these mutineers! There can be no mercy for men who shoot you if you spare them.

Sultanpore, October 16, 1858.

We have had a day's rejoicing here; two of our non-commissioned officers have been promoted to ensigncies for gallant conduct in the field. Of course from the very moment the *Gazette* arrived, they were relieved from their positions as sergeant-major and quartermaster-sergeant, and had to have a tent pitched for themselves in the officers' lines. It must have been strange to them, leaving all their old companions, and feeling that now a bar existed between them that was impassable. The Colonel and officers requested the pleasure of their company at dinner that night, and the band was in attendance. They were placed in seats of honour, and after dinner their healths were drunk by the party after a neat and appropriate speech from the Colonel. Of course now they are as much at home as they ever will be. I do not, as a general rule, advocate promotions from the ranks, simply because I think it is rather a curse than a blessing in most instances to the unfortunates—in the Queen's service almost always. I do not object to the idea of having as companions men who have risen by their own merits; but I know from experience that few can afford to live on ensign's pay, even if bachelors, and they are generally Benedicts, and, even if money was showered on them, they would scarcely feel comfortable mixing so intimately with people whose spheres and ideas are utterly different from their own. At Hythe I met five of this class: one did credit to it, but I believe only two were happy. In India it is different, and there is more sense in such appointments. A man promoted can live on his 202 rupees a month, as indeed do most ensigns; then again, instead of being sent to a new regiment as junior ensigns, they are sent to irregular regiments as adjutants, and so their pay becomes very much increased; added to which, in an irregular regiment with only three or four officers in it, they need not mix in society more than they like, or belong to a mess. Our new ensigns are very good fellows.

If you look at the map you will perceive that Oude is really a sort of triangle, formed by the rivers Gogra and Ganges meeting down towards Ghazipore or Durapore. Both these rivers are very broad and deep, only fordable in a few places, and even then I fancy only in the dry season. Well, we have our enemy hedged in by these rivers, and our object is to prevent their crossing into any other district. Their game is to go about in small bodies, and try to escape, or join the Begum at Bairaitch, or somewhere out in that direction. The consequence is that our whole operations this season will be in chasing small bodies. Already they have had some very heavy punishments. At Selimpore they lost upwards of 700 men, at Sundela they lost 900, and report says that they have been again discomfited. This cannot go on long; they lose ammunition and guns in every action, so it will tire them at last. I fancy that if they had a chance they would come in, but they doubt our sincerity, and not without cause. There is much cause for their detestation of us; but still Mr. Layard is wrong, and has no idea of anything connected with the Mutiny; he got his information from *native gentlemen*, and inspectors of education, men full of theories and Utopian ideas. I have read most of his answers to the Indian Press, and I do not see that he has bettered his case; he has trickily got out of a few, but still he cannot get over his denial of all cruelty exercised on the part of the natives.

The want of confidence in Lord Clyde still continues unabated; perhaps it is natural to us at a distance from the central place of working of the great machine, but still its influence ought not to be felt throughout the length and breadth of the land.

With Pakenham, Wetherall, Mansfield, and all the members of Council around, there ought to be wisdom, but caution seems too much the order of the day.

If we could only publish statistics, and get the natives to read and believe them, it would work wonders. We should be able to show how much we have done with so little loss. But they do not believe that we lose so few men, and they brag of having hurled hundreds of us into the bottomless pit.

Last night we had an alarm. The new police levies got a panic and sounded the assembly; it was merely momentary, but it reminded me of Alumbagh. Somehow one knows intuitively when there is an alarm; I heard no bugles, but simply the way in which a servant came to my tent for a light showed me that all was not peace.

October 23.—I have had another rather severe attack of fever, and it has weakened me very much. I felt so weak that I made a desperate effort, and screwed up courage enough to ask Dr. Arthur to send me away. He would not make any promise; he said he was about to make arrangements for the sick, and, if they were to proceed to Allahabad, it would be an opportunity for me to go with them. I know perfectly well that I shall be miserable when my doom is sealed, and I have to go, for I hate the idea of the regiment being engaged and my not being present.

October 25.—The whole force moves to-morrow towards Amathee, and I am to go away. The doctor has consented; I get a certificate and a copy of my case, then go to Allahabad, there to appear before a medical board. It will depend entirely on them whether I am sent away permanently. One thing I can conscientiously say: and that is, I have tried to get well, and have given the doctors every chance; moreover, I am very unwilling to go away.

Everything is tending to a general smash. One rajah gave himself up the other day, and the enemy let us take a couple of splendid horse artillery guns with everything complete without a feint at a struggle.

Benson's Hotel, Allahabad,
November 1, 1858.

Thus far I have prospered on my journey, and it gives me hope that all will be also well ended.

I started from Sultanpore very early on the morning of the 29th ult., and arrived at Lowe's outpost, a distance of fifteen miles, very comfortably. Colonel Lowe asked me to breakfast with him, and excitement and joy at my deliverance from despair made me happy. I dare say that I was in a good humour, and that things appeared *couleur de rose*, but certainly I did think the trees looked giantlike, and the crops more green and luxuriant than usual.

I started at 12 p.m., allowing my baggage to get on two hours before me, reached Pertabgunj, a large station, and one of the points of concentration for Amathee, at an early hour. Here I met a wing of the dear old 5th Fusiliers coming in, and saw Byng, Carden, etc.; they told me I was looking very ill, and I was not surprised at it.

Here I got a touch of fever again. I went on next morning at 1 a.m., to a place in the jungle called Bysepoor, a miserable, desolate place, not a soul near me, and no guard. I was really very ill.

I determined to make a twenty-two mile march right into Allahabad, but the difficulty arose as to whether bearers or camels could manage it. I cut the knot by saying it must be done. I thought the fatigue of five or six extra miles better than another day's exposure to fever, and I got in without difficulty. The bearers were a little distressed, but not much.

On arrival this morning I procured a room here, which is luxurious and heavenly compared with anything I have been in for a year. The people of the hotel stared terribly at such a pale, lame being, and thought me a ghost. I could see the effect very plainly, for they came to lift me out of my dhoolie—a thing that no one would do except to a cripple or great invalid.

To-day, the assumption of the reins of Government by Her Majesty has been celebrated by fireworks.

The amalgamation of the two services has been sadly mismanaged; the Company's men were handed over by a stroke of the pen like a pack of bullocks, or a lot of commissariat stores. The men are very sore on the subject; they say they not only won India for the Queen, but greatly helped to retain it for her.[1] They urge that by the Articles of War they bound themselves to serve *in India* so long as they were wanted. To oblige a man with a wife and half-a-dozen children to go to England on English pay is a hardship; but every hardship would have been gladly borne, if the transfer had only been accompanied by a few kindly words. The men are absolutely loyal and devoted to the Queen. The Governor-General has been too much

---

[1] Lady Canning in her diary remarks that the neck of the Mutiny was broken by the Company's troops before relief had come from China, or England.

surrounded by useless busybodies, who do not understand Europeans.

November 3.—I have had much trouble here, and am very tired. Dr. Arthur sent me here with an utterly useless certificate; it simply authorized my coming here, and never said for how long, or why or wherefore, so that when I took it to the superintending surgeon, and he said it was useless, I was well nigh broken-hearted. Fortunately he was a kind man, and saw that I had been very ill, and he said he would tell his assistant to make out new ones.

Now, the said assistant-surgeon is an old friend of mine, who knew me at Nawabgunj when I was with the Bengal Fusiliers, so he came over, and together, I supplying the dates, etc., we made out a fresh case. He certified that I was in a delicate state of health, and recommended two years to England; this, however, at my request the committee will, I hope, alter to the Neilgherries. There is still another committee to pass at Calcutta, so I am not yet safe, but I think a recommendation to Europe for two years can hardly be cut down to less than a year to the Hills. I feel the necessity for the change more than ever, for I am quite done up with any exertion.

P. and O. s.s. Bengal, *Nov.* 11.

I forgot to mention that on arrival at Calcutta, which I did after jolting for four days and nights in a wretched desert van, in which, however, I had a bed made up and fitted up tolerably, I went to the great hotel called Auckland House. I arrived very late, and had only time to wash my hands and face before dinner, when my old school-fellow, Kent of the 77th, came. He kindly stayed and dined with me, and we had a most charming afternoon, excitement quite overcoming fatigue; but our joy was somewhat clouded at first by the presence of a madman. He sat opposite me, and spoke in a most singular manner at first, but subsequently he asked me if I knew what "eternal damnation" was, and broke into a most extravagant tirade about hell and sin and crime; he then took up a carving-knife and began to brandish it about, and finally took up his hat and stick, and went off singing loudly. I was so relieved. I have generally plenty of nerve with such people, but illness has quite altered my system, and I could almost have cried when he went. I was unable to eat or do anything in his presence, and so nervous was I that I locked my door that night.

Next morning after breakfast I went down to the ground-floor to get some few necessaries for my voyage, when to my horror I saw my lunatic. He saluted me most courteously. He was dressed in a most extraordinary fashion, and had on his head a grey wideawake with some peacocks' feathers in it, and on his breast one of Bass's beer-labels. I fled as quickly as possible.

At Calcutta I went to the senior surgeon, and to my horror I found out that it was Tuesday, not Monday, and that I was a day too late for the Board. Sending up my card I gained admittance and told my tale, and the good old gentleman promised to do all he could; he was impracticable about changing the certificate, saying that my finances had nothing to do with his estimation of the requirements of my health. I told him that the Neilgherries got the sea-breeze, and at last cajoled him.

My next business was to get an order for departure from the Adjutant-General, and then a passage from the Quartermaster-General.

I got on board at 10 p.m., nearly dead with fatigue and worry. Next morning the first person I met on board was my madman. I sent for the purser, and asked if the man was a first-class passenger, and being informed he was not, I requested he might not be allowed to come on our part of the vessel.

November 13.—I was obliged to stop writing on the 11th, owing to an attack of fever; it lasted four days, and has left me very weak. My poor madman is very quiet; so I no longer fear him, and often talk to him.

By some wonderful stupidity we made Madras on the 14th, but the captain did not know it and passed it, taking us on to Cuddalore. I was by no means annoyed by the mistake, for having shaken off fever, I was improving under sea-air. We turned back from Cuddalore, and made Madras on the fifteenth afternoon; but as it was monsoon, and the surf so high and the rain so heavy, I determined not to land.

Madras Club, November 17, 1858.

I landed yesterday full of hopes; scarcely a cloud seemed to shadow the meridian fullness of my sun of happiness. But scarce had I entered the club, when I heard that my dear friend Hart had been cruelly murdered. The shock was very great.

It appears that he had gone to Vellore to act as commissariat officer for another man, and that during the night of the 13th a Mussulman sepoy, who had intoxicated himself with opium, had gone about, and killed one European and wounded several others.

A lady taking alarm had gone over to Hart's house for protection, fearing a mutiny. Hart, on hearing the disturbance, went to collect his *peons* (watchmen) to apprehend the madman, when he was shot through the neck. I believe he never spoke. Dear, dear Douglas, I could almost have spared a brother better.

November 30.—I have been before the Medical Board, and they have changed my certificate from Europe to the Neilgherries. They were so kind. Nothing I asked was looked upon as a favour; they said after such work I was entitled to a good rest.

I have been very bad again. This time the fever was followed by an awful attack of sciatica; I could not turn in bed without help. I have a rope from the ceiling, by which I manage to help myself in turning.

December 3.—As I am able to go out now, Mrs. Colbeck calls for me every evening in her carriage, and I go to the beach, propped up with pillows. Colbeck is Chief Magistrate, and hearing an officer of the Madras Fusiliers was ill at the Club, he sent his card, and has been most civil ever since.

December 26.—Solomon has given me a beautiful pair of silver muffineers. He is very proud of being made butler. I must tell you the history of these muffineers. When we were in one of the palaces, after the taking of the Kaiser Bagh, Solomon came to me one day with a bundle of tawdry clothes, which I took to be theatrical properties, and asked if he could have them. I told him that he might, but remembering the lice on a former occasion, I told him that they were not to be placed near anything of mine. It turned out that they were part of the robes of the King of Oude, and very valuable. Solomon stripped off the gold and silver lace, and from the produce had the muffineers made by a Madras jeweller. I value them greatly.

Lord Harris, the Governor, has been very kind in asking me to several parties.

Here my letters end, and I take up my narrative chiefly from memory.

The regiment arrived at Madras on February 22, 1859, *en route* to Bangalore. I had secured a very nice bungalow from one of the officers of H.M. 60th Royal Rifles, and my wife had joined me. My duties were those of Musketry Instructor, and very interesting they were.

Cholera broke out very severely at this time, and we lost several old hands. I do not remember ever having seen it more rapid in its action. One woman dropped down dead in the barrack-yard, whilst going to the hospital.

We lost poor Captain Menzies. I well remember the night before he died. I was at mess, and, as he was captain of the day, he begged me to sit up as late as I could to keep him company, until the time came for him to go rounds. Next day, about 2 p.m., I was sent for to see him; he tried, but could not speak, and was dead that same evening.

Strange to say, none of the recruits got it, and my theory is, that, as they were then engaged in the firing period of their musketry instruction, the smoke of the gunpowder acted as a disinfectant.

My wife and all my household wore flower of sulphur about them; the natives in little bags under their armpits, and we in our stockings. No one connected with us got it, and I subsequently took the same precautions during a severe outburst at Malta, when no one who adopted my plan was seized. It is, I think, an American remedy. I mentioned it to several doctors, and of course they laughed at it; but I remember that subsequently the principal medical officer got the General to fire salvoes from big guns to windward of the cantonment, and the cholera ceased.

I now come to a personal matter, which caused me considerable annoyance at the time, but which readers can skip if they like. It may be remembered that I was Assistant-Quartermaster-General of a Division in the Crimea. I had been promised before the force broke up that my name should be sent in for a decoration. Some time after the capture of Lucknow I found out that the *Gazette* containing the names of recipients had been published, and that mine was omitted. Of course I wrote as soon as ever I could, but was told that the list was closed, and that I should have applied sooner. How on earth a man cut off from the outer world, fighting for his country, could have applied earlier, I never could make out! Sir John Michel, the Chief of the Staff, wrote thus to Colonel Wetherall:

"I subsequently made out a provisional list of merit, in which I put down Parry's name, as he well deserved it." Sir Robert Vivian and Sir John Michel tried to get the error corrected, but the answer always was "Too late." My grievance was that it was unfair to punish me for a delay, the cause of which should have acted in my favour rather than against me. I have the testimony of the two Generals above-mentioned that my name was included in the list and must have been erased. A man junior to me in my own department, and in army rank, got the decoration.

My days at Bangalore were very happy ones, and I liked my work. Sir John Inglis commanded the Division for a time; but his health had been completely undermined by his anxieties during the defence.

Sir Mark Cubbon, who was the Chief Commissioner in Mysore, was most hospitable to us all, and published a very spirited welcome to us. He also caused a copy of the complimentary General Order of the Governor-General to be given to every man and woman in the regiment.

Solomon now reigned supreme, and was invaluable. One day he came to my wife with a sheepish grin and said: "Missie, please, I want to make marriage business." Of course leave was given, and he went off to fetch his bride. On arrival she was brought before us, a trembling little mass of white muslin. Solomon ordered her to show her face: she was quite a child. She then went off to the godown outhouses to take up her residence.

Some months afterwards my wife heard crying in the godown, and asked the matee what was the matter. The answer was, "Solomon beat his wife." Of course Solomon was instantly paraded and interrogated. "Yes," he said, "I give her one slap; she naughty girl, and no take her medicine." He was told there must be no more slaps. Poor little thing, she soon died. I never saw grief so indelibly depicted on a human face as on Solomon's; his face turned an ashen grey. For some time he was eternally neglecting his work to "make poojee business" for his wife.

I must finish off Solomon here. When we left Madras I gave him my London address, feeling sure I should never see him again, and told him to write to me if he was ever in want. I did not hear for years. One day a letter from him came through my bankers. He told me he was well and married again, with grown-up daughters, who were placed with English ladies to learn sewing and other duties. He said he was not *quite* a Christian, for he could not run counter to the prejudices of his relations, but he added, "I believe in master's God all the same." He wrote several times to me, but never asked for anything.

My days at Bangalore, with its charming climate and lovely flowers, was about to draw to an end. My wife got a letter to say that her father was dangerously ill and wanted to see her. I went to the General, who was kindness itself, and forwarded my application for a year's leave on urgent private affairs. All my goods were disposed of, and we set off for England. I knew it was a case of good-bye to India for ever, and I own I was somewhat sad. Looking back over a vista of years, I can most truly say that nowhere have I ever met such kind friends and true gentlefolk as in India, and more especially at Bangalore. I never have forgotten, and never shall forget, them.

CHAPTER XIII

ENGLAND—MALTA—RETIREMENT

ON arrival we found that the health of the invalid was such that a return to India would be almost an impossibility, the more so as there were objections to taking the children out. My own health was not as good as it might have been, and, after having suffered so often from dysentery and fever in Burmah and at Lucknow, I was not very keen about returning. Add to all this the new and pressing home duties to attend to, and the situation may be realized. I could not afford to sell out just at that time, so an exchange was my only alternative. Luckily a man in the 8th King's Regiment had a brother in Ours, and wanted to join him; so we exchanged. Before the exchange was completed I went to the depôt at Chatham, a miserable place, where we were quartered in some old Crimean wooden huts.

. On joining the 8th I was ordered to Templemore. Soldiering there was a solemn sham! Luckily for me, my brother-in-law, Colonel Meredith, late of the 41st, came as Major to the depôt battalion; so I had the society of my own belongings. My stay was brief, for I had to join head-quarters at Malta.

Here I became Acting Inspector of Musketry, and had a jolly time. I constantly acted as Town Major for Colonel Mitford, who was an old friend. On such occasions, with other duties, I had to serve on a committee which regulated the affairs of the Opera, which in Malta received a subsidy from Government. This gave me the use of the directors' box, which was admirably situated, and had a huge mirror facing the stage, in which we could see all the acting reflected without the glare of the footlights, and also get a full view of the house. It also gave me the *entrée* behind the scenes, and brought me into contact with very interesting people. They were very stand-offish at first, but as soon as they found me sympathetic became good comrades.

We had two *prima donnas*, and they took it in turn, I think, week about. The utmost etiquette had to be preserved in all matters connected with their duties; ordinary quarrels or disputes we could settle, but professional ones were referred to Milan.

One very charming *prima donna* was a great favourite, and received everywhere in society. It so happened that the *Ballo in Maschera* was to be played, and in it there are parts for two *prima donnas*, one being a page having of necessity to wear a boy's dress. We thought that perhaps the lady would not care to don masculine attire, so gave the part to a *seconda donna*.

The bills had been scarcely published, when I heard a demand at my office for an instant interview. It was my pretty young friend, who pointed to a bill which she held in her hand. She was furious. I asked the cause of her resentment, and found she claimed the part as a right. I was in a fix. I said, "Of course you know the dress; we thought perhaps you might object to a male costume." She glared at me, and said, "Art is art; never mind the dress." So she took it, and looked lovely. I found out afterwards that she was particularly proud of her feet and legs.

I occupied very good rooms, and had a quartett every Friday, in which Ruxton of the 29th, commonly known as Handel, took part with three professionals, and a septett on Saturdays, in which Grenfell of the 60th Rifles played second fiddle (I guess he don't play second fiddle now to any one). His name reminds me of his splendid caricatures. I have one that will live for ever of old Mitford.

I must tell one musketry story before I close this section. A company of the 84th was out at skirmishing practice. Amongst them I noticed poor Clayton's servant, and on examining the targets found that his target had decidedly the greater number of hits. On my telling Clayton this, he laughed and said he did not believe his man could hit a haystack. A few days after, he said to me: "If you won't say anything, I'll tell you about that good shooting." I promised, and then he told me that his servant, knowing his incompetence in the matter of shooting, had selected a first-rate shot as a partner, and had handed him over his rounds whenever he could do so unobserved, so that the good marksman fired off an extra number of rounds, and thus made a good target. I could not help thinking that in action his wisdom would have met with approval.

I had now served my time for retirement, and sold out. Sir East Apthorpe, my old Colonel, tried to get me a brevet on retirement; but I had not lived within one hundred yards of the Horse Guards, and therefore any recognition of my service was declared impossible.

So ended my military career. I was offered by private individuals good appointments in the Militia and Volunteers, but I had had enough of soldiering and declined them. Curiously enough, my career seemed to run in triplets. I had held commissions in three different armies, served in three campaigns, and held three Staff appointments. This gave me a fair insight into the military system of my day, and has perhaps induced me to speak somewhat openly of my seniors; not half as decidedly as I could have wished.

India no doubt made our best soldiers, but the practice of keeping regiments out there for ten to twenty years was ruination to smartness.

As to regiments, every one had its own peculiar special excellency, and all had the merit of thinking themselves superior to all others. *Esprit de corps* is the key-note of the British Army; it is made up of trifles, but trifles sacred in the eyes of Tommy Atkins and his officers.

Soldiers are emblem worshippers. Why interfere with a harmless idiosyncrasy? Too much is done in that way under the guise of making the soldier more comfortable. Men worked in the Punjaub, in Burmah, and during the Mutiny without blue spectacles or mosquito curtains, and all such trash will go where it ought to go after a couple of days of real campaigning.

The British Army is, I think, better to-day than it was when I left it; the men are better looked after, and the officers very much better up in professional matters. As to fighting, the men will fight as well in 1900 as they did in 1800; it only wants twenty-four hours of bullets flying about to make the men of to-day as good as those who won Waterloo, held Inkerman, and captured Delhi and Lucknow.

Only one more word. The Indian Army in my day was, I think, more free from favouritism than the Queen's; a man without a particle of interest could by merit get on. There were no back stairs; or if there were, they were not so broad as the Horse Guards'. I can now speak only from common report, but it seems that favouritism still exists, though it runs in a different channel.

CHAPTER XIV

HOME. 1868

I HAD now settled down in my Welsh home, and, as the home farm had to be held in hand, I took up farming. In doing so I determined to give my new calling the same attention as I had given her Majesty's interests whilst receiving her pay, and, though I had much to learn, and had to buy experience at first somewhat dearly, I have never found farming a losing concern. When amateurs devote two days a week to shooting, two to hunting, and two to market, which mean billiards, I can imagine the thing would not pay; and as to tenant farmers, they are just as likely to tell you that farming is a thriving trade as a parson is to tell you that you have no need of his services. But the farmer really has a hard time, and everything falls on land. If the money wasted on an Agricultural Department and in grants to agricultural colleges, which only teach young men how to spend other men's money, was only spent in reducing the farmers' taxation, it would do some good.

But farmers themselves are greatly to blame; for the sake of some political or religious fad, they send men to represent them in Parliament, who not only have no knowledge of, or interest in, agriculture, but are often absolutely hostile to measures in the direction of benefit to the farmer.

I became a magistrate almost immediately on taking up my residence. The work was interesting, and of course my army training in the matter of courts-martial was a help.

I have sat on some very curious cases, and have had all kinds of birds, beasts, and fishes in the witness-box. As a visiting justice I made acquaintance with all sorts and conditions of men and women.

Once a case fairly puzzled us. My cousin, John Vaughan, used to go with me to the county gaol as a visitor. The Governor reported that a prisoner managed to shave himself: that meant he had some sharp instrument concealed somewhere. He had been stripped as usual for his bath on entering, and his clothes taken from him, but nothing had been found. We moved him to another cell, and punished him; all in vain—we could not solve the mystery. As a joke one night, he shaved only one side; he was a funny fellow, and I liked him.

Eventually he was released, but in a short time came back again for another short period. Again the shaving took place. Finally he took to good ways, got employment in the town, and I often had a chat with him. He confessed that his shaving was effected with a piece of a watch-spring, sharpened like a razor, which he hid under his tongue when he came into prison.

We had another constant inmate in the person of a young girl, who robbed men under curious circumstances. I think it was on the third occasion of her being committed for trial, that just before the court sat we visited her, and she then voluntarily confessed her guilt, and said she intended to plead guilty. Next day Vaughan and I were on the grand jury. The case came on, and there was a very considerable difference of opinion as to whether a true bill should be found or not. A question arose in our minds whether we ought to tell the grand jury what the girl had said; we consulted in private, and determined to treat her confession as a private matter. No true bill was found, and of course she got off. The question on which the jury split was to my mind a childish one, but that made no difference to us in the matter that perplexed us. I have often wondered if we were right or wrong in our decision.

In 1871 I was High Sheriff. The expenses in those days were very considerable, but one had to grin and bear them. I was lucky in my first Judge, Mr. Justice Mellor. His son had been my subaltern in the 8th at Malta. After I had done salaam, and seen his lordship safe in his lodgings, I told him this, and his civility was unbounded. It so happened that this son was most seriously ill with fever at Malta, and a brother came out to nurse him. Sir John Mellor referred to this, and told me he never could forget the kindness of the doctors and officers of the King's to his sons.

As I said, his civility to me was most marked, and on finding I was married he invited my wife to sit beside him on the Bench, and asked her to lunch—a most unusual thing for a Judge to do on circuit. In speaking of this kindness to another son, who was his marshal, I was amused at his saying: "Oh yes, it's all right of my father to do the civil, but what the deuce am I to do for sweets for dinner to-night?" It was the custom in those days for the Judge to invite the High Sheriff, the chaplain, and magistrates to dine with him. We had used certain of the sweets at lunch that were intended for dinner, and young Mellor was at a loss how to supply their place in a small county town. Hence his tears.

The Judge was *very* complimentary to my chaplain. I remarked on this to the son. "Oh, all right," he said, "I know, whenever the sermon is less than twenty minutes, my father thanks awfully." Let us hope it really was the *admirable discourse,* not the brevity, that took the Judge.

Amongst other things I put to the Judge the vexed question of precedence between the Lord-Lieutenant and the High Sheriff. His answer was characteristic. "I really have never thought which takes precedence, but this I know, the High Sheriff can hang the Lord-Lieutenant, and the Lord-Lieutenant cannot hang the High Sheriff."

My second judge was Sir Montague Smith; such a charming man—his friendliness was very gratifying. I had rather a nasty shock just before the Assizes. I was having a happy day at the Crystal Palace, when I met a Welsh friend, who told me there had been a most brutal murder committed in Cardiganshire. Of course that meant a hanging job for me. It turned out that a mad gamekeeper had shot an old man of seventy, who was game enough to recover; so there was no murder, and the man did not even come up for trial: he was, poor man, already detained at Broadmoor.

I do not think anything of further interest occurred during the year of my shrievalty. Not only had I to put my hand deep down in my pocket, but Government were mean enough to tax me for a hired extra servant, who was necessary, though his services were of only two days' duration. About this time I was made a Deputy-Lieutenant.

Time passed happily enough until 1878, when I had an accident out hunting that put a stop to my riding and shooting. My health was affected, and my nerves shaken. I took a voyage round the world, the incidents of which I published in a book entitled *My Journey Round The World*.[1] The most amusing result of this was the extraordinary number of letters I got from would-be travellers. I made many life-long friends.

Amongst other curious applications received by me in consequence of publishing, was an invitation by the Balloon Association to give a lecture at the Aquarium. As I had never been up in a balloon, I did not quite see where my *locus standi* came in. However, I have since wiped out the reproach by going up in a balloon, but alas! only a

[1] Hurst & Blackett, London.

captive, not a captivating one. I do not care for the sensation, and dislike looking down on people.

My Bohemian life of early days left a restlessness behind, and I soon tired of too monotonous a life. I had always taken an active part in the politics of my country, and when the Primrose League was started, applied for and got the appointment of District Inspector. This was another of the mistakes of my life, for I know I lost caste by accepting it, especially in my own neighbourhood, because it was commonly reported that I was fabulously paid for my services, and the Welsh do not care for paid political speakers; they say that they speak to order, and not from conviction. As a matter of fact, I was considerably out of pocket when I took up my duties in my Welsh district.

The Primrose League was, and still is, to my mind, the link that was so much needed to bring the richer and more pronounced Conservative into touch with his more humble brethren, who are unselfishly Conservative, but for obvious reasons not demonstrative. As an organization it has done wonders from an educational point of view. The lying trash that was disseminated from platform and press is now exposed, and even the boldest speaker does not use arguments now that were familiar before the Primrose League took action.

The first batch of Inspectors were, I think, a valuable lot: they certainly were gentlemen, and took office out of sheer love of the cause. They gained the reproach of more than one Radical paper on account of their all having what was termed "double-barrelled names." I do not think the fact of their being all men of a certain social position was ever fairly recognized at head-quarters, where they were treated somewhat cavalierly by the officials.

My first district comprised Somersetshire, Gloucestershire, Devonshire, Cornwall, and Monmouthshire—a good allowance. However, I did fairly well in it, and had nothing to complain of, even in the matter of salary. The hospitality shown me was truly splendid, and to my dying day I shall remember the many kindnesses I received. The only drawback was chairmen. I got chairmen on the brain. Whenever one told me in confidence that he never made a speech, "only introduce the speakers, that's all," I knew I was in for a good forty minutes, and frequently I had to alter my whole address on the spur of the moment to avoid repeating what my chairman had already said. I well remember one genial Irishman saying to me as we walked to the meeting: "Bedad, ye know I never make a speech, it's not my line; I merely tell them who you are, and where you come from." I was young at my work in those days, and believed him. Alas! when on the platform he blundered out a few opening sentences, and then took a Primrose League pamphlet from his pocket and commenced reading it aloud. It took just forty minutes, and forestalled all I was about to say. It gave me, however, time to make headings for a new address.

Lengthy addresses and sermons remind me of dear old Baron Channel, who told me he one day attended Divine Service in the cathedral at Chester with Baron Gurney. The select preacher gave them a forty-five minutes' sermon. As they were returning in the Sheriff's carriage, Baron Gurney thanked the chaplain for his admirable discourse, adding dryly, that it contained subject-matter enough for at least six sermons. Baron Channel, with a twinkle in his eye, assured me he always told this anecdote to the various chaplains *on their way to church*, as a hint to use moderation.

When I was Sheriff I had printed sermons sent to me by nearly every sect in England, with a request that I would use my influence to get my chaplain to advocate the writer's views.

My second division comprised Carmarthenshire, Cardiganshire, Pembrokeshire, and Radnorshire. This was by far the most difficult and expensive area to work, and, if I had not had my own carriage and horses, I could not possibly have done it. The absence of any railway system was the great drawback, causing extra expense and much loss of time. I made a point of visiting the wildest and remotest parts, not sticking to the populous centres where I could get good audiences and so send in flourishing reports.

It is no exaggeration to say, I held forth on the very mountain tops, and at one meeting poor old Geoffrey Hill, the chairman, told me if I looked out of the window I should find grouse listening to me. At this same meeting a farmer told me I was "a little man, but I could make a deal of noise." It was intended as a great compliment.

I did not get on well with head-quarters while working this division. They never to my mind recognized sufficiently the services of ruling councillors working under the very greatest difficulties. Flags and honours of all kinds were given to habitations in England, where, according to my experience in five counties, there was no difficulty in rallying thousands, but no credit was given to those who in little gallant Wales gathered their neighbours in tens and twenties.

In three years I spoke about 300 times, and travelled some 30,000 miles. I held forth in tan-pits, malt-houses, and granaries. The largest audience I ever had was at Bristol, computed at 4000; the attraction was Lord Plunkett. My smallest was at Raglan—only nine, of whom six came with me. They were too sound there to need a physician.

As a rule, wherever I was told that the place was full of Radicals, and that I should not get a hearing, I always found the meetings most enthusiastic.

I never had one uncivil word said to me in the whole course of my lecturing.[1]

I cannot leave this subject without referring to the extreme hospitality I received on all hands, and the assistance rendered to me in organizing meetings in Devonshire by Mr. Lane Fox, and especially by Miss Mallock. I now only speak by invitation at meetings organized by old friends.

My recollections cannot be brought to a close without referring to one of the crowning incidents of my life, namely, having been the guest of the gallant survivors of the Defence and Relief of Lucknow.

The chair was taken by that William Olpherts whom Lord Napier described as "never going into action without deserving the Victoria Cross."

It was the greatest compliment that could be paid me. I fully appreciated the honour of associating with so many old comrades, who had been lucky enough to share in operations which I missed, though I did my best to arrive in time for them; and it gives me no small satisfaction to record in this narrative my appreciation of services which, to my mind, have been but indifferently acknowledged by the powers that be.

There was not a man amongst them who had not been, not days or weeks, but months, under continuous fire from heavy guns, with a network of mines running almost under his very feet; not one who had not by his own individual exertions helped to protect and sustain the poor helpless creatures, who by dire misfortune had become their precious charge; not one who could not grasp his comrade's hand and honestly say, "We did our best for one and all."

Where could such a bond of union, such brotherhood as this be found elsewhere? Yet these men, with medals on

---

[1] I must in justice acknowledge the courtesy shown me on all occasions by my political opponents.

their breasts, aye, and scars beneath them, have had but scant reward. How do they stand by the side of recipients of the D.S.O.[1] (two hundred and fifty of which have been awarded in the last ten years)? Why, simply superseded.

To give men, some of whom have barely smelt powder, precedence socially over the men who, by dint of hard fighting in the Punjaub, Burmah, and elsewhere, first won an Empire, and then at Delhi and Lucknow maintained it, seems to me not only humiliating but an injustice.

Yet, in spite of official neglect, these heroes have their reward. They have the satisfaction of knowing that Lucknow day—

> "shall ne'er go by,
> From this day to the ending of the world,
> But we in it shall be remembered."

My day is past and gone. I desire no more than to be left alone with sweet memories; but for my dear old comrades who won and held our glorious Empire, I truly feel—

> "If it be a sin to covet honour
> I am the most offending soul alive."

---

[1] The D.S.O. comes after the Royal Victorian Order, and before the Victoria and Albert, the Imperial Order of the Crown of India, and the Victoria Cross. For the social precedence, see *Burke*.

THE END

www.ingramcontent.com/pod-product-compliance
Lightning Source LLC
Chambersburg PA
CBHW020809100426
42814CB00014B/384/J